Teaching The Online Catalog User

Library Orientation Series

Number

(Most volumes are still in print;
the two out-of-print volumes are designated.)

Teaching The Online Catalog User

Papers and Work Session Notes Presented at the Second Biennial
LOEX Library Instruction Workshop held at
Eastern Michigan University,
9 & 10 May 1985; and Numerous Examples of Current Instructional
Materials Collected in late 1987

edited by
Carolyn A. Kirkendall
Director, LOEX Clearinghouse
Center of Educational Resources
Eastern Michigan University

Published for the Center of Educational Resources,
Eastern Michigan University
by
Pierian Press
Ann Arbor, Michigan
1988

ISBN 0-87650-250-8

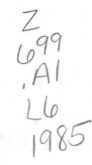

Pierian Press
P.O. Box 1808
Ann Arbor, Michigan 48106

Table of Contents

Articles   1

Poster Session Abstracts   101

Discussion Group Handouts and Sample Materials
from the LOEX Clearinghouse Collection
125

Bibliographies
225

Participants
249

Preface

In 1985, the LOEX Clearinghouse sponsored its second workshop for bibliographic instruction librarians--Teaching the Online Catalog. For several years, Clearinghouse staff had received requests for treating this topic at its annual May meeting. By 1985, a considerable number of BI librarians could be identified who had experience in this area, and who had also developed recognizable, evaluated programs and projects in their own academic libraries.

The session was labeled a workshop, and participants--sitting eight to a table--were expected to be familiar with a short list of suggested readings before attending, and to work together after each presentation in hands-on exercises, assignments and discussions, applying the recommendations they heard from each speaker to their own campus situations.

Because of the practical and informal format of the workshop, proceedings of the meeting were initially not intended to be printed. However, after the two-day session, it was decided to collect and reprint the comments and worksession notes from most of the workshop speakers and leaders, and to also include many samples of printed handouts relating to teaching online catalog use. These latter samples were of great help to participants who were eager to see and adapt existing academic library guides and materials, rather than 'reinvent the wheel.'

Those who attended received selective (now outdated) bibliographies of recommended background readings and of user reactions and responses to OPACs. Revised reading lists are still available by writing to the LOEX Clearinghouse.

Participants seemed interested in solving the following potential problems when online catalogs arrive on campus: how to prepare for the change from cards to terminals; which methods are best for teaching specific library users; what is the best format for a user's manual; common pitfalls to anticipate; advice on handling the complexities and staffing when expanding the BI program to include instruction in OPAC use.

Workshop speakers collectively emphasized that teaching students and faculty how to use the online catalog needs to be kept in perspective, and not overemphasized in the total BI program...an admonition that instruction librarians have kept in mind for years: teach search strategy and process, not tools without context. (See Bill Miller's article, "Instructing the Online Catalog User," in the Spring 1986 issue of *Research Strategies*, for a subsequent succinct comment on this recurring temptation.) Gratitude toward the helpful EMU Hoyt Conference staff, Vicky Young of Xavier University for her competent annual assistance to LOEX, and to all loyal LOEX Clearinghouse users and workshop participants is sincerely extended.

Carolyn A. Kirkendall
Former LOEX Director

Educating the Online Catalog User

Betsy Baker

GENERAL PRESENTATION
OUTLINE/MATERIALS

Advance preparation for the session will ensure that: 1) the equipment is operational, 2) a sufficient supply of handouts, worksheets, and other materials is available, and 3) the classroom is organized.

I. **Introductory Comments (5 minutes)**
   A. Identify self and position.
   B. If session is voluntary attendance, inquire as to how participants learned of the workshop.
   C. Assess audience familiarity with library and computer catalog.
   D. Briefly describe length and purpose of presentation by noting the following points:
   - Describe the computer catalog
   - Describe relationship between card catalog and the computer catalog
   - Outline efficient ways to search the computer catalog
   - Discuss the scope of the online catalog (monographic publications, serials publications, and so on).
   E. Stress the availability of library staff assistance at all public service desks.
   F. Mention the availability of online instructions in the form of introductory screens, help screens, or other prompts.
   G. If Dial-Access is available to the system, briefly describe this, offering to provide further details after the session is over.

II. **Presentation Content (15 minutes)**
   Describe what the online system represents.

Baker is Bibliographic Instruction Services Librarian at Northwestern University Library.

This corresponds to Program Objective 1--the user understands what the online system represents.

What Is the Computer Catalog

This corresponds to Program Objective 1, part A--the user understands the function and purpose of the online catalog.

Give a brief overview of the system. Emphasize the point that the user interacts directly with the computer's memory and logic when operating the keyboard and terminal. Describe the types of searching capabilities available in the system (e.g., author, title, subject, Boolean). Also mention other types of information provided by the computer catalog (e.g., circulation, cross-references, location, and holdings).

Define the Scope of the Database

This corresponds to Program Objective 1, part B--the user can define the scope of the database in terms of the types of materials included and excluded and the dates of coverage.

1.   What is in the computer catalog

Discuss what types of materials are listed in the computer catalog (e.g., books, periodical titles, microfilm, items on order) with particular emphasis on the initial dates when online bibliographic records for these items were first input into the computer catalog. Be sure to include information about materials from special collections, departmental, or affiliated libraries, if these collections are also available through the computer catalog. Again, emphasize dates of coverage. Note specific kinds of information provided by the online catalog. Note that the phrase "bibliographic record" refers to descriptive information about books and other library materials (e.g., author's name, date, year, and place of publication, author's year of birth, whether the book is illustrated, has bibliographical references, tables, call numbers, location information, circulation status, related subject headings, and so on).

2.   What is not in the computer catalog

To reinforce an understanding of what information is listed in the computer catalog, a synopsis of items not listed in the online file provides a helpful contrast. Mention again the dates when bibliographic records were first input into the system, emphasizing that library materials processed before that date could only be located in the card catalog. If non-Roman alphabet titles are not found in the online catalog, be sure to mention this. Another important point is the fact that journal articles are not listed in the computer cat-

alog. Clarify the distinction between periodical or magazine title and titles of magazine articles.

3.   What is the card catalog

In this presentation, it is helpful to incorporate a description of what types of information can be found in the card catalog, note that author, title, and subject information about library materials is available in the card catalog. As with the computer catalog, it is important to mention whether cards for items currently processed are still being filed for current materials, emphasize both the date when this practice ceased, and the fact that the student must use the online catalog in order to locate this information. Note the existence of cross-references as standard in the card catalog, and explain their importance in helping a researcher move from an unused heading to one that is used to find information on a particular subject. If cross-references do not exist in the computer catalog, discuss alternative strategies for subject searching here (if subject searching is available on the system). Also, if the shelflist is available for public access, describe how it can be used and note whether it is kept current.

4.   What is not in the card catalog

As with the computer catalog, note materials not available through the card catalog (special, departmental collections, government publications, maps, recordings, software, and so on).

Constructing and Formatting a Search

1.   Demonstrate how the equipment is operated (5 minutes). This corresponds to Program Objective 3--the user can operate the equipment accompanying the online catalog such as the terminal, keyboard, and printer.

Define the function of special keys used to interact with the computer (e.g., enter, reset, clear keys), locate them, and demonstrate how they are used. Stress the point that there is no chance of damaging the computer catalog by incorrectly operating the equipment. By the same token, remind students that the computer does not think--it searches for exactly what is input.

2.   Demonstrate how to initiate and format an online catalog search (20 minutes). This corresponds to Program Objective 4--the user is able to structure an online catalog search by correctly choosing, entering, and manipulating appropriate search commands.

Begin with a discussion of structure of the computer catalog's introductory and help screens, demonstrating what type of online assistance (if demonstrating what type of online assistance), if any, is available. Indicate where a search term is displayed on the screen, as a point of reference for the student to use to check his/her search statement throughout a search. Highlight the availability of any system prompts, noting that if the student is unsure of how to proceed at any time, there is always at least an alternative course of action--to request online assistance. Describe the various means available for searching the computer catalog (e.g., author, title, subject, books). Indicate how a search statement is constructed. (These points are most effectively illustrated by the use of examples, which are listed in the following section.)

Demonstration Examples

The selection of good examples is an effective means to illustrate system points that may serve as a source of difficulty for users. (It is useful to make up a list of example searches in advance that best illustrate the various searching methods and techniques that can be used with the computer catalog. In addition, the session runs more smoothly if the instructor has prepared a list of examples, which he/she can be confident will effectively illustrate important points.)

If the design of the system is such that different levels of display appear depending on how much information is retrieved, an example is an effective method for clarifying the distinction between these various levels.

For instance, Northwestern's LUIS system has three possible levels of screen display that might appear during search--guide, index, or bibliographic record. In an author or title search in LUIS, if more than one author or title matches a search request, the screen displays an index that lists titles or author/title combinations that match the word or phrase entered. To see the bibliographic record for any listing in this index, the user must type the number that appears to the left of the title. If more than seventeen authors or titles match a search request, the screen will display a guide that groups the index into sections. From this guide the user may select the number of the author or title that would display the section of the index he/she wished to see. From this index, the user could see a bibliographic record by typing the number to the left of the title he/she wished to see.

Learning Objectives for Online Catalog Education

General Objective

Upon completion of an online catalog instructional activity, a user should have an understanding of the function and scope of the online system and be self-sufficient in using computer catalog public terminals to perform monograph and serial searches.

P = Program Objective: E = Enabling Objective

P1 The user understands what the online system represents.
  A. The user understands the function and purpose of the online catalog.
    E1 The user can define the phrase "online computer catalog," and understands that he/she interacts directly with the computer's memory and logic when operating the keyboard and terminal of the online catalog.
    E2 The user understands that the public terminal, screen, and keyboard are used to transmit a catalog search question on the terminal screen to the computer.
    E3 The user can recognize and define basic computer terms such as command, database, online, terminal, and search term.
  B. The user can define the scope of the database in terms of the types of materials included and excluded and the dates of coverage.
    E1 Given a citation, the user can decide whether to look in the card catalog, the online catalog, or an index to locate the item cited.
    E2 The user can identify the different types of information that are available in the online catalog, such as bibliographic (author, title, publisher, date of publication), circulation, library location symbols, cross-reference provision, and call numbers.

P2 The user understands selected concepts of an online information retrieval system.
    E1 The user can distinguish between subject searching and other searching forms; given a subject search, the user selects terms from LCSH, MESH, or other controlled vocabularies as appropriate; given a search other than subject, the user selects uncontrolled terms in appropriate formats for searching.
    E2 The user understands the purpose of truncation and the way it is implemented in the specific system. She/He demonstrates understanding of truncation by applying it at appropriate times and in the appropriate form.
    E3 Given a list of terms, the user can distinguish between terms that are

meaningful as keywords for searching in the online catalog and those that are not meaningful.

P3 The user can demonstrate how the equipment accompanying the online catalog is operated (e.g., terminal, keyboard, printer).

E1 The user is able to use the alpha-numeric, transmitting, and special function keys (enter key, reset key, clear key) on the keyboard correctly.

E2 The user is able to identify commonly held misconceptions regarding the use of computers and computer terminals, specifically the fear of damaging the system by incorrectly operating the equipment and expecting system correction of inputting errors.

E3 The user is aware of the existence or lack of existence of sign-on procedures required by the online catalog.

P4 The user is able to structure an online catalog search by correctly choosing, entering, and manipulating appropriate search vocabulary.

A. The user can state the existence of the different methods of searching the online catalog.

E1 The user is able to enter each of the commands that retrieve various records from the online catalog correctly. Given an author, title, or subject command, the user is able to choose the appropriate command for his/her information need.

E2 The user is able to combine a search command with an argument.

E3 Given an information need that requires utilizing the subject searching capability of the online catalog, the user will select the appropriate printed source (such as Library of Congress Subject Headings, Sears Subject Headings, Medical Subject Headings), if any, to correctly format the search.

E4 The user avoids common inputting errors and is aware that inputting errors can cause a search to fail.

E5 The user is able to locate a unique bibliographic record, given partial or complete information about the desired item.

E6 Given a choice between initiating an author, title, or subject search, the user will select the most system-efficient search category for his/her information need.

E7 The user can employ special searching features available for the system in the search process such as truncation, key word searching, and use of Boolean logic.

B. The user is able to utilize system features in order to manipulate retrieved data and fully exploit system capabilities.

E1 The user is able to recognize and identify different categories of display within the system.

E2 The user can explain the function of the key data elements provided in each display in order to complete or continue a search.

P5 The user can correctly interpret the results of a search and can identify information from it that is pertinent to his/her information needs.

E1 Given a bibliographic record display, the user is able to identify author, title, publication date and publisher, and call number from the record.

E2 Given a complete citation, the user can locate useful information in the record, such as author birth and death dates and collation.

E3 The user can interpret any online error messages.

E4 Given an error message, the user can return to point at which error was made and proceed correctly.

E5 Given a library location code from a screen of information, the user is able to identify correctly the area of the library in which the material may be found.

E6 The user is aware that online assistance is available for the online catalog in the form of help screens.

E7 The user recognizes the library staff as a source of information about the online catalog and uses if appropriate.

MODEL PROGRAM MATERIALS FOR EDUCATING THE ONLINE CATALOG USER: INSTRUCTIONAL MATERIALS FOR THE MODEL PROGRAM

This document from "Educating the Online Catalog User: A Model for Instruction Development and Evaluation Report," provides a description of the supporting instructional materials developed for the program. These materials are based on the learning objectives that are attached.

The establishment of learning objectives is an essential step in instruction planning, as the objectives specify the expected outcomes of the instruction activity. With these objectives in mind, a workshop approach to teaching the online catalog, and a printed guide were devised for the project. The objectives served as the means for determining the content of these methods. Consensus in the bibliographic instruction field holds that a multi-faceted instruction program, which provides a variety of learning opportunities or teaching methods, best meets the needs of a user community--a diverse population with different learning styles. For the purpose of this project, the two methods that follow were utilized, though the objectives readily lend themselves to other teaching approaches. At Northwestern, the online catalog user education program included a workshop and instructional brochure. The workshop outline and the brochure were modified for use in this project once learning objectives had been developed. The following discussion details the content of these teaching methods.

Workshops

The LUIS Workshops are structured to provide, within a fifty-minute session, basic instruction in the use of LUIS, Northwestern's online catalog. Each session is conducted by a reference librarian, who uses a chalkboard, printed handouts, and three video monitors attached to a single CRT terminal as teaching aids for the presentation. The terminal is linked by cable to the library's computer, and also is connected to the monitors that provide the same display as the terminal screen.

The LUIS Workshop sessions are structured in two parts. The first part is a presentation of concepts, relating the online catalog to the card catalog in order to take advantage of what the students may already know about catalogs in general. It is in this first part that an overview of the system is provided and information is presented that relates to automated retrieval and file structure. The LUIS online system and manual catalogs are compared in order to sensitize students both to the similarities of the two files and to the search strategies that must be adjusted according to which file is approached. This content provides a means of conveying what may be new information about the online system in a way that does not patronize.

The second part of the session focuses on specific features of the LUIS system, highlighting especially those features that seem to cause the most difficulty for users. It is during this part of the session that the monitors are used extensively to provide illustration of system structure along with the major points covered. Throughout the second part of the session, an underlying goal of instruction is to convey the pattern and regularity of the retrieval system and the user interface. Attention is drawn to the location of user prompts and help screens. The constant redisplay of the original search input on every screen is pointed out to give the user a means of self-diagnosis for errors. The basic construction of a search statement is exhibited through the use of a number of specific examples. Attention is specifically directed toward how to manage the size of retrieval through the use of truncation and how to manipulate the system to cope with a large retrieval.

The attached workshop presentation outline is provided to all librarians planning similar programs.

Workshop Presentation Outline

The outline that has been used at Northwestern has been modified and generalized to serve as a convenient instructional framework for other libraries. The suggested presentation outline comprises two main sections: 1) an introductory section, describing the purpose and length of the session; and 2) a four-part content section, which is organized around the five program objectives. This section includes discussion of a) what the computer catalog represents; b) the scope of the computer catalog; c) constructing and formatting a search statement; and d) demonstration examples.

The objectives that form the basis for the instructional session are broad, and therefore should be prioritized according to the needs of the institution and its system. The outline does not attempt to provide a level of detail that includes coverage of each of the enabling objectives. Careful selection of examples, however, can serve as an effective means of assuring that these enabling objectives are incorporated into the workshop. In the presentation outline, program objectives that correspond to the content of the workshop are listed.

After adapting the outline to fit the specific features of a system, the outline can serve as a means to ensure continuity in instruction. While each instructor will be able to personalize his or her approach and style to presenting the workshop content, the basic objectives in the outline will remain consistent.

Printed Material

The availability of printed instruction saves constant repetition by library staff of the most basic information about the system. It is generally agreed that the availability of a guide accommodates the user who prefers self-instruction through a printed system overview. A single-sheet printed brochure--"Using LUIS"--was designed to serve as a quick-searching supplement to the instructional program. As with the workshop approach, the searching guide incorporates the concepts represented by the five program learning objectives. The brochure includes the following points:

1. Step-by-step instruction and examples for performing author, title, and subject searches in the online catalog that correspond to Program Objectives 3, 4, and 5.

2. Helpful information about specific system functions and automated retrieval concepts. For example, the following points are made: "Information is sent to the computer only after you press the ENTER key;" "When typing number do not substitute the letter 'o' for the numeral '0';" also provided are specific examples of truncation. These points all correspond to Program Objective 2.

3. An explanation of what the online catalog system represents and what is included in the database is provided. This instruction is related to Program Objective 1.

4. A helpful list explaining abbreviations for codes used in the copy holding statement in the bibliographic record indicates various locations of items in the library.

SECOND BIENNIAL LOEX LIBRARY INSTRUCTION WORKSHOP
TEACHING THE ONLINE CATALOG USER

Attitudes and Behavior of Online Catalog Users

Expectation: Users like the online catalog.

Examples: It's less monotonous than the card catalog.
Circulation status of books is easily accessible. Saves time.

What do you find?

Expectation: Card catalogs have advantages that can't be
included in the online system.

Examples: Browsing is easier with card catalog. You can take
catalog drawer out and sit with it. Sometimes you can stumble
onto something while browsing through a drawer.

What do you find?

Expectation: Users have trouble finding the right subject
headings.

Examples: Subject heading chosen by user is frequently too broad
or too specific. Patrons waste time trying subject after
subject. Often, they have to ask a librarian for assistance.

What do you find?

Expectation: Users envision features to improve subject access.

Examples: Users want "see" and "see also" references to provide other subject headings. Some said they would like more subject headings assigned to each book. Others wanted to see the indexes of books or their book jacket descriptions.

What do you find?

Expectation: Users want online catalog information about other library materials.

Examples: Users want more reference information such as guides to periodicals. How about an online "Reader's Guide". Some say all types of library resources should be cataloged: specific magazine article titles, pamphlets, tapes, vertical files, etc..

What do you find?

Expectation: Users want new online catalog related services.

Examples: Some suggested expanded access to system through computers in dorms, at home, and in classrooms. Others wanted printers to be attached to terminals for hard copy of book information. Some thought being able to put a hold on a book through the system would be convenient.

What do you find?

Educating the Online Catalog User: An Exercise

Preconditions to Teaching

the Online Catalog User

Linda Wilson

When I was hired to teach patrons how to use the VTLS online catalog, my idea of teaching included workshops and demonstrations of the system and perhaps some one-to-one instruction during my hours at the reference desk. Now, after a year and a half in the trenches, my view of online catalog instruction has broadened considerably. Learning to use the system occurs formally and informally; it involves written, spoken, and online instructions, and most of it, I think, occurs without me. Since there seems to be no correlation between attendance at VTLS workshops (mostly scant) and usage of the VTLS terminals (mostly heavy), I am convinced that users teach themselves and their friends, and that most learning probably occurs through trial and error.

There are a number of ways I can view this phenomenon of self-instruction. One way is for me to come away with a bruised ego, realizing how unnecessary I am in the whole process. Another way to approach it, is to understand that my instruction may have to be largely unobtrusive. Viewed in this second way, teaching the online catalog user becomes a challenge: how to teach without really "teaching."

One important aspect of this nonteaching is what I call the preconditions to teaching. Taking a step back from the actual instructional process, I ask the questions: What environmental conditions are conducive to learning to use an online catalog? What measures can we take to enhance the comfort and productivity of the user?

These questions land me squarely in the middle of the new buzz word, "ergonomics." If you have perused a computer furniture or equipment catalog

Wilson is Project Manager for User Education at Virginia Tech.

lately, you have not escaped the term and how embarrassing for you if the chairs you ordered are not ergonomic chairs! Ergonomics is the study of human capabilities and psychology in relationship to working environment and equipment. I would like to address the issue of ergonomics in relation to the online library catalog.

Librarians responsible for the installation of online catalog computer terminals need to make decisions about the kinds of terminals and furniture to be purchased. Instructional librarians with special knowledge of users' needs should share these decisions. Appropriate kinds, quantities and placements of chairs, tables and video display terminals, as well as the design and placement of instructional aids are important preconditions to teaching use of the online catalog.

Furniture

Ralph Caplan, in his book *By Design: Why There Are No Locks on the Bathroom Doors in the Hotel Louis XIV and Other Object Lessons*, gives a fine definition of a chair:

A chair is the first thing you need when you don't really need anything, and is therefore a peculiarly compelling symbol of civilization. For it is civilization, not survival, that requires design.[1]

Because chairs are such a fixture of civilization, it is difficult to think of them in a fresh way. Chairs for the online catalog should have castors for noise control and ease of movement. As for legs, a center rod with five spokes does not tip as easily as one with four spokes. Arms on chairs tend to get in the way and unnecessarily use up space. You'll want padded chairs with good support that are adjustable. Since online catalog terminals are usually conveniently located and therefore very visible, you'll probably want attractive chairs that make a good impression.

We learned through experience to buy more chairs than terminals. We observed that chairs (like hangers in clothes closets) tend to reproduce overnight. People seem to work together at catalog terminals and an extra chair here and there accommodates this cooperative effort.

Perhaps the most important consideration in choosing tables for catalog workstations is the size of the table top. A minimum size of 30" x 40" will usually accommodate books, bookbags, scrap paper, jackets, purses, and other assorted materials. The nationwide survey of online public catalog users sponsored by the Council on Library Resources (1983) reported, "The primary problem experienced by users of the online catalog was the lack of sufficient writing space adjacent to the terminal."[2]

Make sure that plenty of leg room is available as well. If the chairs are adjustable in height, there is no need for the tables to adjust. A height of 26" to 27" is optimum. Express terminals, on which searchers have a time limit (usually three to five minutes), should be on tables approximately 42" high so patrons can stand while using them.

Video Display Terminals

Terminals should be chosen for ease of maintenance. They need to be sturdily built and easily repaired. When response time is slow, users (including librarians) tend to pound the keys for faster response. The main ongoing maintenance problem is dust clogging the keyboards. Small hand vacuum cleaners are available to ameliorate the problem and a regular cleaning schedule is highly recommended.

In addition to simple and rugged design, simplicity of operation is an advantage. Choosing a "dumb" terminal for public use is a smart thing to do. Select terminals with a minimum of extra function keys. This protects the integrity of your database and less programming is required to disengage specific keys.

Security issues are of primary importance. Switches and wiring should be internal or covered. Keep in mind that terminals with detachable keyboards are about the same size as bookbags.

We have noticed that the glare of lighting on monitors or screens can be a problem. The best solution is to cut down on lighting, but antiglare screens are also available from vendors for attachment over the monitor. We have not found them to be terribly satisfactory as they are constructed of a very fine mesh that gets dusty and is very hard to clean. Some monitors come equipped with a nonglare glass matte finish, which is, however, harder to clean than smooth glass. Another solution is to purchase monitors with amber letters rather than the standard green letters. The amber color reflects less light, but costs more.

Other things to look for in monitors are high contrast between lettering and background as well as good resolution, which refers to how distinct and well-formed the letters are. Another option, which may be important, is the availability of an auxiliary port on the terminals in the event you wish to attach a printer.

Placement of Terminals

The CLR survey referred to previously (1983) reported that, "The majority of users (64%) first discover that the library has an online catalog by simply observing the terminal in the library."[3]   It makes sense, then, to place terminals in a conspicuous place and also to locate a number of them near the card catalog if both kinds of catalogs are in use. Some terminals should be placed near reference points so librarians are available to help users. We have found, however, that most users want some privacy so that close proximity to librarians may inhibit searching.

We have placed an express terminal in the library lobby with a sign requesting patrons to limit their searches to three minutes. We also have a number of other express terminals in the reference area for quick searches. These terminals are placed on high tables so users do not sit down and settle into searching.

As patrons become accustomed to using automated library systems, they will begin making requests for additional services. They will ask for access to the library's catalog from their dorm rooms, offices, and homes via personal computers or perhaps via strategically placed library terminals. Placement of terminals beyond the walls of the library is an issue that most libraries will eventually face.

Number of Terminals

One of the trickiest challenges in moving to an online catalog is the decision regarding the number of terminals that will be needed. There is no precedent in libraries to provide guidelines for resolving this problem. The card catalog has a number of physical access points, which may be used concurrently, while the online catalog provides only one terminal per user.

Research studies with queuing theory as the basis of analysis have been done with card and online catalogs. Two recent studies, one at Northwestern University Library (Knox and Miller, 1980-81) and one at the Dallas Public Library (Borgman and Kaske, 1980), looked at the average arrival rate at the computer terminal and the average search time. These variables were then specified in terms of probabilities with the researchers asking the question: What is the probability of having to wait for a terminal?

The results of a queuing study in one library are not, of course, generalizable to other libraries since the variables are dependent on location. This kind of research would no doubt prove worthwhile in your own library if you have the time, expertise, and willingness to do it. Otherwise, you may do what most libraries seem to be doing: install a number of terminals based on space and budget constraints as well as on your best guess. Several librarians I have talked to have mentioned the figure of one terminal per one hundred users

as a quick and dirty initial estimate.

There are a number of things to consider when you are faced with the decision of how many public terminals to install. I have already mentioned space and cost. You should also realize that usage varies over time and that online catalog usage will most certainly increase over time. Keep in mind too that terminals break down and may have to be replaced temporarily.

Instructional Materials

I'd like to stretch the word ergonomics to include not only furniture and equipment but also the written and online instructional aids for using the online catalog. I have discovered a Murphy's Law that goes something like this: "The longer written instructions are, the less likely they are to be read." The presenters of a paper at the 1984 meeting of the Human Factors Society reported that first time users of online catalogs "...appear to make very rapid judgments as to when they have read enough information to meet their needs."[4] Robert Waite came to a related conclusion: "When people have to operate a new piece of equipment, they learn in the way that requires the least effort."[5]

Based on users' surveys and what we know about human learning and memory, we can come up with a list of characteristics for ergonomic instructional materials. There should be many different kinds, both written and online, because users bring a variety of experiences and learning styles to the online catalog. Written instructions should be as brief as possible; active rather than passive verbs should be employed; examples should be shown and small print and jargon should be avoided. Graphics, underlining, and use of thematic titles help to simplify and organize information.

There seems to be a proliferation this year at LOEX of the flipchart format for point-of-use manuals. To me, this format makes sense because it gives the illusion (correctly or incorrectly) of simplicity. A large amount of information can be packed between its covers and each page can be designed to look uncluttered.

Online help screens have real benefits over written instructions, especially for more sophisticated computer users who are accustomed to online help messages. Having online tutorials abbreviates the need for users to switch formats, from screen to written page, when help is needed and provides help directly at the point the trouble occurs. Some design considerations for written instructions apply to screen design as well. Users will ignore screens that are wall-to-wall words; so, brief is better. Natural language and ample spacing between lines are also important features.

I have addressed some environmental conditions

that can enhance our efforts to teach the use of the online catalog. While the selection and placement of furniture and equipment may seem merely tangential to the teaching of the catalog, studies of catalog use reveal that users themselves are very aware of the human factors involved. It's important to keep in mind that good decisions regarding these environmental conditions may cost no more than bad decisions. In addition, these factors are usually more easily within our control than other things we're called upon to do--for instance, it's impossible to predict or control the number of users who will attend a workshop on the online catalog. Thoughtfully designing this aspect of our education program ensures that users, even when they're teaching themselves, are supported by a user-friendly environment.

NOTES

1. Ralph Caplan, *By Design: Why There Are No Locks on the Bathroom Doors in the Hotel Louis XIV and Other Object Lessons.* (New York: St. Martin's, 1982).

2. J.R. Matthews, G.S. Lawrence, and D.K. Ferguson, *Using Online Catalogs: A Nationwide Survey.* (New York: Neal-Schuman, 1983), 108.

3. Matthews, 103.

4. P.J. Smith, B. Janosky, and C. Hildreth, "Study of the Errors Committed in the Use of an Online Library Catalog System," *Proceedings of the Human Factors Society*, 28th annual meeting, 639-642. (1984).

5. Robert Waite, "Making Information Easy to Use," *ASIS Bulletin* 9 (1982): 34-37.

REFERENCES

Borgman, C.L. and N.K. Kaske, "On-Line Catalogs in the Public Library: A Study to Determine the Number of Terminals Required for Public Access." In *Proceedings of the 43rd Annual Meeting of the American Society for Information Science*, 273-275. 1980.

Knox, A.W. and B.A. Miller, "Predicting the Number of Public Computer Terminals Needed for an On-Line Catalog: A Queuing Theory Approach," *Library Research* 2 (1980-81): 95-100.

Workshop Exercise: Ergonomics and User Education

The Lower Outer Eastern Xanadu (LOEX) University Library has recently installed an automated library system. The original purchase of five public computer terminals has proven to be inadequate to meet the demands of users.

You are a consulting team from the Eastern Innovative Ergonomics Institute of Oswego (E.I.E.I.O.). The LOEX library has hired you to conduct a study and submit a report recommending the appropriate number of terminals needed.

What questions will you ask the librarians in order to determine how many computer terminals are needed for their online catalog?

Preconditions to Teaching the Online Catalog User: Handouts

Selected Bibliography:

Ergonomics and User Education

Borgman, Christine L. and Nela K. Kaske. "On-line catalogs in the public library: A study to determine the number of terminals required for public access." *Proceedings of the 43rd Annual Meeting of the American Society for Information Science* 17 (1980): pp. 273-275.

Crawford, Walt. "VDT checklist: Another look at terminals." *Information Technology and Libraries* 3 (1984): pp. 343-353.

Farkas, David L. "Computer furniture...an expert's guide on how to be comfortable at your micro." *Online* 8 (1984): pp. 43-49.

Kaske, Nela K. and Nancy P. Sanders. *A Comprehensive Study of Online Public Access Catalogs: An Overview and Application of Findings*; Final Report to the Council on Library Resources, Vol. III. Dublin, OH: OCLC, 1983.

Knox, A. Whitney and Bruce A. Miller. "Predicting the number of public computer terminals needed for an on-line catalog: A queuing theory approach." *Library Research* 2 (1980-1981): pp. 95-100.

Markey, Karen. "Offline and online user assistance for online catalog searchers." *Online* 8 (1984): pp. 54-66.

_____. *Online Catalog Use: Results of Surveys and Focus Group Interviews in Several Libraries*; Final Report to the Council on Library Resources, Vol. II. Dublin, OH: OCLC, 1983.

Mason, Robert M. Ergonomics: "The human and the machine." *Library Journal* 109 (15 February 1984): pp. 331-332.

Smith, Philip J., Beverly Janosky, and Charles Hildreth. "Study of the errors committed in the use of an online library catalog system." *Proceedings of the Human Factors Society, 28th annual meeting (1984): pp. 639-642.*

Tolle, John E. *Current Utilization of Online Catalogs: Transaction Log Analysis*; Final Report to the Council on Library Resources, Vol. I. Dublin, OH: OCLC, 1983.

Waite, Robert. "Making information easy to use." *ASIS Bulletin* 9 (1982): pp. 34-37.

Wilson, Linda. "Designing point-of-use instruction for the online catalog." *Library Instruction Round Table News* 7 (1984): pp. 5-6.

Yeaman, Andrew R.J. "Microcomputer learning stations and student health and safety: Planning, evaluation, and revision of physical arrangements." *Educational Technology* 23 (1983): pp. 16-21.

Preconditions to Teaching the Online Catalog User: Handouts

V T L S

(VIRGINIA TECH LIBRARY SYSTEM)

VTLS is an online* catalog which provides access to approximately one-third of the items in the University Libraries. All currently received books and periodicals are in VTLS, as well as most books added or circulated since 1978.

Although the card catalog is still the most complete listing of items in the University Libraries, VTLS has several features which provide additional information for the library user. VTLS can show:

1) whether a books is "available," checked out (and the due date), on reserve, missing, or at the bindery;

2) which volumes of a periodical the library owns, and in what format and location;

3) a list of books in call number order as they would appear on the shelves;

4) whether a "recall" has been placed on a book.

VTLS can be searched by:

```
AUTHOR    (see page 2)
TITLE     (see page 3)
SUBJECT   (see page 3)
CALL #    (see page 4)
```

An easy way to learn to use VTLS is to sit at one of the public terminals and do the sample searches described on the following pages.

First, familiarize yourself with the keyboard. Locate:

1) the 'RETURN' key. This key must be pressed after every command in order to send the message to the computer.

2) the 'BACKSPACE' key. Use this key to correct typing errors.

3) the '/' (slash) key. This is the slash used in search commands.

Another way to learn to use VTLS is to use the 'HELP' screens. Entering '/HELP' retrieves a screen of basic instructions for the various search commands. Entering 'HELP' (without a slash) retrieves a detailed explanation of any screen on display. Look for messages at the bottom of a screen which suggest what to do next. Whenever you have questions about VTLS, please ask a librarian at any of the reference desks.

*Online means that the user can communicate directly with the computer that stores the information.

Preconditions to Teaching the Online Catalog User: Handouts

Sample Author Search

What books does the library have by Ernest Hemingway?

Entering 'A/Hemingway' retrieves a menu of authors with the last name Hemingway. Although entering only the last name of an author is sufficient for searching, adding a comma, space and the first name or initial will result in a more precise retrieval.

Entering '2' (line # of selection) will retrieve a menu of titles by Ernest Hemingway.

```
* A/Hemingway
  --------------------------------- QUALIFYING AUTHORS

  1.     1 Hemingway, Andrew.
  2.    41 Hemingway, Ernest, 1899-1961.
  3.     1 Hemingway, Gregory H.
  4.     1 Hemingway, John.
  5.     1 Hemingway, Leicester.
  6.     1 Hemingway, Mary Moon.
  7.     2 Hemingway, Mary Welsh.
  8.     1 Hemingway, Patricia Drake.
  9.     1 Hemingway, Samuel Burdett.

  PLEASE ENTER NEW COMMAND OR LINE # OF SELECTION
```

LINE #'S.   # of items by this author in VTLS

This screen shows the first 4 of the 41 titles in VTLS by Ernest Hemingway, in alphabetical order by title.

Entering 'NS' (next screen) would retrieve more titles. Entering 'PS' would retrieve the previous screen.

Entering the line # '4' retrieves the ITEM SCREEN for Death in the Afternoon.

```
* 2
  --------------------------- PUBLICATIONS BY SELECTED AUTHOR

  Author:      Hemingway, Ernest, 1899-1961.

  1. Title ------- ACROSS THE RIVER AND INTO THE TREES
     Main author - HEMINGWAY ERNEST 1899-1961

  2. Title ------- BY LINE ERNEST HEMINGWAY SELECTED ARTICLES AND
                   DISPATCHES OF FOUR DECADES EDITED BY WILLIAM WHITE
     Main author - HEMINGWAY ERNEST 1899-1961
     Pub. data --- NEW YORK SCRIBNER 1967

  3. Title ------- COLLECTED POEMS OF ERNEST HEMINGWAY
     Main author - HEMINGWAY ERNEST 1899-1961

  4. Title ------- DEATH IN THE AFTERNOON
     Main author - HEMINGWAY ERNEST 1899-1961
     Pub. data --- NEW YORK SCRIBNER 1932

                                         ENTER 'NS' FOR MORE

  PLEASE ENTER NEW COMMAND OR LINE # OF SELECTION
```

This screen shows the call number for locating the book and notes that its status is CHECKED OUT and due on 11/17/82.

If the book was not checked out, the status line would read 'AVAILABLE.'

```
* 4
  --------------------------------------- ITEM SCREEN

  Call Number - GV1107 H4
  Author ----- Hemingway, Ernest, 1899-1961.
  Title ------- Death in the Afternoon.
  Item Number - 1000088488
  Copy Number - 1               ......HISTORICAL DATA.......
  Location ---- Newman          Entry date into system: 01/01/81
  Loan Period - 90              Circulation count to date:  14
  Status:  CHECKED OUT ON 10/18/82   DUE 11/17/82
  PLEASE ENTER NEW COMMAND OR 'HELP' FOR ASSISTANCE
```

Corporate authors also may be searched on VTLS. As shown here, entry of the main body or group retrieves that group as well as any of its subdivisions which have authored works that are in VTLS.

```
* A/VIRGINIA EMPLOYMENT COMMISSION
  --------------------------------- QUALIFYING AUTHORS

  1.    27 Virginia Employment Commission.
  2.     1 Virginia Employment Commission.  Division of Research and
           Analysis.
  3.     1 Virginia.  Employment Commission.  Labor Market Information
           Unit.
  4.    35 Virginia Employment Commission.  Manpower Research
           Division.
  5.     2 Virginia Employment Commission.  Office of Research and
           Analysis.
  6.     1 Virginia.  Employment Commission.  Research, Statistics
           and Information Division.

  PLEASE ENTER NEW COMMAND OR LINE # OF SELECTION
```

*These are commands entered by the user.

Preconditions to Teaching the Online Catalog User: Handouts

Sample Title Search

Does the library have the book From Genesis to Genocide?

To search by title, enter the command 'T/' followed by the entire title. Or, to save key strokes, use the title search keys. For titles of three words or less, enter a 3 2 1 key: first 3 letters of the first word (space), first 2 letters of the second word (space), and first letter of the third word (return key). For titles of four words or more, use a 5 2 1 2 2 key for the most precise retrieval.

In this example, the title search key 'T/FROM GE T GE' retrieves a menu of four different titles. Entering '3' for line #3 retrieves the ITEM SCREEN, indicating the call number, location and status.

To find more complete bibliographic information on this book, entry of the command 'CA' retrieves the bibliographic (or card) screen.

```
* T/FROM GE T GE
- - - - - - - - - - - - - - - - - - - - - - - - - - - - QUALIFYING TITLES
  1. From Generation to Generation; Age Groups and Social Structu
  2. From generation to generation : how to trace your Jewish family
     history and genealogy / Arthur Kurzweil.
  3. From genesis to genocide : the meaning of human nature and
     the power of behavior control /  Stephan L. Chorover.
  4. From Geography to Geotechnics.

PLEASE ENTER NEW COMMAND OR LINE # OF SELECTION
* 3
- - - - - - - - - - - - - - - - - - - - - - - - - - - ITEM SCREEN
  Call Number - HM73 C49
  Author ------ Chorover, Stephen L.
  Title ------- From genesis to genocide : the meaning of human nature...
  Item Number - 1000362319
  Copy Number - 1            ......... HISTORICAL DATA ...........
  Location ---- Newman       Entry date into system: 01/01/81
  Loan Period - 90           Circulation count to date:  0
  Status:  AVAILABLE
PLEASE ENTER NEW COMMAND OR 'HELP' FOR ASSISTANCE
* CA
- - - - - - - - - - - - - - - - - - - - - - - - - BIBLIOGRAPHIC SCREEN
  HM73 C49

  Chorover, Stephen L.

  From genesis to genocide :  the meaning of human nature
  and the power of behavior control / Stephan L. Chorover.
  Cambridge, Mass. :  MIT Press, c1979.

  xiii, 238 p. ;  24 cm.

  Includes bibliographical references and index.

  SOCIAL CONTROL.
  HUMAN BEHAVIOR.
  POWER (SOCIAL SCIENCES)

PLEASE ENTER 'C' FOR CIRCULATION INFORMATION
```

Sample Subject Search

What books does the library have on human behavior?

First, identify the correct subject to use. By using the Library of Congress Subject Headings (LCSH--found near any reference desk or the card catalog), the appropriate heading can be found. Personal names and place names not in LCSH may also be searched on VTLS. Items can only be retrieved by subject by using the subject headings assigned to them.

As shown here, entry of 'S/HUMAN BEHAVIOR' retrieves that subject heading and any subheadings attached to that subject.

Entering '1' retrieves the first three of the 37 titles on the general subject 'Human behavior' in VTLS.

```
* S/HUMAN BEHAVIOR
- - - - - - - - - - - - - - - - - - - - - - - - - - QUALIFYING SUBJECTS
  1.   37 Human behavior.
  2.    1 Human behavior -- Bibliography.
  3.    7 Human behavior -- Congresses.
  4.    1 Human behavior -- Genetic aspects -- Congresses.
  5.    1 Human behavior -- Juvenile literature.
  6.    1 Human behavior -- Mathematical models.
  7.    1 Human behavior -- Mathematical models -- Congresses.
  8.    2 Human behavior -- Nutritional aspects.
  9.   11 Human behavior -- Periodicals.
 10.    1 Human behavior -- Study and teaching.

PLEASE ENTER NEW COMMAND OR LINE # OF SELECTION
* 1
- - - - - - - - - - - - - - - - - - PUBLICATIONS ON SELECTED SUBJECT
   Subject:    Human behavior.

  1.  Title ------ ARCHITECTURE FOR HUMAN BEHAVIOR COLLECTED PAPERS
                   FROM A MINI CONFERENCE
      Main author - BURNETTE CHARLES
      Pub. data --- PHILADELPHIA AMERICAN INSTITUTE OF ARCHITECTS
                    PHILADELPHIA CHAPTER 1971

  2.  Title ------ ATTENTION AND SELF REGULATION A CONTROL THEORY
                   APPROACH TO HUMAN BEHAVIOR / CHARLES S CARVER
                   MICHAEL F SCHEIER
      Main author - CARVER CHARLES S
      Pub. data --- NEW YORK SPRINGER VERLAG C1981

  3.  Title ------ BIOLOGY AND SOCIAL BEHAVIOR BY ALLAN MAZUR AND
                   LEON S ROBERTSON
      Main author - MAZUR ALLAN
      Pub. data --- NEW YORK FREE PRESS 1972
                                       ENTER 'NS' FOR MORE
PLEASE ENTER NEW COMMAND OR LINE # OF SELECTION
```

These are commands entered by the user.

Preconditions to Teaching the Online Catalog User: Handouts

Sample Call Number Search

How many copies of TA645 G65 1978B does the library have? Where are they?

To search by call number, enter 'C/' followed by the entire call number (note spacing).

This screen indicates that copy 2 is on Newman Reserve, copies 1 and 3 are available, and copy 4 is checked out from the Architecture Library until 1/12/83.

```
* C/TA645 G65 1978B
--------------------------------- MENU OF COPIES AND VOLUMES

Call No:  TA645 G65 1978B
Author:  Gordon, James Edward, 1913-
Title:  Structures: or, Why Things Don't Fall Down/J.E. . . .

    LOCATION         STATUS          ITEM-ID       COPY      UNITS
1.  Newman           Available       1000396040    c.1
2.  Newman           Newman Reserve  1000396041    c.2
3.  Newman           Available       1000396042    c.3
4.  Architecture     Due 1/12/83     1000128945    c.4
PLEASE ENTER NEW COMMAND OR LINE# OF SELECTION
```

Sample Call Number Browse

What books are in the call number area BF575 S75, which covers the subject of stress?

Entering 'C/' and a portion of a call number retrieves a listing of books in call number order as they would appear on the shelves if all of the books were available.

```
* C/BF575 S75
--------------------------------- QUALIFYING CALL NUMBERS

1.  BF575 S75 P3
    Parad, Howard J.    /Crisis Intervention: Selected Readings.
2.  BF575 S75 P33
    Parrino, John J., d/From panic to power : b the positive use of s
3.  BF575 S75 R68
    Rourke, Byron P.    /Explorations in the Psychology of Stress and A
4.  BF575 S75 S44
    Selye, Hans.        /Stress Without Distress.
5.  BF575 S75 S76
    Stress and Anxiety.

                        ENTER 'NS' FOR MORE

PLEASE ENTER NEW COMMAND OR LINE # OF SELECTION
```

Sample Holdings Search

Where are the back issues of the periodical Nation (call number AP2 N2)?

'H/' followed by the call number is the command for a holdings search. This screen indicates main location (Newman) and that Nation is currently received.

<u>Lines 1 & 2</u>: The library has, in bound volumes, v.5 no.11-v.231, except that "scattered holdings" indicates numerous breaks in the holdings. Consult a librarian to find out exact holdings.
<u>Line 3</u>: Volumes 188 through 233 are also available on microfilm.
<u>Line 4</u>: The location of the bound volumes held in the v.5-220 range is Cheds, the off-site storage facility.
<u>Lines 5 & 7</u>: The locations OMI and SMI indicate "ordering missing issues" and "searching missing issues," respectively. The issue numbers for v.232 and v.233 can be obtained by consulting a librarian.
<u>Line 6</u>: Volume 234 is at the bindery and will be available 9/14/82.

Under 'S' (Special Status), line 1 indicates that volume 121 (year 1925) was declared missing from Cheds on 4/11/82.

*These are commands entered by the user.

```
* H/AP2 N2
--------------------------------- HOLDINGS SCREEN
AP2 N2
Nation.
LOCATION:  Newman          MBR 08/01/74
HOLDINGS:                  CURRENTLY RECEIVED.
1.  v.5 no.11-v.231, Aug.15, 1867-1980,
2.  scattered holdings.
3.  Film, v.188-233, Jan.1959-1981.      Micro/Newm
4.  Cheds, v.5-220                       Cheds
5.  v.232, no.1-2, 4-25                              OMI
6.  v.234                                    AT BINDERY 09/14/82
7.  v.233 no. 1-6, 8-22                      SMI
PLEASE ENTER NEW COMMAND OR 'C' FOR CIRCULATION INFORMATION
PLEASE ENTER 'S' TO DISPLAY ITEMS WITH SPECIAL STATUS
* S

    ITEM ID     COPY   LOCATION    STATUS    DATE    REP   UNITS
1.  1000138120   1     Cheds       MISSING   04/11/82 01   v.121 1925
PLEASE ENTER NEW COMMAND OR 'HELP' FOR ASSISTANCE
```

(These line #'s will not appear on your screen)

Preconditions to Teaching the Online Catalog User: Handouts

Teaching The Online Catalog:

Mankato State University

Sandra K. Ready

In the fall of 1980, Memorial Library became the first operational site of the Minnesota State University System Project for Automated Library Systems (MSUS/PALS, known as the PALS system). It was at this time that the Mankato State University librarians began grappling with the problem of user instruction for online catalogs. Possessing a brand new, essentially untested public online catalog (the OLC), they faced the prospect of educating a university community of over 14,000 untrained catalog users.

The PALS catalog is a command-driven system offering five different basic search types:

1. author (last name, first name, middle initial);
2. title (first four title words);
3. combination author-title (author's last name, first title word);
4. subject (Library of Congress subject heading); and
5. term (word/s out of context)

Boolean word and set searches are available; letters, words, and phrases may be truncated; and searches may be limited by date of publication, format of material, and language of text.

Since all seven Minnesota State University libraries are PALS users and are linked via computer, searches may be conducted on the home library collection, on any other member's collection, or on the entire systemwide collection.

In the summer of 1985, the online circulation module for the system was added. From any public terminal, users are able to learn the building location and availability of any bar coded item. The circula-

Ready is Department Chair and Bibliographic Instruction Librarian at Mankato State University.

tion module also enables users to place reservation holds on items currently circulating.

The PALS system, together with its microfiche back up, is the only materials catalog in use at Mankato State. The card catalog was frozen in the fall of 1980 and removed by the fall of 1981.

ONLINE CATALOG INSTRUCTION

Introduction

Initially, all library professionals and paraprofessionals were involved with catalog-use instruction. Catalogers, technicians, and acquisitions and data processing personnel joined with reference, instruction, and circulation staff in an attempt to provide as much instruction and information about the catalog as possible.

Rather than schedule classroom instruction sessions, library staff offered large public demonstrations to anyone interested. A catalog terminal equipped with a video monitor was set up in the library's main catalog room. Librarians and paraprofessionals took turns staffing the demonstration unit while the library was open. Demonstrations were presented to groups ranging in size from three people to more than twenty. This demonstration schedule continued for several weeks.

Eventually, peak demand periods were identified, demonstrations were scheduled and publicized, and drop-in attendance was encouraged.

The main thrust of the OLC demonstrations during the first year was to show the audience how to operate the terminal, how the commands were structured, and how to conduct a simple information search. Demonstrators explained the searching help available from the OLC itself, and pointed out the printed materials available as well. Members of the audience were encouraged to return to the library to experiment with the new system and to ask for assistance whenever they felt they needed it. The twenty-five public-use terminals (all in the library) were geographically placed near staffing points to facilitate such requests.

Recognizing that a goal of personally instructing over 14,000 users would be unrealistic, librarians at Mankato State have developed numerous vehicles for providing instruction in online catalog use. Printed materials, workshops, credit courses, and self-instructional tapes provide a wide variety of instructional opportunities.

Printed materials include a one-page basic introductory sheet (Example A), a one-page reserve reading sheet (Example B), a brief terminal attachment (Example C), and a basic user's guide

(Example D). These materials are available to all users. Help is also available online in the PALS catalog.

Each fall at the opening of the school, workshops are offered to new faculty, entering freshmen, and transfer students. In addition a one-hour, drop-in workshop is offered weekly throughout the school year to enable any user to attend.

To meet the needs of those unable to attend workshop sessions, four self-instructional tapes, which allow users to be introduced to the OLC through an audiotaped orientation, have been developed. The tapes are available in all areas of the library.

CLASSROOM INSTRUCTION

As might be expected, requests from university faculty for bibliographic instruction skyrocketed with the installation of the OLC. Faculty members volunteered that while, in the past, they had assumed their students knew how to utilize the library's card catalog, the new OLC demanded that they have special instruction in appropriate searching techniques.

For over eight years, the library staff had included two full-time librarians dedicated solely to instructional services. At the installation of the OLC, each was spending approximately thirty percent of the time in course-related and course-integrated instruction. By shifting some of their additional responsibilities to other staff members and adding a half-time librarian to the Instructional Services staff, the library director enabled classroom instruction to be expanded. During the OLC's first year, Instructional Services librarians spent over sixty percent of their time doing classroom library instruction. With the cooperation of other library staff members, they were able to cope with the increased demand.

Content of Instruction

In order to determine what to teach and the order of presentation of the concepts, librarians began by examining how library staff had learned to use the catalog. Like children who must learn to walk before they can run, staff needed to learn the basic searching strategy before limiting, set searching, or system searching skills could be added. Basic searching skills provided the foundation for more sophisticated techniques. Working from this principle, librarians examined skill levels and the order for their presentation.

Based on the skill building principle, three general levels were identified. At the basic level, a beginning user with little or no prior experience with the OLC would be introduced to the simple search procedure and to the five major search approaches available (author, title, combination, subject, and term). Once the basic level was understood, search limiting and word or phrase truncation could be added. Finally, when a user had mastered basic searching and search limiting, he would be prepared for Boolean set searching and system searching. The levels would be presented when the user was ready, by virtue of prior experience with the catalog, to learn them.

Librarians assumed that all three levels of skill could not be taught in one session. All system capabilities could be demonstrated, but a user could not be expected to absorb them all in one sitting. Time and practice would be needed between skill presentations before a user would be prepared to progress.

It was also assumed that all instruction required the use of a terminal and actual interaction with the system. To accommodate this need, library classrooms were equipped with terminals and television monitors adapted for computer display. Librarians decided that all group instruction in the use of the OLC would always take place in one of the specially modified classrooms.

Determining the skill level of a particular group poses an especially difficult problem. Invariably, with the exception of entering freshmen, a class will contain a mixed level of skills. A session typically is begun by asking the group, "How many of you have used the online catalog successfully more than twice?" If the majority does not raise their hands, the basic level is presented; if the majority of hands are raised, the basics are reviewed and the instruction focuses on search limiting and truncation. The primary goal is to have the majority of users comfortable through the second skill level, which makes use of the advantages of the technology.

The information needs of a particular group also affect the instruction. While freshmen rarely need Boolean set searching or system searching to conduct their research, upper division students often do. Graduate students must always use more sophisticated searching techniques to conduct their research adequately. No instruction is presented until the faculty member has been consulted to determine the needs of the group. If the assigned research project would require the use of typical card catalog materials (e.g., books), the OLC must be included as a part of the session. On the other hand, if a project would require exclusively information sources not typically found in a card catalog (e.g., journal article references), the OLC would be excluded from the lecture.

Any presentation including instruction in use of the OLC must also include a brief explanation of the contents of the OLC database, and more importantly, what is not included in the database. This is especially important, since users tend to assume the computer will list "everything there is to know" about a topic, when, in reality, it currently lists only information sources one would typically expect to find using a traditional card catalog.

Believing that information retrieval is a process and should be taught as such, Mankato State instruction librarians are concerned that too much emphasis not be put on just one of the tools used in the process and that equally important tools not be overlooked. They are convinced that what users learn ought to be transferable--students ought not to learn how to use a specific library, but rather should learn how to use libraries in the information gathering process, rather than strictly online catalog use.

When planning an instructional session, the first step in determining whether OLC use instruction should be included is to ask, "Does the OLC provide information appropriate to this class on this topic?" If the answer is "yes," the second question is, "What specific strategies will provide what these students need?" The identified strategies, together with suggestions for effective and efficient limiting, truncation, or set searching techniques, are then incorporated into the instruction.

The planning, of course, rarely stops with the OLC. The search strategy approach used at Mankato State necessitates that other reference materials, indexes, abstracts, and a discussion of their relevance to the search at hand be included when appropriate. This is best illustrated by two examples. In one class, a history instructor may assign a class to research a topic related to the American Civil War and require them to use primary information resources. He requests library instruction when he realizes the students are unable to cope with the assignment on their own. A sociology instructor may assign students reading in contemporary social work journals. She requests library instruction since her objective is to familiarize the students with their professional journals and the appropriate tools for accessing them.

In the first case, the library instruction would include a discussion of narrowing the topic, sources for background information, use of the OLC, and other sources for identifying primary literature of the Civil War period. In the second, since the sociology professor's objective is to familiarize the students with journal material and indexing and abstracting tools, the instruction would include a discussion of why the OLC would be an inappropriate tool to use and focus on appropriate strategies for identifying and obtaining social work journal material.

When determining content for instructional sessions, a variety of questions need to be answered. About the catalog itself...

1. What must ALL users know

   - about the database?
   - about the equipment?

2. Where or how does the user get help?

To prepare for the instructional session...

The librarian needs to know

- what are you expected to include?
- how much time is AVAILABLE?
- how much time is NEEDED?
- how skilled will the students be?
- what level of research is expected of the students?
- will the students have a library assignment?
- will the information needed be accessible in the catalog?

LIBRARY
CATALOG ACCESS SYSTEM

BASIC DIRECTIONS

library
mankato state
minnesota

1. To send all messages to the computer, you must depress the "New Line" key.

2. To correct a typing error, press the "Back Space" key and retype.

3. A space is essential after all commands (CO, AU, etc.) and between all words.

4. Do not hesitate to ask a librarian for assistance.

   NOTE: For a complete explanation of all search commands, type: HELP

SEARCHING BY AUTHOR AND TITLE

When you know both the author and title of a work, the combination search is the best way to find out if the library has the work.

To search by author/title combination:

1. Type: CO AUTHOR'S LAST NAME, FIRST TITLE WORD
   (leave off "a", "an", or "the" at the beginning of the title)

2. Depress the "New Line" key.

For example, to search for Ernest Hemingway's, <u>The Sun Also Rises</u>, type:

   CO HEMINGWAY SUN

SEARCHING BY TITLE

To find out if the library has a book when you know only the title:

1. Type: TI TITLE OF BOOK
   (leave off "a", "an", or "the" at the beginning of the title)

2. Depress the "New Line" key.

For example, to search for the title, <u>The Old Man and the Sea</u>, type:

   TI OLD MAN AND THE SEA

SEARCHING BY AUTHOR

To obtain a list of books that the library has by an author:

1. Type: AU LAST NAME, FIRST NAME, MIDDLE INITIAL
   (if you know only part of the name, enter as much as you know)

2. Depress the "New Line" key.

For example, to search for the author Ernest Hemingway, type:

   AU HEMINGWAY ERNEST

Teaching the Online Catalog: Handouts

BASIC DIRECTIONS, CONTINUED

✻ SEARCHING BY SUBJECT

Before conducting a subject search, it is a good idea to consult <u>Library of Congress Subject Headings</u> (a large, red two-volume set of books located near the terminal) to be sure your subject heading is used. Subjects you can use are printed in bold type ————————————

To get a list of books we have in our library on a subject:

    1. Type:

      SU SUBJECT HEADING FOR YOUR TOPIC #

    2. Depress the "New Line" key.

For example, to search for information on the topic "learning handicaps", type:

      SU LEARNING DISABILITIES #

Always type the # sign after your subject heading for best results.

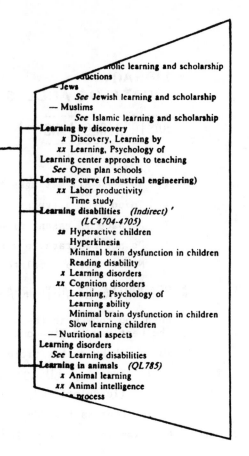

— ...holic learning and scholarship
    ...ductions
— Jews
      See Jewish learning and scholarship
— Muslims
      See Islamic learning and scholarship
Learning by discovery
    x Discovery, Learning by
    xx Learning, Psychology of
Learning center approach to teaching
    See Open plan schools
Learning curve (Industrial engineering)
    xx Labor productivity
        Time study
Learning disabilities *(Indirect)* '
      (LC4704-4705)
    sa Hyperactive children
        Hyperkinesia
        Minimal brain dysfunction in children
        Reading disability
    x Learning disorders
    xx Cognition disorders
        Learning, Psychology of
        Learning ability
        Minimal brain dysfunction in children
        Slow learning children
— Nutritional aspects
Learning disorders
    See Learning disabilities
Learning in animals *(QL785)*
    x Animal learning
    xx Animal intelligence
    ...process

✻ SEARCHING BY TERMS

Use term searching when you do not know the Library of Congress Subject Heading or when you wish to broaden your search. Searching by "term" means that you have the computer look for specific words supplied by you. You may instruct the computer to look for a single word or for several words.

SINGLE TERM SEARCH

    1. Type: TE WORD YOU HAVE CHOSEN

    2. Depress the "New Line" key.

For example, if you are interested in "wolves", type:

                TE WOLVES

MULTIPLE TERM SEARCH (using 2 or more words)

    1. Type: TE WORD AND WORD AND WORD ...

    2. Depress the "New Line" key.

For example, if you are interested in "discrimination against women in employment", type:

    TE DISCRIMINATION AND WOMEN AND EMPLOYMENT

It is possible to form other search combinations using Boolean operators (and, or, not) - see the Librarian.

NOTICE - Any record displayed tells you the subject heading for your topic. You may want to do a Subject Search using this subject heading.

10/81

Teaching the Online Catalog: Handouts

LIBRARY
CATALOG ACCESS SYSTEM: RESERVE READING MATERIALS

HOW TO LOCATE RESERVE READING MATERIALS

---

1. To send all messages to the computer, you must depress the "New Line" key.

2. To correct a typing error, press the "Back Space" key and retype.

3. A space is essential after the reserve command (RES) and between all words.

4. Do not hesitate to ask a librarian for assistance.

   NOTE: For a complete explanation of all reserve search commands, type: HELP RES

⁑ SEARCHING BY INSTRUCTOR

To locate reserve reading materials listed by instructor:

   1. Type: RES INSTRUCTOR LAST NAME, FIRST NAME

   2. Depress the "New Line" key.

For example, to search for reserve reading materials listed for classes taught by Professor Joseph Lee, type:

   RES LEE, JOSEPH

NOTE: Reserved readings can be found using an instructor's last name when first name is not known. Be aware that this may result in matches for professors in addition to the one you seek.

⁑ SEARCHING BY DEPARTMENT NAME

To locate reserve reading materials listed by department name:

   1. Type: RES DEPARTMENT NAME

   2. Depress the "New Line" key.

For example, to search for reserve reading materials listed for classes taught in the Economics Department, type:

   RES ECONOMICS

Teaching the Online Catalog: Handouts

HOW TO LOCATE RESERVE READING MATERIALS, CONTINUED

⁑ SEARCHING BY DEPARTMENT NAME AND INSTRUCTOR

To locate reserve reading materials listed by department name and instructor:

1. Type: RES DEPARTMENT NAME and INSTRUCTOR

2. Depress the "New Line" key.

For example, to search for reserve reading materials listed for classes taught by Professor Joseph Lee in the Economics Department, type:

RES ECONOMICS LEE

NOTE: A reserve reading search may be done on any on-line catalog terminal. Reserve readings are available at the 2nd Floor Circulation Desk.

⁑ SEARCHING BY TITLE

To locate reserve reading materials listed by title:

1. Type: RES TITLE

2. Depress the "New Line" key.

For example, to search for reserve reading materials listed by the title of the reading, type:

RES GRIEVANCE GUIDE

⁑ SEARCHING BY COURSE NAME

To locate reserve reading materials listed by course name:

1. Type: RES COURSE NAME

2. Depress the "New Line" key.

For example, to search for reserve reading materials listed by the name of the course, type:

RES GOVERNMENT REGULATIONS

9/85

Teaching the Online Catalog: Handouts

EXAMPLE C

Mankato
STATE UNIVERSITY

Library
MSU Box 19
Mankato State University
Mankato, Minnesota 56001
(507) 389-5952

ONLINE CATALOG COMMANDS

BE Begin
HELP Help online instructions

SEARCHING
AU Author (last name, first name, middle initial)
TI Title (first four title words)
CO Combination author/title (author last name, first title word)
SU Subject (LC Subject Heading only)
TE Term* (word from any indexed field)
AT Author term* (except personal names)
TT Title term* (word from subject heading)
ST Subject term* (word from subject heading)
  * use *and, or,* or *not* between words
BR Browse alphabetic sequence (use search keys—BR TE trees, BR AU Smith)

LIMITING (enter searching command prior to limiting search)
Publication Date:
GT Greater than (publication year after year inserted— e.g. GT 1974)
LT Less than (publication year prior to year inserted— e.g. LT 1945)
EQ Equal to (publication year identical to year inserted— e.g. EQ 1980)
Language of Text: (use first 3 letters of language desired—e.g. LA GER)
Format of Material:
FO Format (use with 2-letter abbreviation—e.g. FO MO)

AV Audiovisual	**MA** Map	**SE** Serial
BO Book	**MI** Microform	**SL** Slide
DI Disk (floppy)	**MO** Motion picture	**SO** Sound recording
FI Filmstrip	**OT** Other	**VI** Video recording
KI Kit	**SC** Score	

BA Back up to search results preceding limiting command

DISPLAY (enter searching command prior to displaying results)
DI Display (use with item numbers—DI 1-10 or DI 14 or DI 1-3, 7)
  Length Option (use with item number)
  S Short (location, author, title—DI 3 S)
  M Medium (usual format—DI 5)
  L Long (full bibliographic information—DI 5 L)

DS Display status (enter after display of individual record. Retrieves information about availability of item.)

HLD Hold (places reservation on desired items which are currently checked out.)

RE Recall brief entry listing

PRINTING BIBLIOGRAPHIES
PRINT Order overnight printing

an affirmative action/equal opportunity university

Teaching the Online Catalog: Handouts

Library Users and Online Systems:

Suggested Objectives for Library Instruction

Deborah Masters

Prepared for the Direct Patron Access to Computer-Based Reference Systems Committee, Machine-Assisted Reference Section, Reference and Adult Services Division, American Library Association, January 1985.

INTRODUCTION

The widespread use of personal computers in the home and in the office, combined with the increasing availability of various types of automated information systems in libraries, have opened up an important new area of user education. In libraries, many of these automated information systems are used directly and do not required the personal assistance of librarians as intermediaries between the library user and the information. Librarians want the users of these systems to be self-reliant and successful in accessing needed information. There is an expanding need to instruct library patrons who directly use online catalogs, online circulation systems, and other bibliographic and nonbibliographic databases. Librarians have a responsibility to develop instructional programs that will enable users to be successful with all types of online systems through the effective use of learned information access skills. During the 1982 Annual American Library Association Conference, the Direct Patron Access to Computer-Based Reference Systems Committee undertook a project to establish learning objectives for training direct users of computer-based information systems. The members of the committee developed a draft of generic learning objectives for training searchers. Comments on the draft were solicited from the RASD membership by means of

Masters is Head of Reference and Bibliographic Instruction at George Washington University.

an announcement placed in *RASD Update*.

SCOPE AND PURPOSE

The objectives developed are designed to serve as guidelines for library instruction where any online system is used directly by patrons. They are intended for librarians who have responsibility for devising instructional programs for online systems in school, special, public, or academic libraries. These objectives provide an outline of general topics and skills to be covered in classroom or individual instruction. They may also be used by librarians who are seeking guidance for preparing printed or online instructional aids. A selected bibliography for further reading about online searching and the training of users follows the objectives.

INSTRUCTIONAL OBJECTIVES

1. *Understanding the system*
1.1 The user will know which online systems are available and what each system represents.
1.1.1 The user will understand the relationships among the various online and manual systems provided by the library and will be able to choose the most appropriate system to satisfy a particular information need.
1.1.2 The user will be able to define the scope of each system in terms of the types of material included and the subjects and time or other periods covered. The user will also know which kinds of information are unique to a particular system.
1.1.3 The user will be aware of any fees incurred in using a particular system.
2. *Planning the search strategy*
2.1 The user will be able to analyze each information need and develop a search strategy appropriate to the need and the system.
2.1.1 The user will be able to identify the various files that are available in the system.
2.1.2 The user will know which access points may be used within a particular file to retrieve information.
2.1.3 The user will understand the syntax and function of Boolean operators and will be able to use them to search the files in the system.
2.1.4 If the online system is under authority control, the user will understand the relationship between the authority file and other

files in the system and will be able to identify and use authoritative access points to search the system.
2.1.5 The user will understand the difference between free text and controlled vocabulary searching and will be able to determine which approach to use for the best search results.
2.1.6 The user will know how to select the search strategy that is the most efficient and uses the least amount of machine resources.
2.1.7 The user will understand how to narrow or broaden a search strategy.
2.1.8 The user will be aware of significant limitations of the online system.
3. *Operating the system*
3.1 The user will be able to operate the system in an efficient manner.
3.1.1 The user will be able to operate the terminal and any auxiliary equipment or devices.
3.1.2 If necessary, the user will be able to log-on and log-off the system.
3.1.3 The user will be able to access the various files within the system.
3.1.4 The user will be able to enter search commands correctly.
3.1.5 If a choice is available, the user will be able to select the appropriate display format.
3.1.6 The user will be able to use the appropriate command(s) to page through a list of display results or to move forward or backward in the system.
3.1.7 The user will be able to comprehend and to respond appropriately to error messages and to other system prompts.
3.2 The user will be able to obtain assistance in the use of the system.
3.2.1 The user will be aware of available online help commands and will be able to use them as needed.
3.2.2 The user will be aware of any available written aids or human resources that may be consulted for assistance.
3.2.3 The user will know when it is necessary or appropriate to refer a search to a search intermediary.
4. *Interpreting the search results*
4.1 The user will understand how to interpret the search results and how to obtain the needed information.
4.1.1 The user will be able to identify the elements of a search display and will be able to determine which elements are relevant in retrieving the needed information.

4.1.2 When more than one item of information is retrieved in the system, the user will understand the order in which items are displayed.

4.1.3 The user will understand any instructions or procedures necessary to obtain the information or the sources of information retrieved as a result of the search.

SECOND BIENNIAL LOEX LIBRARY INSTRUCTION WORKSHOP: TEACHING THE ONLINE CATALOG USER

Library Users and Online Systems: Suggested Objectives for Library Instruction
Follow-Up Work Session: Applying Objectives to Systems

1. *Understanding the system*
1.1 What online systems are available in your library? What online systems are available in other area libraries that users might have previously experienced? Keep in mind that COM catalogs in public libraries may be easily confused with an online catalog.

1.1.1 How does your online catalog or circulation system relate to your card catalog? Does the online system include full MARC records? Is full cataloging information readily available to users of the online system in a user-friendly format? Are there unique access points in the online or manual system?

1.1.2 Does the online system exclude any particular categories of material (e.g., non-Roman alphabets) that users must locate in other catalogs? Are government documents included in either the manual or the online catalog?

2. *Planning the search strategy*
2.1.2 What access points are available in the online catalog? Author? Separate personal and corporate author fields? Title? Combination of author and title? Call number? Subject? Other? Key word approach to title and/or subject? Controlled vocabulary for subject headings?

2.1.3 Are Boolean operators available? Are codes or symbols used to represent these? How can the effect of Boolean operators on the search results best be explained to the user?

2.1.4 Does the online system have authority control? If so, how does the user identify authorized headings?

2.1.6 Which searchers are most efficient on the system? Given several pieces of information (e.g., author, title, call number), what should be the user's first choice in trying to retrieve the record from the system?

2.1.7 What methods are available to narrow or broaden a search? Can search results be limited by date? By language? Can the user browse call numbers or subject headings? Can he or she browse "see and "see also" reference in subject headings?

2.1.8 What limitations should the user be aware of in using the system?

3. *Operating the system*
3.1.1 What particular features of the terminal or auxiliary devices require explanation? Is the "return" or "enter" key clearly labeled? Is the backspace key indentifiable? If there are printing capabilities, is the use of the printer self-explanatory?

3.1.2 Does the system require the user to log-on or log-off?

3.1.3 Is there more than one file available on the system? If so, how does the user select the needed file?

3.1.4 What are the requirements for entering search commands? Is particular spacing required? Is punctuation required? Does a search code identifying the type of search precede or follow the information for that search?

3.1.5 What display formats are available? How does the user select a display format?

3.1.6 What commands enable the user to move back and forth in the system? How are these commands entered?

3.1.7 What kinds of error messages or system prompts can the user expect? What response is expected to these prompts?

3.2.1 What help screens are available? How does the user retrieve these help screens?

3.2.2 What written aids or library staff assistance are available? When should the user use these resources?

4. *Interpreting search results.*
4.1.1 What are the elements of the search display? Are different elements included in different displays? What elements are necessary for the user to locate the item in the library? How are they identified on the screen?

4.1.2 In what order are search results displayed? What influence does that order have on the user's search strategy or interpretation of search results?

4.1.3 Once the user identifies the needed items from a search, what does he/she do next?

BIBLIOGRAPHY

Association of Research Libraries. *User Instructions for Online Catalogs in ARL Libraries.* System and Procedures Exchange Center. (SPEC Kit 93). Washington, DC: Association of Research Libraries. Office of Management Studies, 1983.

Borgman, Christine L., Dineh Moghdam, and Patti K. Corbett. *Effective Online Searching: A Basic Text.* New York: Marcel Dekker, 1984.

Hildreth, Charles R. *Online Public Access Catalogs: The User Interface.* Dublin, OH: OCLC, 1982.

Matthews, Joseph R., Gary S. Lawrence, and Douglas K. Ferguson, eds. *Using Online Catalogs: A National Survey. A Report of a Study Sponsored by the Council on Library Resources.* New York: Neal-Schuman, 1983.

Ritch, Alan. "Teaching MELVYL: A Research Study." *DLA Bulletin* 4, no. 2 (October 1984): 4-7.

SECOND BIENNIAL LOEX LIBRARY INSTRUCTION WORKSHOP

TEACHING THE ONLINE CATALOG USER

Library Users and Online Systems: Suggested Objectives for Library Instruction

Followup work session: Applying Objectives to Systems

In order to facilitate organizing groups of people whose libraries
are currently using or plan to implement common systems, please identify
the online catalog or circulation system used in your library:

____ Advanced Library Concepts (AdLib)

____ Biblio-Techniques (Biblio-Techniques Library Information System BLIS)

____ C L Systems, Inc. (CLSI)

____ Comstow Information Services (Biblio-Tech Library Software)

____ Data Phase (ALIS)

____ Data Research Associates (ATLAS)

____ Dynix

____ Electric Memory Inc. (EMILS/3000)

____ Geac

____ Georgetown University Medical Center Library (Library Information System)

____ Innovative Interfaces (INNOVACQ)

____ Library Control System (LCS)

____ M/A-COM Information Systems, Inc. (formerly M/A-COM Sigma Data) (DATALIB)

____ Northwestern University (NOTIS)

____ OCLC Local Systems (LS/2000)

____ Pennsylvania State University Libraries (Library Information Automated
        System LIAS)

____ Sedna Corporation (Sedna Information Management System SIMS)

____ Sirsi Corporation (Unicorn Collection Management System)

____ Sperry Corporation (PALS Automated Library System)

Library Users and Online Systems: Handouts

Library Users and Online Systems: Suggested Objectives for Library Instruction

Followup work session: Applying Objectives to Systems

____ Sydney Dataproducts Inc. (Easy Data Library System)

____ Systemhouse Business Systems Ltd. (MINISIS)

____ Systems Control, Inc. (SCICON)

____ Universal Library Systems (ULISYS)

____ Virginia Tech (VTLS)

____ Washington University School of Medicine Library (Bibliographic
        Access & Control System BACS)

____ Other (Please specify) _____

Are bibliographic utilities available for direct use by patrons in
your library? If so, please check below the systems available this way:

____ OCLC

____ RLIN

____ Other (Please specify) _____

Thumbing the Cards:

The Online Catalog,

the Faculty and Instruction

Marcella Stark and Mary Anne Waltz

The decision to call the presentation "thumbing the cards" was made quickly, flippantly, and with a sense of irony. But when we thought seriously about which of our experiences in teaching the online catalog to faculty we could share with you beyond what was reported in *College and Research Library News*, the title suddenly seemed apt. As any of you who have observed online catalog users or studied the transaction logs of those catalogs can attest, mentally thumbing cards while pressing an "enter," "search," or "return" key is exactly what many users of the online catalog are likely to do. Can one generalize that the longer an individual has used libraries and their catalogs, the more likely one will automatically transfer those skills and techniques to the online catalog?

In the case of university faculty, it has been generally assumed that they approach the library catalog to locate items they have heard about from other sources such as personal networks or footnotes, and the local library is nothing more than a warehouse. Even so, it can be argued that instruction sessions on online catalogs directed at faculty is a necessary library service. This was really brought home to me as I watched a formidable senior professor look through a list of some thirty items to locate one specific title. When I approached him and asked if he had tried a search that would pinpoint the exact title, he looked at me and said, "You're used to thinking this way and I'm not." I felt further vindicated, when early in 1985, in an article in the New York *Times*, Rutherford Rogers, then recently retired as Yale University librarian, remarked that the research of many faculty members indicates they have lost control of the information

Stark is Coordinator of Instructional Services and **Waltz** is Anthropology/Geography/Maps Librarian at Syracuse University.

sources in their field. He went on to say that many faculty never mastered the card catalog, the advent of the online catalog is imminent, and failure to master it will further affect their research and scholarship. Finally, we could note that most students will be around our libraries for four or five years at most, faculty will be around for a much longer period of time, so that the payoff, both in terms of faculty satisfaction with the library and for their own research, will be greater.

Syracuse University is a medium-sized yet diverse university. It has an overall student body of approximately 21,000 and a faculty of approximately 800. While the College of Arts and Sciences representing the traditional disciplines is the largest school, there also are vigorous undergraduate and graduate programs in management, engineering, education, communications, and nursing.

SULIRS (Syracuse University Libraries Information Retrieval System) became available to the public in January 1981. In doing that, we proved that you can put an online catalog in place with minimal user preparation and that most users will take readily to the change, if only because an online catalog is new and more fun to use. There were (and are) the usual misconceptions; a faculty member publicly observed that an online catalog cannot be browsed and students were (and are) often observed searching periodical citations in the catalog.

It should be pointed out that in 1981, when the catalog was put in place, and in 1983, when the seminar was designed, Syracuse did not have a formal library instruction program. (I am happy to report that this has now changed.) Most faculty were not used to having librarians doing presentations, and the concept of the library doing a presentation specifically for them was probably even more foreign.

However, as was pointed out in the article, we had done successful presentations for faculty at the annual campuswide Seminar on Teaching, sponsored by the University Senate Committee on Instruction. In fact, after our initial presentation, the committee invited us to appear at this popular program.

Working with the Senate Committee had shown us how important the participants' sense of ownership is to the success of any program. In order to make the seminar attractive, we needed to appeal to the faculty on their terms. Therefore, we decided to capitalize on the reputation of the Senate Committee, and asked if they would co-sponsor our program. They agreed, as we were going to do all the work. Therefore, we advise, if you're thinking of doing something similar, look around, see who your friends are, and ask for help.

There was another event that contributed to the seminar's attractiveness. Even since SULIRS became an online catalog, people asked if it were possible to use it from other terminals on campus. This became feasible that fall. Syracuse is often rainy or snowy; now one could learn how to check to see if an item was available in the library from the comfort of one's office or at least from the building that houses one's office.

As good librarians, we felt the program should take place in the library. However, we did not have equipment to do a program for a large group. We contacted the university's computing center to see about borrowing terminals or their projection system. They suggested we do the program in their fully equipped classroom. We agreed; it would underscore the fact that the library's catalog was available everywhere on campus. This defined the program's format--a lecture demonstration.

We thought we needed two hours to teach and answer questions. In the article, we implied that we surveyed faculty about length and time of program. Actually, we asked a few people, who said they would consider coming if the program lasted an hour. We reconsidered and decided if we were tightly scripted we could cover everything in an hour.

Faculty schedules determined the times and date the program was offered. We aimed for late September, after the flurry of the opening of school died down, but before everyone got deeply involved in committees and grading papers. Once we moved to the computing center, we had to settle for October dates as that was when the classroom became available. The late afternoons on Tuesday, Wednesday, and Thursday reflect class schedules, as well as the days most people stay on campus after class.

We decided to ask potential participants to make reservations. First, the classroom held about forty people and we did not know how popular the seminar would be. Secondly, reservations create an aura of importance around an event. We were curious as to who would sign up and what areas of the university would be represented.

All of this planning is reflected in the letter that was sent to the faculty and deans. You have a copy in your packet.

The article notes that good-sized groups signed up for the first two seminars. We had a script, knew our equipment, and had rehearsed. But things did not go according to plan with the first group: it was our first appearance before an audience; our speaker was not forceful; in the audience were individuals who were not regular library users, who interrupted the presentation with idiosyncratic questions, which we tried to answer, and on it went. The experience brought home the fact that we were working with people who speak before groups frequently. If a lecture format is used, the speaker must be forceful and not let the audience define the presentation. A (different) more forceful speaker did the second presentation, the audience was more homogenous, and the entire program was exactly as we planned.

As noted earlier, we kept lists of who had signed up for the seminar. As expected, the College of Arts and Sciences had the largest representation, including some biologists and physicists, as well as people from humanities and social sciences. The professional schools were represented by management, nursing, education (the largest group present), and communications. Groups that did not express an interest in the seminar were the College of Engineering, the School of Computer and Information Science, and the School of Information Studies (the latter is the Library School at Syracuse). The seventy-five attendees at the three seminars represented approximately twelve percent of the eligible faculty at the university.

Since 1983, we have not made another campuswide effort at a library program for faculty. The 1983 evaluations indicated that there are people who were interested in a program on a topic such as database searching, but we have not attempted to find a larger audience and develop a program. I would like to develop a topic and offer the program over the lunch hour to see if faculty would find that attractive. The major reason we have not done another campuswide workshop on the online catalog is that it has not changed significantly in the past two years. It is an accepted library service at Syracuse. Even one of the most begrudging faculty critics confessed that the real reason he does not like the online catalog is that items once only he knew how to find were now discovered by others and were no longer in the library when he wanted to use them.

The *SULIRS User's Guide*, of which you have a copy, is the third edition, the second was written partly because of our experiences with the seminar. Likewise, we continue to offer twenty-one hours per week of point-of-use online catalog instruction during the academic year. As we are developing a program of library education, we try to incorporate online catalog instruction into all appropriate classes and workshops.

Faculty outreach has been directed towards new faculty. We offer a ninety-minute orientation program, which includes about twenty minutes of online catalog instruction. The Senate Committee on Instruction is our co-sponsor, the program is offered twice late in the day to give a choice of day and times. The program is tightly organized and attendance has increased each year. We are training new faculty to think in terms of an online catalog and online searching, a process that should become easier with each year and generation of faculty.

The techniques and strategies that we presented to the faculty in our seminar emphasized the unique features of online searches and especially the differences between card catalog and online catalog searches. We had encountered a number of enlightening questions and comments on the system during the two previous Seminars on Teaching Sessions, the one-to-one SULIRS assistance program provided at our Reference Desk area, and our day-to-day reference work. We felt we had a sense of the misconceptions and misunderstandings that our users had developed about searching an online catalog. Our experiences led us to believe that SULIRS users were still, in effect, "thumbing" through the cards, albeit online.

The points we stressed fell into two general categories--those aimed primarily at improving search strategies for known items, such as a specific author or title; and those aimed at stimulating, as well as improving, search strategies for "unknown" items, that is, materials on a particular subject, but with no specific author or title.

We chose four general problems associated with searching for a specific author or title that we believed would techniques for an online search.

The first problem we highlighted was that of *word order*. We explained that one need not key in author or title information in given order, as required by a filing system. One can, and indeed should, manipulate word order to reduce response time, a primary source of user frustration. In order to shorten SULIRS response time, we encouraged the faculty to search for the least common word first, whether author or title. While this technique does not affect the eventual accuracy of the search, it is a more efficient use of time and the system.

Example

```
ENTER SEARCH:  AU; JOHN, GERAINT          (in card catalog
SEARCHING "AU; JOHN "                      order produces a
SEARCHING "AU; GERAINT "                   long response
STILL SEARCHING                            time; 12 still
```

```
STILL SEARCHING                    searching
STILL SEARCHING                    messages)
STILL SEARCHING
STILL SEARCHING
STILL SEARCHING
STILL SEARCHING
STILL SEARCHING
STILL SEARCHING
STILL SEARCHING
STILL SEARCHING
STILL SEARCHING
     10 ITEMS.  PRESS RETURN FOR DISPLAY, OR S AND RETURN FOR NEW
     SEARCH:

ENTER SEARCH :  AU; GERAINT JOHN        (less common
SEARCHING "AU; GERAINT "                word first finds
SEARCHING "AU; JOHN "                   hit immediately)
     10 ITEMS. PRESS RETURN FOR DISPLAY, OR S AND RETURN FOR NEW
     SEARCH:
```

The second problem we addressed was that of *trying to key in too much information* for a search. Aside from the fact that most words, beyond a few key words in author and/or title fields, are unnecessary, we explained that the more words entered (as in long titles), the greater the chance for a spelling error to occur. Inexperienced users seem unaware that SULIRS is, as most systems are, "dumb," and for the most part unforgiving --the system will search exactly what it is given, mispellings and all. More importantly, a lengthy search increases the chances that a record might be missed. For example, it is not uncommon for a book published both in Great Britain and in the United States to have the same title, but different subtitles, or even slightly different versions of the same title.

Example:

```
ENTER SEARCH: TI; THE GLORY THAT WAS GREECE, A SURVEY OF HELLENIC
CULTURE AND CIVILIZATION
SEARCHING "TI; GLORY "                    (does not find the record)
SEARCHING "TI; THAT "
SEARCHING "TI; WAS "
SEARCHING "TI; GREECE "
SEARCHING "TI; SURVEY "
SEARCHING "TI; HELLENIC "
SEARCHING "TI; CULTURE "
SEARCHING "TI; CIVILIZATION "
NO ITEMS FOUND FOR THE SEARCH: TI;GLORY    TI;THAT
   TI;WAS   TI;GREECE   TI;SURVEY   TI;HELLENIC
   TI;CULTURE   TI;CIVILIZATION
TYPE HELP FOR FURTHER GUIDANCE

ENTER SEARCH: TI; GLORY GREECE
SEARCHING "TI; GLORY "
SEARCHING "TI; GREECE "
1 ITEM: PRESS RETURN FOR DISPLAY, OR S AND RETURN FOR NEW SEARCH:

   1. STOBART, JOHN CLARKE, 1878-1933
   THE GLORY THAT WAS GREECE, A SURVEY OF HELLENIC
```

CULTURE & CIVILI<u>S</u>ATION   (finds the record civili<u>s</u>ation)
LONDON, SIDGWICK & JACKSON LTD, 1915
DF77.S7 1915; 5TH FLOOR-BIRD

We also acknowledged the problems presented by *initials*. The bane of online searching must be initials, whether they be authors' first and middle initials, or acronyms of corporate bodies. And faculty members seem to be more likely than any other user group to be searching for books that were cited in bibliographies. These citations all too frequently provide only the author's last name and initials. We tried to provide examples of all possible strategies for searching such an author. These strategies included not only tricks peculiar to SULIRS, but also more general applications such as finding another book by the same author with the use of a subject search, and in that way determining the appropriate entry for that author.

Example:

```
ENTER SEARCH:  AU; BERRY B. J. L.           (finds no records
SEARCHING "AU; BERRY "                       for this author
SEARCHING "AU; BJL "                         of numerous
NO ITEMS FOUND FOR                           books on
THE SEARCH: AU;BERRY                         planning and
     TYPE HELP FOR FUTHER GUIDANCE           geography)

ENTER SEARCH:  AU; BERRY                     (finds 278 records)
SEARCHING "AU; BERRY "
     278 ITEMS.  PRESS RETURN FOR DISPLAY, OR S AND RETURN FOR NEW
     SEARCH:

AND WD; GEOGRAPHY                           (to find 7 books by the
SEARCHING "WD, GEOGRAPHY "                   author and his full name)
     7 ITEMS. PRESS RETURN FOR DISPLAY, OR S AND RETURN FOR NEW SEARCH:

     1.  BERRY, BRIAN JOE LOBLEY, 1934-*
     SPATIAL ANALYSIS; A READER IN STATISTICAL GEOGRAPHY ENGLEWOOD
CLIFFS, N.J, PRENTICE-HALL, 1968 GA9.B53; 5TH FLOOR-BIRD
```

Finally, we considered the problem of *finding too many hits*. One of the most frustrating situations we have had to experience is that of watching a user who has found 97, or 231, or 643 hits on a search and who stands there and "thumbs" through all those records online. The hits may be the result of keying in a single prolific author, a common title search, or a broad subject search. In this seminar, we suggested search strategies that would modify such unnecessarily lengthy searches and help the user define the search appropriately. Our suggestions included a combination search such as adding a search for a few key title words or using an "anding" function to narrow a subject search. (At this time, we did not yet have our "not" feature in operation.)

Example:

```
ENTER SEARCH:  AU; EDMUND WILSON      (produces 81 hits)
SEARCHING "AU; EDMUND "
SEARCHING "AU; WILSON "
     81 ITEMS. PRESS RETURN FOR DISPLAY, OR S AND RETURN FOR NEW
```

```
SEARCH:

AND TI; CASTLE                                    (finds the appropriate
                                                 title immediately)
SEARCHING "TI; CASTLE "
3 ITEMS. PRESS RETURN FOR DISPLAY, OR S AND RETURN FOR NEW
SEARCH:

   1.  WILSON, EDMUND, 1895-1972
   AXEL'S CASTLE : A STUDY IN THE IMAGINATIVE LITERATURE OF 1870-
   1930 LONDON, COLLINS, C1959
   PN771.W55 1959; 3RD FLOOR-BIRD
```

Our impression was that faculty and students had different search strategies. Faculty members were more likely to be searching for given items, while students, especially undergraduates, were more likely to be on "fishing expeditions" for information on subjects--nonetheless, we included a segment on strategies for subject searching online. Here, too, we sought to stress the differences between online and catalog searching. Again we concentrated on four specific problem areas.

For a broad subject approach, we explained our *truncation feature* that performs a search for all words with a given root, in the fields designated. The feature not only allows for broad subject searching capabilities, but is also occasionally a way around the difficulties caused by alternate and British/American spelling differences.

Examples:

```
ENTER SEARCH: WD; WOMEN MARX+           (finds Marxist and
SEARCHING "WD; WOMEN "                   Marxism)
SEARCHING "WD; MARX+"
STILL SEARCHING
STILL SEARCHING
STILL SEARCHING
STILL SEARCHING
7 ITEMS. PRESS RETURN FOR DISPLAY, OR S AND RETURN FOR NEW
SEARCH:

   1. REED, EVELYN
   PROBLEMS OF WOMEN'S LIBERATION; A MARXIST
   APPROACH 5TH AND ENL. ED, NEW YORK, PATHFINDERS PRESS, 1971
   C1970
   HQ1122.R42 1971; 4TH FLOOR-BIRD

   2. FOREMAN, ANN
   FEMININITY AS ALIENATION: WOMEN AND THE FAMILY IN MARXISM AND
   PSYCHOANALYSIS LONDON, PLUTO PRESS, 1977
        HQ1154.F616; 4TH FLOOR-BIRD; IN CIRCULATION -
        DUE 5/15/86
```

Another method of rather broad subject searching we explained was the *call number approach*. This was a new approach for most faculty as they were not familiar with searching a shelf list. With the call number of at least one subject-appropriate book in hand, a call number search can usually produce a general subject bibliography (if one ignores such possible quirks as analyzed series), and allows the user to "browse" the shelves without or before going to the stacks.

Example:

```
ENTER SEARCH:  CN; DD247.H5              (finds works about Hitler)
SEARCHING "CN; DD   247   H5+ "
  113 ITEMS. PRESS RETURN FOR DISPLAY, OR S AND RETURN FOR NEW
  SEARCH:


  1. HOFFMANN, HEINRICH, 1885-1957 *
  DAS ANTLITZ DES FUEHRERS BERLIN, BUECHERGLIDE GUTENBERG, 1939
     DD247.H5H62; 5TH FLOOR-BIRD


  2. HITLER, ADOLF
  ADOLF HITLER-SEIN LEBEN UND SEINE REDEN
  MUNICH, DEUTSCHER VOLKSVERLAG, N.D.
     DD247.H5A41; 5TH FLOOR-BIRD
```

One of the most powerful capabilities of subject searching online that we hoped to impress upon the faculty was that of *combining subject searches*. This is an aspect of online searching with which the card catalog cannot begin to compete. Combining various subject terms or combining subject terms with title words allows a researcher to locate those relevant books/periodicals immediately without "thumbing" through possibly hundreds of cards.

Examples:

```
ENTER SEARCH:  SB; COLONIAL PERIOD STATES     (Library of Congress Subject
SEARCHING "SB; COLONIAL "                      Heading: United States--
SEARCHING "SB; PERIOD "                         History--Colonial period,
SEARCHING "SB; STATES "                         CA. 1600-1775)
  218 ITEMS. PRESS RETURN FOR DISPLAY,
  OR S AND RETURN FOR NEW SEARCH:


ENTER SEARCH: SB; TERRITORIAL EXPANSION       (LSCH:  United States--
SEARCHING "SB; TERRITORIAL "                    Territorial expansion)
SEARCHING "SB; EXPANSION "
  59 ITEMS. PRESS RETURN FOR DISPLAY,
  OR S AND RETURN FOR NEW SEARCH:


ENTER SEARCH: AND SB; COLONIAL PERIOD          (Combined search)
STATES
SEARCHING "SB; COLONIAL "
SEARCHING "SB; PERIOD "
SEARCHING "SB; STATES "
  3 ITEMS. PRESS RETURN FOR DISPLAY, OR S AND
  RETURN FOR NEW SEARCH:


  1. DARLING, ARTHUR BURR, 1892-
  OUR RISING EMPIRE, 1763-1803 N.P, ARCHON BOOKS,
  1962 C1940
     ED301.D22 1962; 5TH FLOOR-BIRD
```

The last problem we presented was that of *terminology*. Every online catalog has a thesaurus--ours in the Library of Congress Subject Headings (LCSH), "those two big red books" found near all our terminals. Our online system seems to invite free text subject searching, so a great deal of our effort in online catalog instruction has been directed at educating our users to apply approved

LCSH in subject searches. In order to address the problem of searching the terminology of so-called "unknowns," we had to seemingly contradict ourselves and suggest that users try their own terms, but in title search or combined searches only. We recommended this strategy for such specific instances as when the user is looking for new terminology that may not yet be in LCSH; or the user may be dealing with jargon from an unfamiliar field. Such searches would be quite complicated, if possible at all, in a card catalog.

Example:

ENTER SEARCH: SB; INTERFERON   (recently added as LCSH)
SEARCHING "SB; INTERFERON "
    8 ITEMS. PRESS RETURN FOR DISPLAY, OR S AND RETURN FOR NEW SEARCH:

ENTER SEARCH, WD; INTERFERON "   (includes word in title
SEARCHING "WD ; INTERFERON "   used before LCSH
    19 ITEMS. PRESS RETURN FOR   approval)
DISPLAY, OR S AND RETURN FOR NEW SEARCH:

The question/answer periods and the hands-on sessions provided additional information for the librarians involved concerning the kinds of searches that faculty members used and their expectations of an online catalog. Although there have been no follow-ups to this series of seminars, this information has not been neglected. It has been incorporated in new features of the SULIRS system (such as the "NOT" operator and an "adjacency" feature); improved HELP screens; revised handouts; and more appropriate online instruction modules for library instruction in classrooms.

NOTES

1. Stark, Marcella. "Using the Online Catalog Effectively." *College & Research Libraries News* 45 (June 1984): 301-305.

2. Campbell, Colin. "Torrent of Print Strains the Fabric of Libraries." *The New York Times* (25 February 1985): A10.

3. Bullard, Gregory N. "The Syracuse University Libraries Information Retrieval System." *Research Libraries in OCLC: A Quarterly* no. 7 (1982): 1-2.

4. Samples available from LOEX Clearinghouse for Library Instruction, Center of Education Resources, Eastern Michigan University, Ypsilanti, MI 48197.

SYRACUSE UNIVERSITY

SENATE COMMITTEE ON INSTRUCTION

September 23, 1983

Dear Colleague

It is a truism that libraries are one of the most rapidly changing components of the University. Syracuse University Libraries have long been a national leader in computerized information services. SULIRS is one of the first on-line public access catalogs in the United States.

Unlike the relatively static card catalog, an online catalog is continuously being refined. New HELP messages were added in recent months. It is important for users to keep abreast of changes in order to use the system effectively. In recognition of these circumstances, the Senate Committee on Instruction and the Syracuse University Libraries are co-sponsoring a Seminar on SULIRS for the faculty of Syracuse University. This is timely, as SULIRS is now available from any terminal on campus and on a dial-up basis as well.

The Seminar will begin with a demonstration of searching techniques and strategies using SULIRS. Time will be allotted for discussion and questions. Terminals will be available for demonstration and hands-on experience. Participants will be urged to share successful strategies using SULIRS and problems encountered with the system. The Seminar will last approximately one hour.

The Seminar will be offered on Wednesday, October 12, Tuesday, October 18 and Thursday, October 20. All sessions will begin at 3:30 p.m. and will be held in Room 215 Machinery Hall.

Reservations are needed and can be made by calling Marcella Stark at X4158.

Seminar Date	Reservation Due
October 12	October 7
October 18	October 14
October 20	October 17

We hope the information shared will help you in your teaching and research. The library hopes that information gained will help improve an already advanced system.

SENATE COMMITTEE ON INSTRUCTION

Carole A. Barone	F. Reed Hainsworth
James Collins	Lore L. Heath, Chair
Robert M. Diamond	Henry Levinstein
Marvin Druger	Patricia Mather
John D. Eggert	Robert S. Pickett
Marc Ellenbogen	George A. Polson
Michael Freedman	John Britton Saylor
Patricia Gates	Marcella Stark

SYRACUSE UNIVERSITY LIBRARIES

Donald C. Anthony, Director
Elaine Coppola
Caroline Long
Marcella Stark
Charles Tremper
Mary Anne Waltz

njh

Thumbing the Cards: Handouts

SURVEY - SULIRS SEMINAR

To help the Library improve this presentation, please evaluate the items listed, using this five-point scale:

1. Excellent
2. Good
3. Adequate
4. Poor
5. Unsatisfactory

	1	2	3	4	5
Usefulness of content presented					
Effectiveness of the method for presenting information					
Adequacy of discussion leaders' knowledge					
Opportunity to personally participate in the session					
Adequate time allotted for the presentation					
Room was adequate for presentation					

If the scheduling of the presentation (late afternoon, mid-week) posed problem, would you suggest a more convenient time.

What suggestions do you have for future SULIRS seminars?

What other library-related topics could be addressed in future seminars?

10/83

Thumbing the Cards: Handouts

Assumptions, expectations and the reality of existing online catalogs

1. Ragnhild Hatton, the historian, recently published a piece with the title "a new look" or "new light" on the age of George I.

2. There are twelve items listed for Ruth Benedict but her Tales of the Cochiti Indians is not there. Does that mean the library does not have it?

3. There has been recently published a newly discovered manuscript by Mark Twain. Looking under "Clemens, Samuel" will tell me if the library has a copy?

4. I would like to find all the publications on city planning published in the Soviet Union during the last eight years that are held by the library.

5. A reference from the Slavonic Review. "Zagoskin, M. N. Jurji Miloslavskyi:ili russkye v 1612 godu.

6. The library does not seem to have the Journal of Church History, published in Germany.

7. I am going through the reading list for the LOEX meeting. Does the library own the summer 1984 issue of Research Strategies?

8. When I looked for Carnaval in Romans, the computer responded with Carnival in Romans. What does this mean? However, when I looked for Le Territoire de l' Historien, I found this title as well as The Territory of the Historian. What is going on here?

Thumbing the Cards: Handouts

Marcella Stark and Mary Anne Waltz   **45**

Some explanations, possibilities, etc.

1. Hatton's "New light on the reign of George I appeared in
    England's Rise to Greatness. U. of California, 1983.
    If the on-line catalog uses the MARC record, and all fields
    of the record are searchable, this item is still not re-
    trievable. Contents notes were not made for this collec-
    tion of essays and Hatton is not an added entry.

2. Tales of the Cochiti Indians was published in 1931. Unless
    holdings are completely retrospectively converted, not
    all materials in the library will be in the online catalog.

3. Old and New (AACR2) forms of the entry may be searchable.
    They may be linked so that, all items appearing under
    either entry will be retrieved.

4. Gorod (City)

    a. Truncation is useful for searching an inflected language
        such that as Russian. Use the root form of the word in a
        title search and combine with their subject heading
        "City Planning".

    b. Combine an imprint search with a subject search.

    c. Subject and language search combination may be a
        possibility.

    d. "Or" concepts together.

5. Two things occur here. The author's established main
    entry is Nikhail Nikolaevich Zagoskin and the translitera-
    tion system being used is not that of the Library of
    Congress (used in the MARC record).

    a. If the system is not friendly, an author search
        using initials will not retrieve the item. Could
        use truncation with initials or as the name is
        uncommon, the last name only.

    b. If system has keyword title searching, truncate
        Miloslavsk* and russk*.

6. Easy, the online catalog as same as card catalog shows
    titles in their language of publication. "Zeitschrift
    für Kirchengeschichte".

7. Online catalog may or may not list serial holdings. Most
    are working towards that feature.

8. The concept of the uniform title is operant. Since AACR2,
    all cataloging records of works in translation have included
    the original title as well as the translated title. If
    there are linked in the online catalog's program, inputting
    either, will retrieve any records that includes both titles.
    Carnaval in Romans is held only in translation while
    Le Terriotoire de l' Historien is held in the original
    French and in translation.

Thumbing the Cards: Handouts

An INTRODUCTION to

SULIRS and

the CARD CATALOG

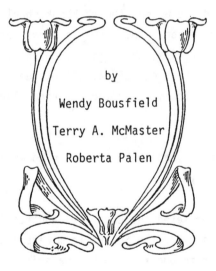

by

Wendy Bousfield

Terry A. McMaster

Roberta Palen

SYRACUSE UNIVERSITY LIBRARIES

Thumbing the Cards: Handouts

I. OW TO USE THIS WORKBOOK

Texts: Self-guided tour of Bird Library, an audio-cassette available at
         the Reserve Desk.

         A Guide to Syracuse University Libraries
         SULIRS User's Guide
         An Introduction to SULIRS and the Card Catalog (this workbook)

Before coming to the library to begin this workbook, take the
audio-cassette tour and read A Guide to Syracuse University Libraries.
These will familiarize you with the physical locations of library
departments as well as library services, policies and resources.

If you have read the Guide, the workbook should take you about an
hour and a half to complete. Come to Bird Library equipped with the
Guide to S.U. Libraries, the Syracuse University Libraries SULIRS
User's Guide and these exercises. All three are available free from
your instructor. You may ask the reference librarian for help at
any point.

Completed workbooks should be turned in to your instructor, who
has the answer key.

When you have completed the exercises and reading, you will
--be skillful users of the SULIRS terminals and card catalog;
--be able to locate books and other materials by call number;
--understand both the Library of Congress and older Dewey Decimal
   systems of classification;
--be sensitive to ways in which you can help keep library books,
   periodicals and research materials clean and damage-free.

Thumbing the Cards: Handouts

II. RELIMINARIES

Read: Guide to Syracuse University Libraries: "Overview," P.4;
        "General Information," p.5; and "Library Policies," p.5.

Exercise 1

1.   What general subject area is housed on the 4th floor of Bird
     Library?

     _____

2.   Where are the science books?_____

3.   You left your keys on one of the Bird Library study tables, but
     they are no longer there.   Where is the Lost and Found?

     _____

4.   If you need help finding something in Bird Library, you should

     a.   call the campus information telephone extension.
     b.   follow a student who seems to know where he is going.
     c.   meditate.
     d.   ASK A LIBRARIAN.

Thumbing the Cards: Handouts

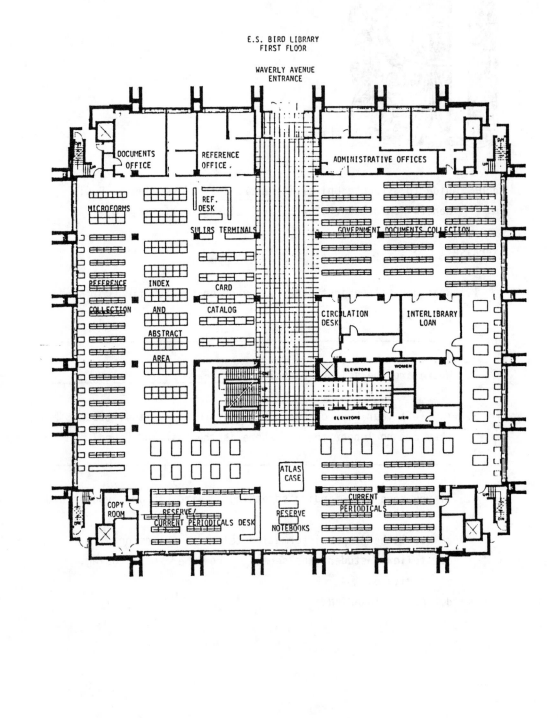

Thumbing the Cards: Handouts

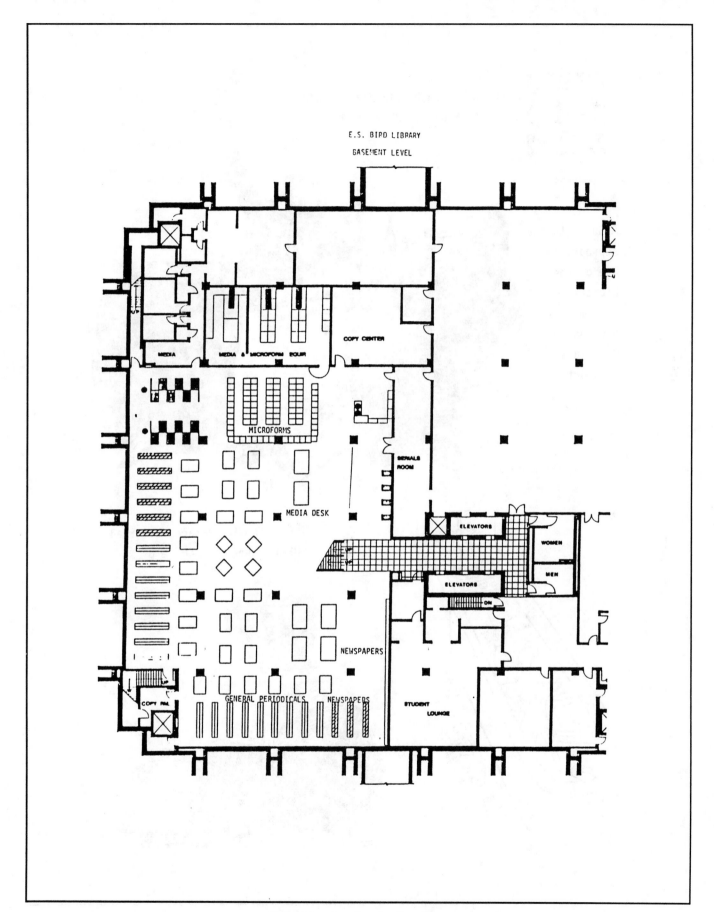

Thumbing the Cards: Handouts

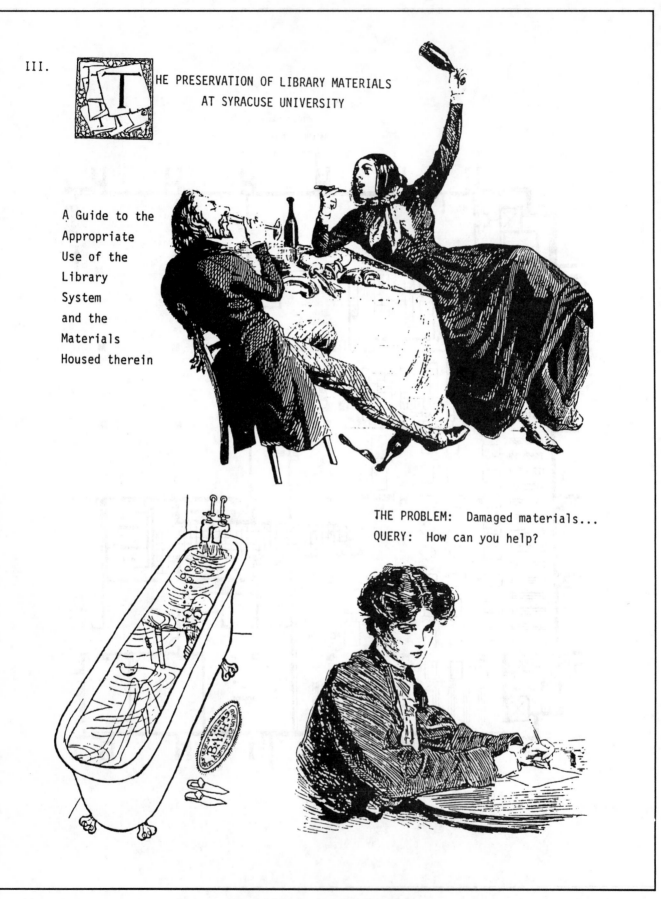

III. THE PRESERVATION OF LIBRARY MATERIALS
AT SYRACUSE UNIVERSITY

A Guide to the
Appropriate
Use of the
Library
System
and the
Materials
Housed therein

THE PROBLEM: Damaged materials...
QUERY: How can you help?

Thumbing the Cards: Handouts

Library materials receive wear and tear through normal use.
In addition, you can help by

--not marking or writing in or on
   materials;

--not eating, drinking or smoking
   except in the lounge;

--handling books with care.

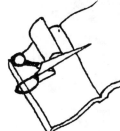

It is infuriating to find
that the most important
article on your research
topic has been torn out
by a thoughtless patron.

Thumbing the Cards: Handouts

Smoking can cause
fire or activate
smoke detectors.

Food and drink can damage library
materials and can attract paper-
eating insects.

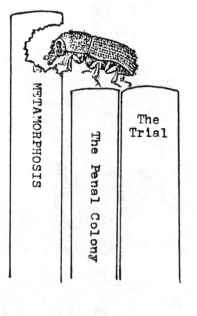

With your help, books and
journals will be there for
others to use, and we will
have a clean, quiet place
to study.

Thumbing the Cards: Handouts

IV.

 CCESS TO THE COLLECTION

CALL NUMBERS

Read: <u>Guide to S.U. Libraries</u>: Introduction to "Access to the Collections," "Call Numbers," and "Classification Systems," p. 6.

<u>Finding the Correct Floor</u>

The call number provides the book's "address," or location in the collection. Most works in the social sciences and humanities are located in the "stacks," or general collection on floors 2-5 of Bird Library. Materials in medicine, science and technology are housed in the Science and Technology Library and the various branch libraries devoted to specialized subjects--Mathematics, Physics, and Geology (see map, p. 10).

In the Syracuse University Libraries, books are found under two classification systems. Most books are arranged by Library of Congress (LC) call numbers. The first letter or letters in an LC call number generally determine the floor or branch library at which the book is located.

Older works may be classified by Dewey Decimal numbers. It is easy to tell a Dewey call number, because it begins with a number rather than a letter. The number or numbers before the decimal point (<u>813</u>.257 K16) determine the floor on which it is shelved.

The following chart outlines the arrangement of the collection. The dashes between letters or numbers mean "through": that is, C - CT means that books with call numbers beginning C, CB, CC, CD... through CT are located on the 5th floor.

Thumbing the Cards: Handouts

Location of Library Materials

Library of Congress	(LC) Call Numbers	Dewey Decimal Call Numbers	
A - AI, AN	3rd floor Bird	000 - 299	3rd floor Bird
AM	2nd floor Bird	300 - 399	4th floor Bird
AP1 - 7	Basement Bird	400 - 489	3rd floor Bird
AP8 - 300	5th floor Bird	490 - 499	5th floor Bird
AS - AZ	4th floor Bird	500 - 570	Science Libraries
B - BX	3rd floor Bird	571 - 573	5th floor Bird
C - CT	5th floor Bird	574 - 649	Science Libraries
D - DX	5th floor Bird	650 - 659	4th floor Bird
E	5th floor Bird	660 - 699	Science Libraries
F	5th floor Bird	700 - 709	2nd floor Bird
G - GB 397	5th floor Bird	710 - 711	4th floor Bird
GB 398 - GC	Science Libraries	712 - 789	2nd floor Bird
GD - GV	5th floor Bird	790 - 799	3rd floor Bird
GV 398	Science Libraries	800 - 889	3rd floor Bird
H - HX	4th floor Bird	890 - 899	5th floor Bird
J - JX	4th floor Bird	900 - 999	5th floor Bird
K - KX	4th floor Bird		
L - LT	4th floor Bird		
M - MT	2nd floor Bird		
N - NX	2nd floor Bird		
P - PF	3rd floor Bird		
PG - PL	5th floor Bird		
PM - PZ	3rd floor Bird		
Q - QR	Science Libraries		
R - RZ	Science Libraries		
S - SK	Science Libraries		
T - TP	Science Libraries		
TR - TT	2nd floor Bird		
TS, TX	Science Libraries		
U - UH	5th floor Bird		
V - VH	5th floor Bird		
Z	3rd floor Bird		

Thus,
HT
111
.M96 would be on the 4th floor of Bird.

RC
209
.P7 would be in the Science Libraries.

296
M53 would be on the 3rd floor of Bird in the Dewey section.

Thumbing the Cards: Handouts

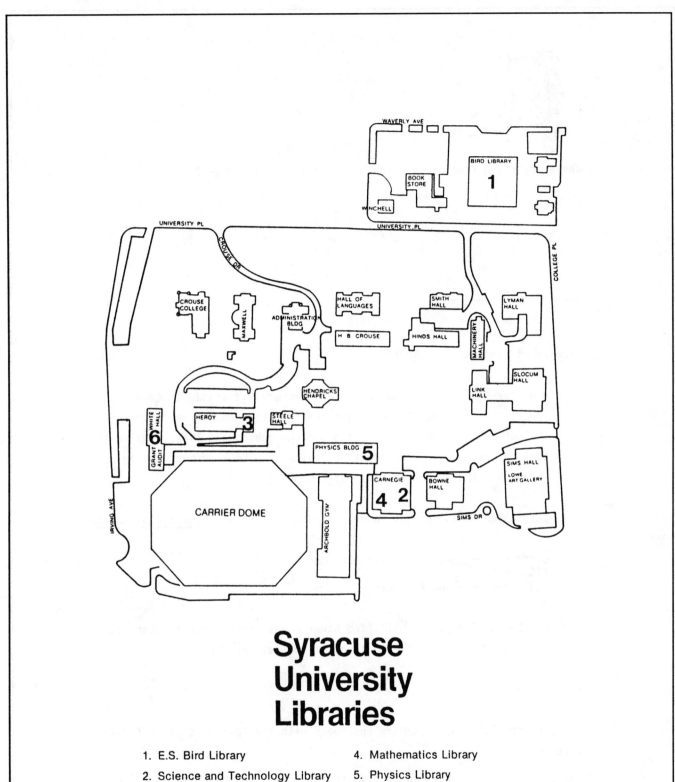

Syracuse University Libraries

1. E.S. Bird Library
2. Science and Technology Library
3. Geology Library
4. Mathematics Library
5. Physics Library
6. William C. Ruger Law Library

Thumbing the Cards: Handouts

xercise 2

Where would you find books with the following call numbers?

E	813.49	BF	HD	QP	ML
21	M97sp	699	30.412	376	111
.R938		.M43	.M36	.P7	.T88
			1982		

_____ _____ _____ _____ _____ _____

Library of Congress Call Numbers

A different Library of Congress call number is assigned to each book. The first two lines, called the classification number, represent the subject of a book. The third and any subsequent lines, called the book number, are an alphabetizing device; the book number usually represents the author or title of a book.

The following is the call number for Shigeru Egami's The Way of Karate:

GV ————————→ classification number
476
.E35 ——————— book number

On the 5th floor, you will find other karate books next to Egami's, all with the same first two lines of the call number.

Exercise 3

While on the 5th floor, examine the books with the following classification numbers:

E 51 to E 99   What subject is represented by these classification numbers?_____

Thumbing the Cards: Handouts

Arrangement on Shelf

The first line of an LC call number consists of 1 or 2 (in one subject area 3) capitalized letters of the alphabet. As might be expected, arrangement is alphabetical. Thus,

```
P                                    PT
32        is found on the shelf before   2
.M4                                  .A56


BF                                   BS
87        is found on the shelf before   9
.Q6                                  .C72
```

The second line is a whole number from 1 to 9999.0. It may include a decimal point. Thus,

```
 .
PT                                   PT
32.7                                 113
.B972     is found on the shelf before   .R5
M22
```

The third line comes after a decimal point and consists of one letter and a _decimal_ number. There may be a fourth line with another combination of a letter and decimal number. A fourth or fifth line may be added, indicating year of publication. Thus,

```
TR                                   TR
456       is found on the shelf before   456 (because .627 is
.A627                                .A8    smaller than .8.)

GV                                   GV
76                                   76
.R623     is found on the shelf before   .R7
M367
1982
```

Thumbing the Cards: Handouts

Exercise 4

Arrange the following call numbers in the order in which they would appear
on the shelves:

PN	B	PT	PT	B	PN	B
1411	1649	75.2	73	1649	1141	1649
.A14	.R94	.D35	.A648	.R94	.A3	.R932
	A32	1970	J7	B34		
	1967					

____   ____   ____   ____   ____   ____   ____

hat to do when you don't find a book

Not in SULIRS or the card catalog:

If you don't find a listing for the book you are looking
for on the SULIRS terminal or in the card catalog:

1. the S.U. Libraries may not own it; or
2. there may be a problem with the way you are look-
    ing it up.

Since a small mistake in spelling or wording of a title or author's name can
"bury" a book in SULIRS or the card catalog, you should consult a reference
librarian if the book you need doesn't seem to be listed.

Not in the S.U. Libraries

If the book you want is not owned by the S.U. Libraries, you may,

1. ask a reference librarian to help you find books on the same subject; or

Thumbing the Cards: Handouts

2. look for it in the Onondaga County Public Library System or at the Lemoyne College Library. The Public Library will allow students to check out a book immediately if they present two forms of identification, one with a Syracuse address. Lemoyne requires only the completion of a guest borrower form.

Not on the Shelf:

If you checked the shelf and found similar call numbers, but not your book,

1. check SULIRS. The entry should tell you whether a book is checked out and, if so, the date it is due back:

BENNETT, LERONE, 1928-
   WHAT MANNER OF MAN; A BIOGRAPHY OF MARTIN LUTHER KING, JR.
CHICAGO, JOHNSON PUB. CO., 1968, c1964
   E185.97.K5B4 1968 c. 3 ; 5TH FLOOR - BIRD; IN CIRCULATION -
   DUE 5/15/85

The King biography is in circulation, or checked out, and is due back in Bird Library on May 15, 1985.

SULIRS will also inform you if the book has been removed to a special location. For example:

RODGERS, RICHARD
   PAL JOEY
   M1503.R684P3 1962; 2ND FLOOR - BIRD; RESERVE ROOM - 1ST FLOOR - BIRD

2. Check the CIRCULATION INQUIRIES TERMINAL at the Circulation Desk, which contains all books checked out from S.U. Libraries, including those listed in the card catalog but not in SULIRS.

If the book you want is checked out, ask Circulation to notify you when it has been returned and hold it for you. If the book is neither checked out nor on the shelf, you may ask Circulation to hunt for it. Searches for misplaced books take several days.

Thumbing the Cards: Handouts

V. ULIRS

Read: Guide to S.U. Libraries: "SULIRS" and "SULIRS Display," pp. 6-7;
SULIRS User's Guide.

SULIRS includes:

    Books
    Theses and dissertations
    Periodical titles

    Newspaper titles
    Maps
    Films and other audio-visual
      materials

SULIRS does NOT include:

    Articles in periodicals or newspapers
    Essays in collections
    Plays, stories or poems in anthologies
    Telephone directories
    College catalogs
    Annual reports of corporations
    Most U.S. government documents

The reference librarians will help you locate materials not found on SULIRS.
In general, SULIRS includes titles of separately published works, whether they
are in print or another media. SULIRS does not list titles that are part of,
or included in, a longer work.

The following exercises illustrate features of the SULIRS online catalog in the
same order in which they are presented in the SULIRS User's Guide. It would be
a good strategy to read about a particular aspect of searching, then do the
relevant exercises.

Thumbing the Cards: Handouts

Exercise 5.

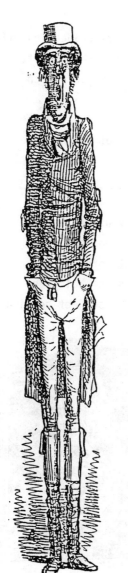

1. HELP

   a. Type HELP END. What do you do when you have reached the end of a list of items and wish to return to a citation displayed earlier?

      _____

   b. Type HELP NEWS. Name one new development in the SULIRS system.

      _____

   c. Type HELP ALL. Select one of the HELP messages and write an example that would help new users of SULIRS understand that particular feature of the system.

      _____

      _____

2. Search Codes

   a. How many books do you find on SULIRS written by Shirley McLaine?_____ Write down the title, place of publication, publisher and date of one of them.

      _____

      _____

      _____

Thumbing the Cards: Handouts

(If you are looking for books by an author who published before 1971, you need to check both the card catalog and SULIRS for a complete list of titles held by the S.U. Libraries.)

b. The fewer words you use in a SULIRS search, the less chance you will have of making an error. Articles ("a," "the") and other short, common words should always be omitted. Usually, a title search need include only two or three words.

   Type: TI; CONSCIENCE TACTICS. What is the title of the book you found?

   _____

c. To search for books by subject on SULIRS, you may use either the prefix WD; or SB;. Since the prefix WD; searches not only the assigned Library of Congress subject heading, but words in the title as well, you will probably get a longer list of holdings than with a SB; search, which calls up works by LC subject heading alone.

   COURTSHIP OF ANIMALS is an LC subject heading. (In searching SULIRS, the "OF" would, of course, be omitted).

   Using a SB; search, how many books did you find?_____

   How many did you find using WD;?
   _____

Thumbing the Cards: Handouts

Write down the author, title, place and publisher of the book or books that appear on the WD; but not the SB; list.

_____

_____

_____

Are any books on this topic checked out or in a special location?

_____

d. On SULIRS, you may search either a whole call number or the first two or three lines. Type: CN; QE522. What is the subject of books in this class?_____

_____

branch library are books in this subject found?

_____

ASIMOV are listed

are on

How many items did you

the plus (+), you may call up both singulars and
PARENT +) or multiple forms of a word (CHILD + for
DHOOD). Using the above example, how many additional
by truncating BOOK (BOOK+)?_____

Thumbing the Cards: Handouts

5. Refining a Search

How many books do you find on SULIRS under the subject heading (SB;)
POPULAR LITERATURE?_____ Using the AND qualifier, limit your
search to the subject SEX in POPULAR LITERATURE. How many items did
you find?_____

6. Expanded SULIRS Display

Job hunters are well advised to consult Richard Nelson Bolles' <u>What
Color is Your Parachute?</u> (HF 5383.B56 1979).

To help find additional books on job hunting
and related subjects, display the record
and write down the subject headings
the Library of Congress has
assigned this book._____

_____

How many entries did you find
on SULIRS under each heading?

_____

_____

Thumbing the Cards: Handouts

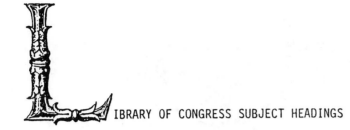

VI

IBRARY OF CONGRESS SUBJECT HEADINGS

There are two ways to find the subject heading or headings that pertain to your topic. First, as you did with the Bolles book, display the record of a recent book on your topic, and try subject searches with the headings assigned it. Second, you may consult the <u>Library of Congress Subject Headings</u>, a two volume set of large, red books, found next to the SULIRS terminals on each floor.

The <u>LC Subject Headings</u> provides terms that may be used both in the subject section of the card catalog and on SULIRS.

For example,

Adoption *(Direct)* *(HV875)*
　sa Children, Adopted
　　Foster home care
　　Interracial adoption
　x Child placing

　xx Children—Law
　　Foster home care
　　Foundlings
　　Guardian and ward
　　Impediments to marriage
　　Parent and child (Law)
　— Domicile
　　　See Domicile in domestic relations
　— Juvenile literature
　— Personal narratives
　— Research　*(Direct)*

Bold face type means that ADOPTION is an LC subject heading.
The "sa" (see also) directs you to additional related headings.
The "x" lists terms that are <u>not</u> subject headings.
The "xx" directs you to broader or more general headings.
The dash "--" indicates compound headings: ADOPTION -- RESEARCH.

Thumbing the Cards: Handouts

xercise 6

1. Having heard about the shooting of four teenagers on a New York City subway, you wish to learn more about gun-control legislation.
   . Using the LC Subject Headings, find the heading or headings you might use to find books on this topic.

   _____

2. Your paleontology term paper is on prehistoric horses. What term or terms does the LC Subject Headings provide?

   _____

Thumbing the Cards: Handouts

VII.

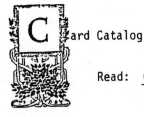

Card Catalog

Read: <u>Guide to S.U. Libraries</u>: "Union Card Catalog,"
pp. 6-8.

<u>Exercise 7</u>

1. Look up "ALLEN, WOODY" in the author/title section of the card catalog. (On SULIRS, an author's name may be entered in any order. In the card catalog, however, you must look under the last name first.)

How many of his books do you find?_____

How many books about "ALLEN, WOODY" do you find in the subject section of the card catalog?_____

2. How many books on KARATE do you find in the card catalog?

_____

3. Look up the <u>Short Story Index</u> in the card catalog. Where is it located?_____

Thumbing the Cards: Handouts

Planning an Online Catalog Workshop:

The Experience of the Ohio

State University Libraries

Noelle Van Pulis

OVERVIEW

The Ohio State University Libraries began offering an online catalog workshop in 1980. The program was planned as a supplement and alternative to other means of learning about the online catalog, or the Library Control System (LCS). Other introductory methods include a brief instructional brochure and a freshman library assignment. The program also was viewed as a public relations tool. The public relations function became particularly important in 1982, when the Libraries froze the card catalogs and LCS became the only catalog for newly acquired materials.

The workshop is planned as a one-hour program, and is offered several times each academic quarter with most sessions being offered in the fall. Sessions are held in the main library and several departmental libraries. The program is comprised of a lecture portion (by a library staff member or as a videotape presentation) and a hands-on portion using a self-test with assistance provided as needed. Content includes the basic catalog searches (title, author, author-title, subject, and call number), interpretation of screen displays, and the relation of the online catalog to other library tools. In 1984 and 1985, fifty sessions reached more than twenty-five hundred users. In addition, less structured demonstration sessions are held in the Health Sciences Library and other locations.

The need for instruction in online catalog use is, in part, due to the original design of LCS as a command-driven circulation system for staff use. Thus, some of the LCS features are not "user-friendly" to patrons. Having long recognized the

Van Pulis is Systems Librarian: Automation Office at Ohio State University.

need to make LCS easier to learn and use for both staff and patrons, a library committee developed proposals and specifications for enhancing the online catalog to make it more self-explanatory. Although these changes will, we hope, help those users who can help themselves, there always will be a need to include the online catalog in the bibliographic instruction program as an element in library use.

THE ONLINE CATALOG ENVIRONMENT

The Ohio State University Libraries is a large, decentralized system, with one main library, two undergraduate and twenty-five departmental libraries distributed throughout the three thousand acres that comprise the Columbus campus. The Libraries serve approximately 50,000 students, 3,500 faculty, and 16,500 staff. The Libraries' online catalog and circulation system also serves the State Library of Ohio.

LCS: EVOLUTION OF THE ONLINE CATALOG

LCS began operation in 1970 as the OSU Libraries' circulation system, using short records converted from the shelflist. Search capability included call number and 4,5 search keys for title and author/title. A number of major changes have been implemented since then. In 1978, LCS was enhanced with the capability for storage and display of full records and for searching subjects and added entries. In 1979, the State Library joined LCS. In 1982, the OSU Libraries froze its card catalogs and LCS became the official catalog for the Libraries.

To date, LCS contains listings for about 2.2 million titles belonging to the OSU Libraries and the State Library of Ohio, with reciprocal borrowing privileges. All State Library titles in LCS have full catalog records and therefore also have subject access. Less than thirty-five percent of OSU titles have full records, primarily titles cataloged before 1974, which a planned retrospective load will move back to 1972. Subject and added entry access to these earlier titles is available through the card catalogs.

The searches, which are taught to patrons, include:

Author, using full or partial name, with cross-reference provided;
Title, using a 4,5 search key and application of a stoplist*;
Author-Title, using a 4,5 search key and stoplist*;

Subject, using LCS subject headings, with LCSH cross-reference; and
Call number, using either a complete or partial call number.

Two searches that we have avoided are series and uniform title, both of which use full words. The series and uniform titles are accessible through the title search and we are concerned that attempting to explain series and uniform titles to our primary user group, the undergraduates, may be more confusing than helpful.

There are two kinds of records displayed by LCS: 1) the location record, which includes brief bibliographic information and holdings (including serial volume holdings), with location and circulation status; and 2) the full catalog record, which contains the information traditionally found on a catalog card (except location). As mentioned earlier, the location, or short record is available for all titles, and the full record is available for all State Library titles and some OSU titles. *[Effective June 17, 1986 users may enter full works; LCS will then apply the stoplist and create the search key, which has been changed to 4,2,2,1 for title and 4,3,2 for author-title.

LCS AND USER EDUCATION

The Libraries established the User Education Office in 1977. In addition to the director of User Education, there are two user education librarians. To supplement this staffing, there are several user education committees, one of which focuses on LCS instruction.

LCS instruction has been a committee responsibility since 1977, although the earliest committees were ad hoc and were not affiliated with the Office of User Education (which was concentrating its initial efforts on developing a Library Instruction Program for 7,000 freshmen each year). LCS public instruction began in earnest in 1977, with the development of the first LCS brochure. A public manual was produced, in limited quantity, in 1979. That year also was the year in which all freshmen participated in the Library Instruction Program, which includes basic information about LCS use.

The LCS committee observed in 1979 that, although the freshmen received LCS instruction, other undergraduates and graduate students did not have an opportunity for a standardized introduction to the Libraries' online catalog. The committee began planning the workshop in the fall of 1979 and offered the first trial sessions in January 1980. Analysis of attendance figures and evaluation forms over the next few months indicated that the workshop filled an instructional void, and was successful in terms of format and content. A more detailed report on the first six months appeared in the fall 1981 issue of *RQ*.

Attendance figures and participant evaluations were collected for several years. Then, the LCS committee decided that the workshop did not require revision and continued to count participation, but discontinued collecting evaluations. This decision was later reversed, and evaluations are once again regularly requested from participants. They have continued to confirm the participants' perception of the value of the session.

We know from several sources (such as a universitywide poll and the recent studies sponsored by the Council on Library Resources) that most online catalog users learn to use the catalog from printed aids. However, printed aids might not provide the most effective instruction. One study of LCS users found that those with the highest success rate were those users who had a year or more of experience with the system and who also had attended an LCS workshop. Users with the same level of experience, but who learned to use LCS in other ways, had much lower success rates. This finding lends support to provision of alternative learning opportunities.

Our analysis of demographic information from the first participant evaluations indicated that about two-thirds of the participants had never used LCS and that most were graduate students. Thus, the workshop reaches its intended audience, those who may prefer "live" instruction to that provided in printed form, and those students who have no other formal opportunity for instruction.

Our attendance levels continue to be gratifying. Of course, the Libraries "push" LCS instruction because LCS is our only catalog for newly acquired materials, and this information is part of the freshman program, the general orientation received by graduate students, and other user education activities. Our major concern with workshop participation is not being able to determine which sessions will be well or poorly attended. Some have very few participants (usually sessions held after Fall Quarter), while others strain our ability to provide hands-on supervised practice. This is a problem for which we have yet to find a solution.

PLANNING AN ONLINE CATALOG WORKSHOP

I have prepared a handout, which provides guidelines for planning an online catalog workshop (see Appendix). I would like to go over briefly the various points I have listed for consideration in the planning process, using the OSU experience as an example.

Needs Assessment

The needs assessment involves consideration of the purpose and/or focus of the workshop. At OSU, we viewed the workshop as both an alternative and supplement to other instruction. At the time the workshop was developed, in late 1979, only the freshman Library Instruction Program required LCS use. For most other library users, the only source of information was the LCS brochure or the manual.

This was, in part, a reflection of the low level of course-integrated instruction available at the time and a staffing situation, which did not (and still does not) encourage extended one-on-one instruction.

Since 1980, we have made some progress in the area of course-related instruction and since 1981, we have offered open "research clinics" for graduate students, which include LCS instruction within a search strategy structure. However, there remains a large number of students for whom the workshop is the best or only way of learning to use the online catalog. The results of the Council on Library Resources study also support the offering of instruction sessions as one alternative for obtaining online catalog information. And, as mentioned earlier, such sessions can serve as a public relations tool, especially when the online catalog is first introduced. We offered many additional sessions when we closed our card catalogs in 1982, and experienced excellent attendance.

Content

The typical workshop format seems to work well for online catalog instruction, particularly in an academic environment where students are used to lectures. It is a good idea for the lecturer to introduce himself and other staff who may be participating, including name and work area. A brief overview of the session format is often helpful, particularly if the demonstration portion will be held in an area other than the lecture room. Our LCS workshop consists of a lecture, with transparencies, lasting about one-half hour, then twenty to thirty minutes of hands-on practice at the public terminals.

The lecture portion provides a brief comparison of the online catalog and the card catalog (which at OSU remains the only source of subject access for pre-1972 material). We also emphasize the advantage of LCS in its provision of circulation status and mention remote availability via dial access. Transparencies are used to illustrate basic searching capabilities and resulting displays. It would be preferable to be able to do "live" demonstrations, but we do not yet have the equipment to do so in the main library building. We do, however, offer live instruction as part of the graduate student research clinics, which are held in a regular classroom lecture hall, which has a large screen projection system attached to a microcomputer with dial access capability.

When the workshop was first developed, the committee drew up a statement of objectives. You might wish to follow the guidelines described by Deborah Masters in the morning sessions in this program, adapting the objectives prepared for library instruction for online systems. We chose, for the LCS workshop, to cover basic searches and mechanics of terminal use. The searches and displays, which are included in the basic LCS workshop, include: title, author/title, author and subject searches, and two call number searches (one which requires a complete, correct call number and one which permits "browsing" in a call number area). Associated follow-up searches are covered, and some explanation of the displays of bibliographic records is provided.

This lecture content is specific to LCS, and would be adjusted according to the system being taught. For example, some systems have menus and extensive online "help," which would affect decisions about lecture content.

Speaking of help, it is a good idea to let the participants know the kind and level of help available. An indication of the availability of online help, printed aids, and staff will reassure attendees. It is a good idea to encourage participants to take advantage of the online help and printed guides if staffing patterns make it unlikely that personal assistance will be readily available.

Following the lecture, demonstrators may be introduced and the participants divided into small groups--no more than three to five per terminal. A brief review of the keyboard layout is essential, especially for those participants who have not yet tried to use the online catalog. You will find that many do not type well and have difficulty finding the correct keys. We have Telex terminals and specifically requested that the RETURN key be labeled ENTER the term we had chosen in 1977 as the equivalent of OCLC's "SEND." We relate this function to the automatic tellers, many of which also use the term ENTER, because we assumed that many of our students would have used the automated banking, a prevalent service in the Central Ohio area even in 1977.

Once the keyboard and associated terminal usage has been reviewed, it is preferable to have each participant work individually at a terminal. We now facilitate this practice by using what is called the LCS self-test, an exercise that requires construction of searches and interpretation of displays. The demonstrators (one of whom is the lecturer) provide guided assistance.

Staffing

It is obvious from the preceding description of the workshop format that it is labor-intensive. There must be strong administrative support for this teaching activity, from the director on down to the immediate supervisor. Our workshop operates on a system of volunteerism. Each session is assigned a lecturer and a backup, plus an estimated number of demonstrators (usually at least three for sessions that are expected to draw a large number of participants). Most lecturers and demonstrators are library faculty rather than support staff, largely I think, because the incentive is greater for the faculty.

The system of volunteerism at OSU encourages all library faculty--in both public and technical service areas--to serve as lecturers or demonstrators. It is suggested that the lecturer, in particular, be knowledgeable about the online catalog, have an acceptable manner to lecturing and, to course, be willing to lecture. Enthusiasm is a highly desirable quality.

It also is a good idea to "prepare" the volunteers for participation in the workshop program. We found it useful to have a review session just before Fall Quarter to go over the workshop format, lecture content, materials, and other related aspects, especially if there have been any system changes that affect the program. We also encourage potential lecturers and demonstrators to attend a session given by someone else, although some lecturers may be uncomfortable (at least initially) with peer observation. Most of us have found that this observation provides an opportunity to learn new lecture techniques, turns of phrase, and other idiosyncracies, which can be adapted to one's own presentations.

All lecturers and demonstrators are given an outline of the workshop content and copies of the transparencies they will be using. Content is prescribed, but lecturers may adjust the session to suit their own style. Due to time limitations, embellishments on the basic content are discouraged.

At OSU, the responsibility for the program resides with the LCS committee mentioned earlier, but the Office of User Education in cooperation with the Automation Office actually prepares the materials, schedules the sessions, and solicits volunteers. These arrangements are, of course, dependent on organizational structure, staffing, and other institutional factors.

Facilities and Equipment

The location in which the sessions are held and the equipment available will vary from library to library. Factors that should be considered in choosing the location include: availability of online catalog terminals, the expected or maximum size of the participant group, the availability of the room, and other site constraints. At OSU, the main library has a large room that is used for lectures and meetings. Although it can hold about seventy-five people comfortably, we prefer not to have groups of more than fifty, (although we occasionally have had more than one hundred students attend a session).

We do not yet have online catalog terminals in the lecture room. Participants are taken out of the room to the large "bank" of public terminals on the same floor. It is hoped that a future reorganization of the first floor will bring the terminals closer to the lecture room. The room does contain an overhead projector and videotape player, which are used for the LCS workshops and other user education activities. It is possible that additional equipment will be acquired next year, to allow live demonstrations of LCS in the lecture room.

Advertising

It is important to advertise the availability of the workshop sessions in a variety of ways. Posting of the announcement/schedule in the library facilities will attract students who visit the buildings. Course-integrated sessions may include the announcement as part of a packet of materials. Some libraries have newsletters, which are distributed to academic departments, and these could be used as an additional vehicle for increasing awareness of the program.

There are a number of opportunities outside the library as well, such as posting the announcement in dining facilities and dormitories (although this requires legwork). If there are standard university mailing lists, these can be used to distribute the information to academic departments, graduate students, or other identifiable groups. At OSU, we also buy advertising space in an early Fall Quarter issue of the student newspaper and inform new graduate students during their Fall orientation. Similar opportunities no doubt exist at your own institutions. Public libraries, which offer similar sessions, will have other opportunities for announcing programs, such as community newspapers. Electronic bulletin boards present new opportunities to communicate with users, particularly those who use the online catalog dial access capability.

Budget

At OSU, there has never been a budget as

such for the online catalog workshop. Staff time is considered as part of the performance of one's duties. Materials generally are inexpensive, in the form of handouts. Audiovisual presentations, however, often require a higher and more visible level of funding. The development of the videotape version of the LCS lecture, for example, was supported with a small university grant.

Equipment may be minimal if transparencies are used for the lecture and online catalog terminals are available in the building. If the workshop is taken "on the road" to a classroom or nonlibrary facility and the online catalog has dial access capability, a portable terminal or microcomputer may be acquired for demonstrations (and may do double-duty for online searching demonstrations).

Advertising and promotion of the program need not be expensive. The greatest direct cost for advertising at OSU is the advertisement in the student newspaper. This is only done, however, at the beginning of the academic year. The extent and cost of the promotion will depend on institutional factors.

Evaluation

One of the difficulties of evaluating "one-shot" programs, such as workshops, is the constraints imposed by this format. If only one hour, maximum, is devoted to the session, pre- and post-tests are not feasible. There are, however, a number of ways of obtaining initial and continuing evaluation of a workshop program. It is useful to have both participant evaluations and others done by the library.

Participant evaluation occurs indirectly in the form of attendance patterns. Poor attendance can indicate too little or low advertising appeal, or that dissatisfied students have told their friends not to bother attending. Informal evaluation also may be obtained by soliciting questions and comments during the actual session. We have found that students will share fears, misconceptions, concerns, and even praise of the online catalog during the brief time we spend with them.

It also is a good idea to devise and collect an evaluation form that solicits some demographic information about the attendees and asks a few questions about their response to the program. Over time, we have made some changes in the content and format based on participant evaluations, which includes their perception of the lecturer's knowledge and style of presentation.

Peer observation is an excellent way for the program organizers to evaluate the lecturers and gather suggestions for improving the program itself. We encourage constructive criticism and try to develop a collegial spirit. This form of evaluation is especially useful at an institution, such as ours, where librarians have faculty status and teaching is considered in the tenure and promotion process.

Continuous review of the program content and format, and supporting materials, is desirable. After six years of offering our online catalog workshop, we are still looking critically for potential improvement.

CONCLUSION

I hope this outline and my comments have provided a framework for developing your own online catalog workshop. Although your program will depend to a large extent on your local situation, the guidelines cover most of the details that must be considered.

REFERENCES

1. Van Pulis, Noelle. *Circulation System to Online Catalog: The Transition at OSU*. Bethesda, MD: ERIC Document Reproduction Service. ED235813, 1984.

2. Thorson, A. Robert and Phyllis B. Davis. "Borrowing Made Easy: Automated Resource Sharing in Ohio." *Wilson Library Bulletin* 53 (April 1980): 502-504.

3. Herndon, Gail A. and Noelle Van Pulis. "The Online Library: Problems and Prospects for User Education." In *New Horizons for Academic Libraries*, pp. 539-544. Edited by Robert D. Stueart and Richard D. Johnson. New York: K.G. Saur, 1979.

4. Pearson, Penelope and Virginia Tiefel. "Evaluating Undergraduate Library Instruction at The Ohio State University." *Journal of Academic Librarianship* 7 (January 1982): 351-357.

5. Van Pulis, Noelle. "User Education for an Online Catalog: A Workshop Approach." *RQ* 21 (Fall 1981): 61-69.

6. Alzofon, Sammy R. and Noelle Van Pulis. "Patterns of Searching and Success Rates in an Online Public Access Catalog." *College and Research Libraries* 45 (March 1984): 110-115.

7. Markey, Karen. *Online Catalog Use: Results of Surveys and Focus Group Interviews in Several Libraries* (Final Report of the Council on Library Resources, Vol. II.) Dublin, OH: OCLC Online Computer Library Center, 1983. See Section 7.0, "User Assistance for Searching Online Public Access Catalogs," pp. 172-205.

LCS SAMPLE SEARCH AND DISPLAYS

AUTHOR & TITLE SEARCH: BOOK

SEARCH: ats/maloagric   [4,5 search key]

RESPONSE:

 PAGE 1   (2 TITLES)
 01 Malott, Deane Waldo   The Agriculture industries   1939
 02 Epp, Donald J.   Introduction to agricultural economics   1981 FBR

SEARCH: dls/2   [for location record]

RESPONSE:

HD1411E6   Epp, Donald J. Introduction to agricultural economics / 80-15888
     2862825   1981   1 ADDED: 820123   FBR
01 ' 001 3 WK   AGI 222543950 0 RNEWD 851031/851209
PAGE 1 END

SEARCH: fbl/2   [for full catalog record]

RESPONSE:

HD1411E6
Epp, Donald J.
   Introduction to agricultural economics / Donald J. Epp, John W. Malone, Jr.
New York: Macmillan,   c1981. xi, 354 p. ; 24 cm.
   Includes index.
SUB: 1. AGRICULTURE--ECONOMIC ASPECTS
AE : 1. Malone, John W.
LC CARD #: 80-15888 TITLE #: 2862825 OCLC #: 06331328 820329 &%q820329
PAGE 1 END

[Note: Effective June 17, 1986 the author-title search allows users to enter
full words. LCS applies a stoplist internally and creates the search key,
which has been changed to 4,2,2,1. The location record display also has been
changed to a labelled format.]

Appendix

Planning Guidelines
for an Online Catalog Workshop

I.   Needs Assessment: Purpose/Focus

     A. Alternative/supplemental instruction
     B. Public relations function
     C. Audience(s)

II. Content

     A. Self-Introduction
     B. Overview of session
     C. Review handouts

          1. General library guides
          2. Online catalog materials
          3. Evaluation Forms

     D. Lecture

          1. Comparison to Other Catalog(s) and Tools

               a. Coverage

                    1. Materials
                    2. Time

               b. Access Points
               c. Availability

                    1. Terminal Locations
                    2. Searches by phone
                    3. Dial access

          2. Searches and Displays

               a. Title

                    1. Book, and Location Record
                    2. Serial and Holdings

Planning an Online Catalog Workshop: Handouts

            b. Author
            c. Author/Title
            d. Subject (including LCSH) and Full Catalog Record
            e. Call number
            f. Special (e.g. Shelf-browsing by call number)

        3. Help options

            a. Online
            b. Printed
            c. Staff

    E. Demonstration/Guided Practice

        1. Keyboard review (special keys)
        2. Self-test/Guided practice

III. Staffing

    A. Administrative support
    B. Requirements

        1. Coordinator
        2. Instructor
        3. Back-up instructor
        4. Demonstrators

    C. Responsibilities of staff
    D. Qualifications of instructor/demonstrators

        1. Knowledge
        2. Style
        3. Willingness/availability

    E. Preparation

        1. Review session
        2. Observation

IV. Facilities and Equipment

    A. Location

        1. Availability of terminals
        2. Size of group
        3. Room schedule
        4. Site or other constraints

    B. Equipment

        1. AV equipment
        2. Portable terminal, phone

    V.   Advertising/Promotion

        A. Library

            1. Postings
            2. BI program
            3. Other

        B. External

            1. Postings
            2. Mailings
            3. Other

    VI.   Budget

        A. Materials (Handouts/AV)
        B. Equipment
        C. Staff
        D. Advertising/Promotion

    V.   Evaluation

        A. Participant evaluation/Attendance patterns
        B. Library evaluation

            1. Observation
            2. Content/materials review

Planning an Online Catalog Workshop: Handouts

OHIO UNIVERSITIES LIBRARY ONLINE CATALOG GOES OUTSIDE THE LIBRARY

Computing Services users can now search Ohio University, Alden or Lancaster, Libraries online public catalog. The catalogs are available to anyone anywhere in the University's computer network with the capability of accessing the Gandalf Port Contention Controller. The Gandalf is accessed through a connection with or by dialing the main computer. For dial in terminals, use the following telephone number: 110 baud, 594-6027; 300 baud, 594-6131; 1200 baud, 594-6761.

- - - - - - - - - - - - - - - - - - - -

TO ACCESS THE SYSTEM VIA THE GANDALF

Your terminal should be set to EVEN parity. Tap the /BREAK/ key followed by /RETURN/. This will produce a series of questions or prompts.

Query or Prompt	Your Response
CLASS	5 /RETURN/
PASSWORD	ALICE /RETURN/

For Alden   :   HELLO ??????,ALICE.GAND /RETURN/
                  The ?????? must be your last name--this will permit
                  port identification in case assistance is needed. Spacing
                  and punctuation are critical.
                  Example: HELLO SMITH,ALICE.GAND /RETURN/

For Lancaster :   HELLO ??????,OWL.GAND /RETURN/
                  The ?????? must be your last name--this will permit
                  port identification in case assistance is needed. Spacing
                  and punctuation are critical.
                  Example: HELLO SMITH,OWL.GAND /RETURN/

This will produce a standard Hewlett-Packard log-on message including the day, date, and time, followed by a pause while the system is called up.

Next there will be a welcoming message from VTLS (Virginia Polytechnic Institute and State University)--designers of the system we call ALICE/OWL.

The system will inquire as to
type of terminal   5 /RETURN/

The public catalog system is now active and can be searched using the same commands as the terminals in the Library. Pamphlets listing the search commands are available in Alden Library. The query "HELP" is also operational.

When the searching is completed, users exit the system by entering: /QUIT /RETURN/
This will log you out of the Gandalf session. You may then return to the Gandalf as you normally would, remembering to change the terminal parity to ODD if you will not be accessing the system.

Any terminal equipped with a printer may also print copies of particular screens or subject bibliographies based on the Libraries online catalogs. To prepare a subject bibliography, the online catalogs should be searched by using the selected subject headings or the call number.

If there is a problem with the computer network, this should be reported to Computing and Learning Services, 594-6961. Most questions about searching on the system can be answered by typing: HELP /RETURN/   If further help with the system is needed, call the Library Reference Desk, 594-5424.

PUBLIC CATALOG "USER" TERMINAL SEARCH CAPABILITIES

A/   Author   Use entire name or just seven letters of authors last name.
                If you qualify by initials or first name, you must type in
                the entire last name.

T/   Title   Use entire title. Omit leading articles (i.e., A, An,
                The, etc.).

S/   Subject

C/   Call #   Example: PS35 A57 -- no space between first two elements,
                          space after each succeeding element. To browse
                          a subject area use just the main class (i.e., PS35).

MA   MARC screen format.

C   From MARC screen to holdings and circulation information.

CA   From MARC screen to card format. Also from Item screen to card format.

/MA   Returns you to the last MARC screen used.

PS   Returns you to the previous screen.

NS   Advances you to the next screen.

BA   Returns you to the intermediate menu screen.

/AM   Returns you to the menu screen.

Help For help screen -- screens vary according to type and stage of search.

———————————————————————————————————
———————————————————————————————————

Upon searching: Author/Title/Subject
                           ↓
                  QUALIFYING SCREEN
         (If linked) ↙   ↘ (If not linked)
    ITEM SCREEN   BIBLIOGRAPHIC SCREEN   (CARD SCREEN)

3/6/84

Planning an Online Catalog Workshop: Handouts

The Ohio State University

LIBRARIES

LCS (Library Control System)

LCS LECTURE

Attached is the revised LCS lecture, including an outline and a list of workshop volunteers' responsibilities. Please feel free to use these materials in whatever way they are most helpful. Questions or suggestions should be addressed to the Chair, Subcommittee on LCS Instruction, c/o the Office of User Education, 224 Main Library, 1858 Neil Avenue Mall, Columbus, Ohio 43210.

July, 1985

Planning an Online Catalog Workshop: Handouts

Instructor's Responsibilities:

1) Make sure room is arranged appropriately.

2) Deliver lecture.

3) Answer questions.

4) Help collect evaluations and place in user education mailbox.

Back-up's Responsibilities:

1) Attend full lecture.

2) Distribute packets to attendees.

3) Take Attendance (head count) and place in user education mailbox.

4) Help lecturer answer questions.

5) Help lecturer guide students through LCS hands-on experience.

6) Collect evaluations and place in user education mailbox.

Demonstrator's Responsibilities:

1) If possible, encourage participants to do self-test at terminals; answer questions as needed.

2) If a large crowd, demonstrate the self-test for small groups at the terminal.

3) Answer questions at LCS terminals as needed.

4) Collect evaluations and place in user education mailbox.

Planning an Online Catalog Workshop: Handouts

LCS Lecture Outline

I. Introduce Yourself

II. LCS

    A. What it does

    B. LCS vs. Card Catalog

III. Show Transparencies

    A. Transparency 1 – Title search
       a) <u>Homes in the Earth</u> – tls/homeearth
       b) Stress checking bottom of screen for instructions.

    B. Transparency 2 – tls/homeearth

    C. Transparency 3 – dsl/l

    D. Transparency 4 – tls/envimanag/ser
       (Journal of Environmental Management)

    E. Transparency 5 – aut/chalmers larry s

    F. Transparency 6 – Author search
       a) Mention variations on one author's name entered into system,
          i.e. Chalmers, John W. ; Chalmers John West.

    G. Transparency 7 – aut/chalmers larry
       a) Desired info. is on line 6. Author's middle initial was needed
          for this search.

    H. Transparency 8 – Author/Title search
       ats/chalhomes

    I. Subject search –
       a) Library of Congress Subject Headings (LCSH) and SAL/ command on
          LCS.

    J. Transparency 9 – sub/earth sheltered houses

    K. Transparency 10 – sub/earth sheltered houses

    L. Call Number Search – dsc/call#

    M. Transparency 11 – dsc/th4819e27c48
       a) Full Bibliographic Record (FBR)

    N. Transparency 12 – LCS Response (FBR)

IV. Review

    A.   Transparency 13

        a) Title search – tls/45

        b) Author search – aut/

        c) Author/Title search – ats/45

        d) Subject search – sub/

        e) LCSH terms

        f) Call Number Search – dsc/

    B.   "Help" key

V. LCS Services offered by the Library

        a) LCS brochures by the terminal

        b) HELP screens

        c) library staff

        d) Library Telephone Center – 422-3900
            1. staff will locate books and charge/renew/save them for you
               by phone.
            2. materials can be sent through campus mail.

VI. Hands-on LCS terminal experience.

Planning an Online Catalog Workshop: Handouts

LCS WORKSHOP

Introduction:

A. Introduce yourself and tell what you do:

Welcome to the LCS workshop. I am _____ and I work at OSU Libraries as _____. In my job, I frequently (use LCS to _____/help students and others new to the libraries to learn to use LCS). I'm happy to have the opportunity to talk with you today about the Library Control System. If you have any questions during the course of the workshop, please don't hesitate to interrupt.

B. Introduce the LCS system and outline the format of the workshop:

. This workshop is especially designed to help the individual who has had little or no experience in using LCS. We're going to talk about what kinds of questions you can ask LCS and what kinds of answers the computer system will provide for you.

Let's talk a bit first about what LCS is and what it can do. LCS is a finding aid. Basically, it helps you find library materials both when you know what you're looking for and also when you don't.

LCS functions as the library's computerized catalog. It contains records for most books, journals and other materials owned by OSU Libraries. When searching LCS, you will also come across records for materials owned by the State Library of Ohio, the Center for Research Libraries and records for items which OSU Libraries have ordered but which are not yet part of the collection. You will probably be primarily interested in finding books and journals at OSU Libraries, and you can search for these materials in a number of different ways on LCS.

Planning an Online Catalog Workshop: Handouts

During this workshop, we will demonstrate how you can successfully locate items by searching the author's name, the title, a combination of both author and title, the call number, and also by searching the subject or topic you are interested in.

Many people want to know when they need to use LCS and when to use the card catalogs. You can do author, title and call number searches on LCS for items in the OSU collection, whether it was published in 1902 or in 1982. However, searches on subjects will locate primarily materials acquired during and after 1974, so you will need to use the card catalog to find items by subject which were acquired before that date. After July 1982, OSU Libraries stopped adding cards to its catalogs, so LCS is the only subject catalog you need to use for any items acquired after this date. Generally, for materials acquired before 1974, use the card catalog for subject searches; for materials acquired after 1974, use LCS.

I said earlier that LCS helps you to find library materials both when you know what you're looking for and also when you don't. This means that when you have some specific information in hand--the author, title or call number of a book or journal--there are certain kinds of searches to use or questions to ask LCS in order to get some specific answers from the system. In addition to telling you whether OSU Libraries owns the item in question, LCS will also indicate what library in the system has the item and whether it is being used at the time or is immediately available. We'll go over these types of searches in the next part of the workshop.

What happens when you're looking for information on a topic, but don't have any specific authors or titles in mind? How can you question LCS and what kinds of answers will you get in return? This is the time when it's appropriate to use the subject search capability of LCS that we mentioned

Planning an Online Catalog Workshop: Handouts

earlier. We'll describe this search and the kinds of displays you can expect to see later in this workshop.

I'm going to show some transparencies which illustrate the basic kinds of searches or questions you can ask LCS and how to interpret the information you receive from the computer. After this, you will have the opportunity to go out to the LCS terminals in the circulation area and do some searches using the self-test we have given you.

The self-test is included in the materials you have been given. The test gives you a chance to try the commands that you learn today and includes additional searching techniques found in the LCS brochure. [SHOW LCS BROCHURE HERE]. Also included are _____ [ask participants to look at these more closely later when basic instruction is finished]. Let's begin to look at some of the searches you can use when looking for specific authors, titles or call numbers on LCS.

Title Search:

[DISPLAY TRANSPARENCY 1]

Transparency #1

User Request: Find a book entitled Homes in the Earth.

Search: tls/homeearth

Let's first search for a title of a book that we already know. We will search LCS to see if the OSU Libraries or the State Library own a copy of the book entitled, Homes In The Earth. When using the LCS title search, we must enter the three letter command "tls" followed by a slash and the first four letters in the title's first significant word, then the first five letters in the title's second significant word. A significant word is any word which is not on the stoplist.

We must avoid using words on the "stoplist" which is taped to the LCS
terminal. The "stoplist" contains words which are commonly found in titles,
and are therefore not helpful in identifying specific books. For example,
when searching LCS for the book entitled <u>Homes In The Earth</u>, we will use the
words <u>Homes</u> and <u>Earth</u> in the search command.

The first step in searching for the title of our book is to type in the
three letter command "tls" plus the slash mark. Then type in the first four
letters of the "Homes" and the first five letters of "Earth." Then press the
ENTER key to begin your search. This is how our search will look:

[DISPLAY TRANSPARENCY 2]

 Transparency #2

 <u>Search</u>: tls/homeearth
 .
 <u>LCS Response</u>:

   PAGE 1   (1 TITLE)
   01 Chalmers, Larry S.   Homes in the earth /   1980 FBR
   END   FOR AVAILABILITY ENTER DSL/ AND LINE NO.

In our example search there is only one title which is retrieved in LCS.
Now if we want to know if that book is available for loan we follow the directions at the bottom of the LCS screen. [These directions are underlined in
red.] On some LCS screens you will see small asterisks or plus signs next to
the line numbers along the left side of the screen. The asterisks indicate
books owned by the State Library of Ohio; the plus signs indicate materials
owned by the Center for Research Libraries.

Planning an Online Catalog Workshop: Handouts

[DISPLAY TRANSPARENCY 3]

Transparency #3

<u>Search</u>: dsl/1

<u>LCS Response</u>:

```
TH4819E27C48 CHALMERS, LARRY S.      HOMES IN THE EARTH /      80-133381
     2732144 1980       2   ADDED: 810130      FBR
01     001  3WK   UND
02     002        ENR  272667027 0 CHGD  840510/840531
PAGE 1 END
```

In our example we follow the directions and enter "dsl/1" and LCS replies with information pertaining to our particular book. The following information appears on the LCS screen:

    Call number [this is underlined in red]
    Author
    Title
    .Publication Date
    Line number
    Number of copies available
    Location of copies and availability
    Existence of a FBR (full bibliographic record). This concept will be
      explained later.

[DISPLAY TRANSPARENCY 4]

Transparency #4

<u>User Request</u>: Title Search for <u>Journal of Environmental Management</u>

<u>Search</u>: tls/envimanag/ser

If we want to determine if the Libraries own a copy of a journal or magazine we use the same basic title search plus the three letter qualifier "ser," which stands for serial. For example we will use the following search to see if the Libraries own a copy of the journal entitled: <u>Journal of Environmental Management</u>. Note that we should use the qualifier "ser" after the title when we are searching in LCS for the title of a journal. Remember, too, that we can search LCS for the titles of journals, but not for titles of articles contained in those journals.

Author Search:

[DISPLAY TRANSPARENCY 5]

> Transparency #5
>
> User Request: Book written by Larry S. Chalmers
>
> Search: aut/chalmers larry s

Now let's consider how to search LCS when we know only the author's name. The author search command, similarily to the title search command, is a three letter command followed by a slash. The command is "aut/" followed by the author's name in reverse order. If we are looking for a book written by Larry S. Chalmers the search would look like this. As we can see the author's last name is followed by a space. Then the author's first name is typed and it is followed by a space and finally the middle initial is typed.

[DISPLAY TRANSPARENCY 6]

> Transparency # 6
>
> ```
> 1    3 CHALMERS, JOHN ALAN
> 2    2 Chalmers, John R.
> 3    1 CHALMERS, JOHN W.
> 4    2 Chalmers, John West
> 5    1 Chalmers, Larry S.
> 6    2 CHALMERS, LIONEL
> 7    1 Chalmers, Louis
> 8    2 CHALMERS, M. D. E. S.
> 9    1 CHALMERS, MACKENZIE D. E. S.
> 10   1 CHALMERS, MACKENZIE DALZELL
> ENTER TBL/LINE no. FOR TITLES.
> ENTER PS- FOR PRECEDING PAGE: ENTER PS+ FOR NEXT PAGE
> ```

After we enter the LCS author search the LCS screen displays an arrow ( ) in the left margin which points to the author's name that we just typed. The number to the left of the author's name indicates how many titles are available under that particular name. There is only one title available by Larry S. Chalmers: [author's name is underlined in red]. It is helpful when doing an author search to note the names of the authors, above and below the one we typed in on LCS. For example, a name could be listed on LCS with only the

first and last name or it could be listed with the first, middle, and last
names. When we do an author search for the name "Larry C. Chalmers" using an
incorrect author's middle initial then this is the response we will find on
LCS.

[DISPLAY TRANSPARENCY 7]

   Transparency # 7

   <u>Search</u>: aut/chalmers larry c

   <u>LCS Response</u>:

   1   3 CHALMERS, JOHN ALAN
   2   2 Chalmers, John R.
   3   1 CHALMERS, JOHN W.
   4   2 Chalmers, John West
   5 NOTHING WAS FOUND UNDER: CHALMERS LARRY C
   6   2 Chalmers, Larry S.
   7   1 CHALMERS, LIONEL
   8   2 CHALMERS, LOUIS
   9 '   1 CHALMERS, M. D. E. S.
   10   1 CHALMERS, MACKENZIE D. E. S.
   ENTER TBL/LINE no. FOR TITLES.
   ENTER PS- FOR PRECEDING PAGE; ENTER PS+ FOR NEXT PAGE

The response indicates there was nothing found under the name Larry Chalmers,
however, on line 16 we can see there is one title under the name <u>Larry S.</u>
<u>Chalmers</u> and this is the author that we are trying to find. We just forgot to
put the correct middle initial in our search.

<u>Author/Title Search</u>:

[DISPLAY TRANSPARENCY 8]

   Transparency #8

   <u>User Request</u>: Larry S. Chalmers' book entitled <u>Homes in the Earth</u>

   <u>Search</u>: ats/chalhomes

   Now let's move on to the author/title search. This 3 letter search command is "ats" followed by the slash. After the slash we type the first four
letters of the author's last name and then the first five letters of the first

significant word of the title. When searching for Larry S. Chalmers' book entitled Homes in the Earth we will use this search. This search command will retrieve the book we are trying to find. The author/title search is important because it is the most efficient search to use on LCS if we know both the author and title of a book. If you know both author and title, this is always the best search to begin with.

Subject Search:

Now let's think about finding information on a certain subject in LCS. Suppose we are interested in finding information on "underground homes." We first need to know that LCS uses a controlled vocabulary. This means certain subject terms are used in LCS. These two volumes of the Library of Congress Subject Headings (LCSH) list many of the terms that are used in LCS. In our case the terms to use in LCS are "earth sheltered houses."

[HOLD UP COPIES OF LCSH]

You can also find your subject terms by using LCS. When doing a subject search, use the instructions at the bottom of the screen to find the SAL/ listings for your subject. More about this later. As in the author, title and author/title searches there is a three letter command for a subject search. The command is "SUB/" followed by the terms used in LCSH. At the LCS terminal we would type in the following:

[DISPLAY TRANSPARENCY 9]

Transparency #9

User Request: Looking for books on underground homes.

Search: sub/earth sheltered houses

LCS will search its subject files for our subject. The response to our search on LCS will look like this.

Planning an Online Catalog Workshop: Handouts

[DISPLAY TRANSPARENCY 10]

Search: sub/earth sheltered houses

LCS Response:

```
1    1 EARTH SCIENCES--UNITED STATES--CONGRESSES
2    2 EARTH SCIENCES-UNITED STATES--MAPS
3    1 Earth sciences--Vocational guidance.
4    1 Earth scientists-United States--Directories
5   17 EARTH SHELTERED HOUSES *(see below)
6    2 EARTH SHELTERED HOUSES--BIBLIOGRAPHY
7    2 Earth-sheltered houses--Congresses.
8    1 EARTH SHELTERED HOUSES--COSTS
9   10 EARTH SHELTERED HOUSES--DESIGN AND CONSTRUCTION
10   1 Earth sheltered houses--Design and construction--Congresses.
ENTER TBL/LINE no. FOR TITLES. *ENTER SAL/LINE no. FOR MORE INFORMATION.
ENTER PS- FOR PRECEDING PAGE; ENTER PS+ FOR NEXT PAGE.
```

Our subject terms appear on line 5 and LCS shows us there are 17 books on our subject.

' Also note that this LCS screen shows us more specific aspects of "earth sheltered houses." For instance if we were really interested in the cost of underground homes we could look at line 8 and note the Libraries have one copy of a book on the cost of underground housing.

If we want to look at the titles of the books on our subject we follow the directions at the bottom of the LCS SCREEN. Notice that you can enter SAL/line no. to display other search terms on your topic. We have underlined these directions in red.

Call Number Search:

Now let's move on to another type of search. We can use the call number search when we know the call number of the book that we are looking for in the Libraries. Let's say we wrote down the call number of a book that we wanted but we forgot to see in what library we can find a copy of the book.

[DISPLAY TRANSPARENCY 11]

Transparency #11

<u>User Request</u>: Find a copy of a book with the call number TH4819E27C48

<u>Search</u>: dsc/th4819e27c48

We can use the three letter call number command "dsc/" followed by the call number of the book. At LCS we would type the following [point to transparency]. LCS will then search its call number file for the call number that we typed in and look for our book. Then LCS will display a list of libraries that hold a copy of our book.

[DISPLAY TRANSPARENCY 12]

Transparency #12

<u>LCS Response</u>:

```
TH4819E27C48
Chalmers, Larry S.
   Homes in the earth / Larry S. Chalmers, Jerry A. Jones ; (Design Concept
Associates). San Francisco :  Chronicle Books, c1980. 112 p. (p. 112 blank)
: ILL. ; 22 x 28 cm.
   Design Concept Associates book."
SUB:  1. EARTH SHELTERED HOUSES
AE :  1. Jones, Jeremy A. joint author.  2. Design Concept Associates.
LC CARD #:80-133381   TITLE #:2732144   OCLC #:6690313 810120  &lq810120
PAGE 1 END
```

Now let's look at a full LCS display for our book and determine just what information is on the screen. This is an example of a full bibliographic record (FBR) on our book entitled <u>Homes in the Earth</u>. This information that we see on the LCS screen is similar to what we would find in a card catalog. One way to display th FBR record is to type "fbc/" and the call number of our book. Press the help key on the right hand side of the LCS terminal for more information on the FBR display.

The call number, which we have underlined in red, is always on the upper lefthand corner of the screen.

The author's name is underlined in this example in blue.

Planning an Online Catalog Workshop: Handouts

The FBR also gives the complete title which is underlined in this example in green.

Also note the name of the publisher is given along with the number of pages in the book. From the FBR we can also see the subject headings used to index our book. This full bibliographic record gives us the most detailed information on our book and is helpful to the user who is compiling the bibliography or writing a term paper.

Review:

[DISPLAY TRANSPARENCY 13]

Transparency #13

1. User Request: A book entitled Homes In The Earth
   Search: tls/homeearth

2. User Request: A book by Larry S. Chalmers
   Search: aut/chalmers larry s

3. User Request: Larry S. Chalmers' book entitled Homes In The Earth.
   Search: ats/chalhomes

4. User Request: A book on underground homes.
   Search: sub/earth sheltered homes

5. User Request: A book with the call number TH4819E27C48.
   Search: dsc/th4819e27c48

Let's review the five different types of searches that we have just discussed. The title search command is "tls/" followed by the first four letters of the first significant word of the title and the first five letters of the second significant word of the title. The author search command is "aut/" followed by the author's name in inverted order. The author/title search command is "ats/" followed by the first four letters of the author's last name and the first five letters of the title. The subject search command is "sub/" followed by the LCSH terms used for our subject. The call number search command is "dsc/" followed by the call number of the book or journal that we are wanting to locate in the Libraries. This transparency outlines the five basic commands we have just discussed.

All of these searches are outlined in the black and white LCS brochure. If we run into problems with one of these searches we can always type in "help" or hit the "help" key on the right hand side of the LCS terminal. The help screens will explain how to do searches on LCS.

Conclusion:

Let's go over some of the features of LCS that we mentioned earlier, now that you're familiar with searching techniques.

1. Remember that LCS can help you find books and journals by author, title, call number or subject, just like the card catalog does. But LCS tells you more than the card catalog can. LCS will also tell you whether an item is checked out and where other copies may be available, including copies held by the State Library of Ohio. And LCS can provide this information very quickly. Because you're seeing holdings of all OSU libraries, the State Library, and the Center for Research Libraries in LCS displays, you can search from any public terminal in the library system and get the same information. And you can have a "save" placed on any item that is being used from any library in the system. Using LCS can save a lot of your valuable time.

2. Remember, too, that LCS provides author, title and call number access to all books and journals owned by OSU Libraries, but that subject searches are generally possible only for items acquired during or after 1974. The card catalog will still help you to find older materials by subject. Then a quick call number search will tell you what library to go to and whether the item is available for use.

Planning an Online Catalog Workshop: Handouts

B. Services

Finally, let's review some of the services which the libraries provide to help you use LCS.

1. In each library, by each terminal, are brochures which illustrate in brief form the techniques we talked about today [hold one up]. You don't need to worry about remembering all of the specific instructions because they're always available by the terminals. After you've had some practice, searching LCS will become easy for you.

2. Remember, too, that help screens are available on each LCS terminal to refresh your memory. Just press the button marked HELP on the right side of the keyboard or type the word "help" and enter. Then select the kind of instruction that you need and follow the instructions on the screen.

3. Please ask for help if you don't find what you're looking for. Each library has staff available who are experienced using LCS and who enjoy answering your questions. LCS is a dynamic system, constantly changing and improving, so please don't hesitate to ask for help at any time if something new or different in the LCS display confuses you.

4. Remember, the Library Telephone Center is just a phone call away. The staff of the Telephone Center are happy to locate specific books and charge them to your ID number, place saves for you or renew books you already have. If you have a campus address, you can request that materials be sent to you through campus mail, or you can pick them up at the library. The phone number of the Telephone Center is 422-3900 [also write on blackboard]. This number is also on the LCS brochures and on the date due slips in the backs of library books. This is the end of our lecture.

C. <u>Questions</u>?

D. Thank you for participating in this workshop. We hope that you feel more confident about using LCS now. [Introduce demonstrators and tell participants that they can proceed to the terminals to try some searches and use the self-test if time permits.]
[ENCOURAGE PARTICIPANTS TO COMPLETE THE EVALUATION FORM AND TO HAND IT IN TO A DEMONSTRATOR AFTER THE HANDS-ON PRACTICE].

Planning an Online Catalog Workshop: Handouts

Online Catalog Guides:

Poster Session Abstracts

SELF-INSTRUCTIONAL FLIP
CHART FOR ONLINE CATALOG USERS

Linda Balsiger and Cecelia Brown

A self-instructional flip chart was developed to teach students at College Library the basics of using the new online catalog.

The online catalog is a command-driven system that has no menus or online help facility. Instructions for new users were developed and arranged in a small flip chart. The flip chart uses a simple example of a catalog search to take the student step-by-step through the search process. It teaches the use of the seven basic search commands and illustrates the necessary keyboard functions. This tool was later expanded to include sections on more advanced searching commands.

The flip chart has served as the primary instructional tool since the start of the online catalog. With the flip chart alone, a new user can generally learn the basic commands and start searching the catalog within ten minutes. In most cases, the students progress to the more advanced search commands with no other instruction.

Balsiger and **Brown** are Instruction Librarians at the University of Wisconsin-Madison.

INTRODUCING NLS AND THE COMPUTER CATALOG
OF THE UNIVERSITY OF WISCONSIN - MADISON LIBRARIES

WHAT IS IT?

The Network Library System (NLS) is a computer system that will
provide a variety of automated library services. For library users
the most important of these services is the online public catalog,
which will be installed throughout the campus libraries over a period
of several years. The first terminals will be available for use by
the public during the fall of 1985. In the Memorial Library these
will be on the second floor, in the lobby area adjacent to the
author/title section of the card catalog (Room 224). There will also
be terminals in other libraries on campus and in other departments of
the Memorial Library.

HOW IS IT USED?

Using the NLS online catalog you may locate books, periodicals and
other material in a variety of ways, including the customary searches
by author, title and subject. An especially helpful feature of this
catalog is that it allows searching by any key word, including
individual parts of a name, or words in a title or subject heading.
You are not limited to searching in strict order, left to right.
Also, it is not necessary to use complete names or titles. At some
terminals, a printer is attached, allowing you to obtain a printout
of your search results. Instructional material and on-site
assistance in the use of the NLS online catalog will be available.

WHAT DOES IT CONTAIN?

The NLS online catalog will initially contain records for more than
800,000 items. It will not entirely replace the card catalog, which
contains records for nearly four and one-half million items. The
records in NLS are primarily for books and periodicals received since
1976. Some material acquired prior to 1976 may also be located using
this catalog. Authors and titles of articles in periodicals are not
included. See reverse for a list of libraries included in this
system.

Balsiger and Brown: Addendum

Illuminating Library Users: Teaching the LUMIN Online Catalog

Goodie Bhullar
University of Missouri Library
Columbia, Missouri 65201

LUMIN (Libraries of the University of Missouri Information Network) is the online union catalog for the four campuses of the University of Missouri. Based on the Washington Library Network (WLN) system, LUMIN has been developed locally since 1981. It became available to the public in January of 1984 at the Rolla campus and in January of 1985 at the main campus in Columbia.

Teaching the use of the online catalog is a high priority of the four campus libraries. Online catalog users learn in different ways and the libraries provide the users a choice of learning the LUMIN system by either:

- attending a LUMIN workshop held twice a week, which also includes hands-on approach
- attending any course-related instruction session
- enrolling in a one credit hour course entitled "Library Skills"
- receiving one one one instruction at the terminals given by the reference staff
- picking up one of the brochures/manuals from the reference desk

LUMIN utilizes two modes to search its database or library records. Menu-driven mode is tutorial with instructions on the screen, while Command mode requires the knowledge of commands. LUMIN workshops make the users aware of the modes of accessing information, the advantages of using the system, library records included in the database, and future enhancements and plans for the system. The main part of the workshops detail the six access points (author, corporate author, title, subject browse, subject term, and call number browse) to information in the LUMIN database. An important feature of the LUMIN online system is the Authority Control linkage--the Authority File is linked with the Bibliographic File. This forces the users to interact with the Authority File. Transparencies featuring the sequence that users encounter using the Authority File during an Author/Subject search would be of interest to librarians.

Poster session display will include workshop text for both in-class and terminal instruction, transparencies used in workshop instruction, enlarged diagrams detailing the internal files of the system, color-coordinated posters and signs, newspaper advertisements, well-designed brochures, detailed manuals, and evaluation forms. Graphic displays of results tabulated from evaluation forms will also be presented.

Bhullar is Reference Librarian at the University of Missouri.

LUMIN
THE ONLINE CATALOG

LUMIN, the acronym for Libraries of the University of Missouri Information Network, is the new online, computerized catalog which is being used by all libraries in the entire University of Missouri system.

Use LUMIN to find any book owned by UMSL, checking the card catalog ONLY after you do not find a pre-1979 published title on LUMIN. Items cataloged since January 1986 are only in LUMIN, and by June 1986 90% of the book collection will be online. By December 1986 holdings for 90% of the library's periodicals will be online. Until then you should continue to use the SERIALS CATALOG to locate periodicals.

The system is designed so that you search for an author, title, or subject, by following the simple instructions given to you on the screen. To start, follow the instructions on the orange card on the keyboard, "press green key, then red key." This will give you the LUMIN "Welcome" screen. From this point on, simply follow the instructions step by step as they appear on the screen. READ THESE SCREEN INSTRUCTIONS CAREFULLY.

Be sure to type accurately!

It is not necessary to use capitals.

ALLOW THE SYSTEM TIME TO PROCESS! After pressing the yellow ENTER key, wait for a change in the screen before proceeding.

IF YOUR TERMINAL BEEPS, check the screen for an error message and press the green key to reset. Beeping is caused by a lockup which results from pressing a key while the system is processing or from typing in information which is incorrect at that point in your search. Read your screen instructions.

If you do not find what you are looking for, be sure to check the regular card catalogs.

Use the SERIALS CATALOG to find periodicals.

If you have any problems or questions, check at the REFERENCE DESK.

Bhullar: Addendum

the survey is currently being compiled.

Small Group Instruction for the Online Catalog

Jayne Crofts
William H. Welch Medical Library
The Johns Hopkins University
1900 E. Monument St.
Baltimore, Maryland 21205

Crofts works in the William H. Welch Medical Library at the Johns Hopkins University, Baltimore, Maryland.

Computerized catalogs have become a common feature of most academic libraries. At the Welch Medical Library, the online catalog, part of the Integrated Library System or ILS developed at the National Library of Medicine, has been available for patron access since April 1983. Prior to implementation, planning began for the development of a systematic training program to introduce library patrons to the unique features of the new system. The primary goals of the training sessions were to 1) make the user feel comfortable using the terminals, and 2) make the user feel confident that he was capable of mastering the system. Over a five-week period, the reference staff offered daily orientation sessions at a specified time. The orientation was not required. The teaching method--small group instruction--was used for three reasons: 1) people are more inclined to ask questions when they are in a personalized setting, 2) group members can watch closely during the lecture/demonstration period and easily see the searches being executed, and 3) all group members can participate through hands-on experience. Each one-half hour session began with an introduction to the online catalog, including a description of the information included in the catalog and a discussion of possible enhancements to the catalog. The introduction was followed by a brief explanation of the terminal keyboard, placing particular emphasis on the special function keys. Each person completed a set of six sample search questions, which illustrated the types of searches he would use to locate a specific type of information. The remaining time was devoted to giving each participant an opportunity to freely search the online catalog. The session instructor was available to provide assistance if necessary. During January 1985, the Welch Library conducted an Online Catalog Patron Survey. The data gathered from the survey will indicate 1) how patrons prefer to search the online catalog, 2) how patrons learn to search the online catalog, 3) what steps are taken by the patron to correct problems encountered while searching, and 4) what additional information and new features added to the ILS system would most benefit library patrons. Data from

Teaching the University of California MELVYL Online Catalog

Dennis Hamilton
University of California
Santa Barbara, CA 93106

The MELVYL online catalog contains over 1.6 million records for books held by libraries in the University-wide system. About 520,000 periodical and other serial titles listed in the *California Academic Libraries List of Serials* (CALLS) may be accessed in the MELVYL system. The online catalog is a user-friendly system and progressively displays online explanations and instructions designed to help the user make effective, independent use of the system to access needed information.

Responsibility for teaching users of the MELVYL online catalog rests with the instruction librarians at the nine U.C. campuses. Librarians at each campus have developed a variety of instructional activities and materials for teaching the library staff, faculty, and students to make effective use of the online catalog.

In February 1984, the six hundred member Librarians Association of the University of California (LAUC) established a Committee on MELVYL Instruction. This University-wide committee, which has a representative from each campus, is serving as the major organizational structure for producing and sharing instructional materials, ideas, and methodologies for training users of the MELVYL online catalog. The MELVYL Instruction Committee works cooperatively with other University offices and library committees responsible for developing, evaluating, and improving the MELVYL system.

TYPES OF READY-REFERENCE QUESTIONS

ANSWERED BY USING

THE UNIVERSITY OF CALIFORNIA MELVYL ONLINE CATALOG

Compiled by

Dennis Hamilton, University of California, Santa Barbara

with assistance from

Alan Ritch, University of California, Santa Cruz and
Catherine Thomas, University of California, San Diego

1. How many books can you find which compare Shakespeare and Sophocles?
   (example of a literary criticism question)

   FIND SU SHAKESPEARE AND SU SOPHOCLES

   Three records at UC libraries compare the two dramatists.

2. A user is looking for a report on mass media written by Robert Baker.

   FIND PA ROBERT BAKER AND TI MASS MEDIA

   Three titles by Robert Baker are retrieved on the subject of mass media.

3. Where was Fra Angelico born?

   FIND TI FRA ANGELICO OR SU FRA ANGELICO

   Fifteen records are retrieved for Giovanni da Fiesole, called Fra Angelico,
   1387-1455.

4. What is Michael Buckland's middle name?

   FIND PN MICHAEL BUCKLAND

   Three records give his full name as Buckland, Michael Keeble.

Hamilton: Addendum

5. What and where is the William James Society?

    FIND CA WILLIAM JAMES

    One record at UC libraries gives bibliographic information that shows that
    the William James Association is a group of prisoners in a Santa Cruz County
    (Calif.) prison who publish prisoner's writings from The Prison Arts Project.

6. What French authors have written works on California?

    FIND TI CALIFORNIE

    Typing the French spelling (californie) retrieves twenty-four records, several
    of which are written in the French language by obviously French authors.

7. What are the Superintendent of Documents numbers for some Veterans Affairs
    Congressional reports on "agent orange"?

    FIND CA CONGRESS VETERANS AFFAIRS AND TI AGENT ORANGE

    Four records are retrieved. By displaying the Marc formats of these records,
    the Superintendent of Documents numbers are given in the 086 field.

8. What pseudonyms has Ken Follett used?

    Search the authority file records: ACF PN KEN FOLLETT

    He has used the names Zachary Stone and Symon Myles.

9. What does the acronym OPEC stand for?

    Search the authority file records: ACF CA OPEC

    Answer: Organization of Petroleum Exporting Countries

10. What are the AACR2 authoritative forms of headings for the Ilias by Homerus?

    Search the authority file by name and title: ACF PN HOMERUS AND TI ILIAS

    Authority record #1 verifies Homer and the uniform title Iliad as AACR2 forms.

11. When did Saint Bernard live?

    FIND TI SAINT BERNARD

    He was born in 1090 or 1091 and died in 1153.

12. When was the American Library Association founded?

    Search the authority file: ACF CN AMERICAN LIBRARY ASSOCIATION

    Authority file record #29 gives the answer: The ALA was founded in 1876.

Hamilton: Addendum

Instruction Strategy for a
Public-Access OCLC Term

Lynn Magdol
University of Wisconsin-Madison Library
Madison, Wisconsin 53706

To encourage library users to search OCLC on their own, point-of-use instructional aids were developed for public-access OCLC terminals at the Reference Desk and the Card Catalog Information Desk.

An ad hoc committee of library staff from various public service departments and from the Orientation Committee was formed. The committee decided to use four forms of printed materials. Two posters previously developed by the Information Desk staff were added to the Reference Desk terminal area. A sample screen with fields labelled and identified was created in poster format, and a brochure published by OCLC was placed in large quantities at the desks.

Use of the OCLC terminals increased, for ILL verifications, to verify obscure citations, and to find additional access points in the card catalog. Because of the resulting increased demand for one-on-one instruction, faculty seminars may be given in the future on the use of OCLC. When the card catalog goes online, the public and library staff will be somewhat better prepared psychologically.

Magdol is a BI Librarian.

Using an Audiotape to Teach
the Online Catalog User

Judith E. Young
University of Central Florida
Orlando, Florida 32819

A twenty-minute audiotape was produced that provided self-instruction for online catalog users. While listening to the tape, the user interacts with the CLSI terminal.

Over one hundred students have listened to the tape and completed evaluation forms. The results of the survey indicate that the students consider the tape to be a valuable learning tool.

Serious students who want to understand how to use the online catalog are willing to spend twenty minutes listening to the audiotape. However, the average student wants immediate help with a specific search and will not read printed instructions or listen to an audiotape. The tape may become a required part of the library self-guided tour for the freshman composition classes.

Young is a Reference Librarian.

ONLINE AT UCF

<u>SYSTEM DESCRIPTION</u>

The current system consists of a CLSI LIBS 100 multi-processor with 3 - 600 Megabyte Winchester fixed disks that supports 28 public terminals and 20 technical terminals. This is an integrated system; i.e., used for circulation and catalog functions.

The Titlequery program allows inquiry by title, author, subject, call number, and location. It was not designed to be a public access catalog, and is not user friendly. Complicated procedures cause frustration to new users. As a result, we have developed a thorough instruction program.

<u>A MULTIFACETED APROACH TO USER INSTRUCTION</u>

** Instruction flipcharts at each terminal
** Catalog assistance desk
** Interactive audiotape: "Introduction to UCF Library's online catalog"
** Instructions available online
** Library self-guided tour
** General library instruction program
** Reference desk assistance
** Catalog demonstrations
** Phone assistance for dial-up access users

<u>CHALLENGES OF THE SYSTEM</u>

User frustration with the unfriendly programming
Inadequate backup for the online catalog
Computer phobia and unrealistic user expectations
High demand for dial-up access

<u>FOR MORE INFORMATION, OR SAMPLES OF OUR PRINTED AIDS, CONTACT :</u>

Ms. Marilyn Snow
UCF Library
P. O. Box 25000
Orlando, FL 32816-0666
Phone: 305-275-2562 SUNCOM: 345-2562

Young: Addendum

INTRODUCTION TO THE UCF LIBRARY'S COMPUTER CATALOG

Music

Welcome to the UCF Library! During this program you will practice using the online catalog with me.

Think of this online catalog as the new card catalog. It is primarily a listing of the general collection and reference books in the library. You will also find a listing of the library's audio-visual materials.

We believe that you will learn more quickly from this "hands on" experience than from simply reading printed instructions. If you need more time to do the search than is allowed by this program, stop the tape by pressing the stop button on the tape player. If you need to hear part of the tape again, rewind it. Ask a librarian to help you if you are not familiar with operating the tape player.

Stop Music

After hearing this program, you should be able to use the online catalog to see if the library owns any books by a specific author, to see if the library owns a specific book when you know its title or to see if the library owns books on a selected subject.

The word "title" followed by a question mark should be the last word on the screen. If this is not on the screen, ask a librarian for help. Don't let the word "title" confuse you. When the computer says "title" it is ready for any new search -- author, title or subject.

The symbol that you type at the beginning tells the computer to do a certain type of search.

The title symbol is a comma.
The author symbol is an ampersand (or "and" sign.)
The subject symbol is an equal sign.

Refer to the blue information sheet for the numbered list of commands you will give the computer during this program. If you do not see the sheet by the computer terminal, ask for a copy at the reference desk.

Young: Addendum

Speak slowly when spelling out title	Let's see if the UCF Library owns a copy of the novel, <u>Slaughterhouse Five.</u> Do the search with me. This is the first command on your information sheet. Type a comma, then type the complete title of the book. (Don't worry about capitalization.) Slaughterhouse is one word. Type s-l-a-u-g-h-t-e-r-h-o-u-s-e, press the space bar, type f-i-v-e. Now type a dollar sign. You must always type a dollar sign at the end of an author, title or subject search. Do not space before typing the dollar sign. After you have typed the request, check your typing. Did you make any errors? If you see a "4" on the screen instead of a dollar sign, you did not hold down the shift key when pressing the correct key. To correct a typing error, hold down the shift key and at the sme time press the rub key to backspace. The rub key is on the lower right section of the keyboard, the second row from the bottom.
Pause	When you are positive that your search has been entered correctly, press the return key. The return key is on the right side of the keyboard-- the second row from the top. The computer will not respond to your request until you press the return key.

If the library does not own the requested item, the computer will answer "not on file." If you left out the dollar sign at the end of the title, or if you mde an error in your typing, you will usually get a "not on file" answer from the computer even if the library owns the book.

As you should now see on the screen, the computer answered with more than one entry for <u>Slaughterhouse Five</u>. When two or more entries match your search, the computer always gives a short entry for each. Let's look at this information: The top line of each entry is a unique number which we call the title ID. The book by Vonnegut has v-o-n-s-f-i-v-nine-nine zero as its title ID.

The next line is the call number. You will need this in order to find the book on the library shelves. Be sure to write down the entire call number. P-S-three-five-seven-two,point 0 five, [pronounced Oh five-not zero five]S-Five, nineteen seventy-nine. |

Young: Addendum

The third line will sometimes have a location symbol. These symbols are important for locating books in the library. Notice that one of the entries has "A-V" as a location symbol. This stands for audio-visual material. You have located a videodisc of the novel as well as the book. The videodisc call number is VD 20 .

If there is no location symbol on the third line, the book is part of the general collection. To determine on which floor of the library an item is located, refer to the last page of the green flip chart booklet entitled "How to use the UCF Library's online catalog."

The next line will usually have the author of the book. Kurt Vonnegut is shown as the author of this book.

The next line is the title. Notice that there is an alternative title -- The Children's Crusade.

This short entry did not give us a complete description of the book. We cannot tell when the book was published, who published it, how many pages it has, etc. from this short entry.

Speak slowly when spelling out title ID

To display additional information, type the title ID and press the return key. You do not need to type any symbol before the title ID or the dollar sign afterwards. Don't worry about capitalizing the letters. Refer to command number two on the information sheet. Type this with me--v-o-n-s-f-i-v-nine-nine-zero.

Be sure that you type a zero--it's on the top row of the keyboard. Do not type the letter "O". Remember to correct a typing error, hold down the shift key and press the rub key to backspace. Press the return key after you have checked your typing.

Pause

Let me explain the parts of this long entry. The first few items are the same as the short entry that you have seen before: the title ID, call number, location symbol, author and title.

Young: Addendum

The new information that you will get this time begins with place of publication, publisher and date of publication.

All of this information is necessary if you plan to compile a bibliography later. This book was copyrighted in 1969, printed in 1979, and published in New York City by Dell Publishing Company.

The next line is the physical description of the book. This book is 215 pages long, has illustrations and is 18 centimeters high.

Next are the notes. These will vary greatly with each title. Notes tell you if the book has a bibliography, if it's part of a series or if it was previously published under another title. This book has only one note--telling us that it is a Dell book.

Next are listed the subject headings assigned to this title. Novels rarely are assigned subject headings so we do not have a subject heading for this particular book.

Following the subject headings are listed the added titles or added authors. In this case, Children's Crusade is an added title. You can find this book in the catalog under the title Slaughterhouse Five or Children's Crusade.

The only item of information useful to you in the next series of numbers is on the line above the Inquiry title statement. Near the end of this line, above the cursor, you will see either the statement "on shelf" or if the book is checked out, the date that it is due. Diagonal or slash marks separate the month, day and year in the due date.

Speak slowly when spelling the title
Let's try one more title search. Enter a request for the title Silent Spring. This is command number three on your information sheet. First type a comma, then s-i-l-e-n-t, press the space bar, type s-p-r-i-n-g. Now type the dollar sign. Check your typing. Press the return key when everything is correct.

Young: Addendum

Speak slowly
when giving
the title ID
You will receive a long entry unless the library has recently added another
book with this title to the collection. If you did not get a long detailed
entry, please type the fourth command which is the title ID c-a-r-s-s-p-r-
nine-nine-zero and press the return key. We should now be examining the
same long entry together.

Notice the three subject headings assigned to this book:

Subject heading number 1 is pesticides dash toxicology
(this means that toxicology is a subheading of the
heading pesticides)

The second subject heading is wildlife conservation.

The third subject heading is insects, injurious and
beneficial dash biological control (again, biological
control is a subheading of the insects heading)

These subject headings are important. You might want to do a subject
search using one of these terms. We'll discuss subject searches later.

Notice that the last two lines above the inquiry title statement are
very similar. Each line represents one copy of the book. When this tape
was recorded, both copies of this book were on the library shelves. Near
the end of the two lines the statement "on shelf" appeared. If either of
these books is now checked out, you will see a due date near the end of
the line. You will be able to recognize it because of the diagonal or
slash marks separating the month, day and year.

To review: If the library has no books with the same title, you will receive
short entries.

If the library has only one book with your title, you will receive a long
detailed entry.

Young: Addendum

The title ID can be copied from the short entry and typed at a later time if you wish to look at a long entry for any book.

Pause

Now we are ready to try an author search.

Remember that the author symbol is an ampersand or "and" sign. This symbol is located above the number six on the keyboard. The most common way to search for an author is to type this ampersand symbol, the author's last name, a comma, press the space bar and type the author's first name. As you did with the title search, you will end the request with a dollar sign.

Speak slowly when spelling out author's name

Try the author search with me. We want to find out which books the library owns by the author Alvin Toffler. Refer to the information sheet for the fifth command. First type the ampersand symbol, then type t-o-f-f-l-e-r, type a comma, press the space bar, type a-l-v-i-n. Now type the dollar sign. Double check your typing. If you have "six" instead of an ampersand, you forgot to hold down the shift key. To correct a typing error, hold down the shift key and press the rub key to backspace. When you have checked your typing, press the return key. When this tape was recorded there were three titles under this search.

But these a e not all of the books that the library owns by Toffler. In order to be sure that you have found all of them, you must do a second author search. Searching the first way-Toffler comma space Alvin did not allow you to identify some of the library's older titles. To identify them, a second author search will be necessary. It will be almost identical to the first one. The only difference is that this time you will not have a space after the comma. Older books are listed in the catalog without a space after the comma following the author's last name. Newer books have a space after the comma. Type the second author search (which is the sixth command) with me.

Speak slowly when spelling author's name

Type the ampersand symbol, t-o-f-f-l-e-r, comma, (do not hit the space bar this time), a-l-v-i-n, type the dollar sign. When you have checked your typing, press the return key.

Young: Addendum

You should now see at least six more titles by Toffler. Since there is more than one title, the entries are short. Remember that you can get a long detailed entry for each book by typing its title ID number.

Let's try the second Toffler search again. This time we will stop the computer during the search. You should locate the control key before we begin. It is located on the bottom left side of the keyboard and is marked C-T-R-L.

Refer to the sixth and seventh commands on your information sheet. Type the ampersand symbol, t-o-f-f-l-e-r, comma, (do not hit the space bar), a-l-v-i-n, type the dollar sign. Press the return key. Now hold down the control key and at the same time type the letter "S" (as in Sam). This should freeze the screen. Let's resume your search by pressing the space bar. The screen should be rolling again now. If it's not, press the space bar.

Pause

In future searches you might find it helpful to freeze the screen so that you can write down the title ID (found on the first line of each entry) and the call number (found on the second line) for each of the books. You will then be able to go directly to the book shelves and browse, or if you find that you would like to see more information about a specific title, you can do a title ID search later.

The last search we will do is a subject search.

Before beginning a subject search, you should check in the large red books entitled Library of Congress Subject Headings to see if your heading is listed. You will find this 2 volume set by the computer terminals.

Written instructions for interpreting the books are nearby. Ask the reference librarian if you need help in selecting your subject.

Young: Addendum

If you want to know if the UCF Library owns a book about job applications, use the Library of Congress Subject Headings book to identify the correct heading. Here you will find that the proper subject heading is "Applications for Positions."

Remember that the subject symbol to be used on the computer is an equal sign.

Speak slowly when spelling the words

Do the search with me. This is command number eight on the information sheet. First type the equal sign (it's above the dash), now type a-p-p-l-i-c-a-t-i-o-n-s, press the space bar, type f-o-r, press the space bar, type p-o-s-i-t-i-o-n-s, now type the dollar sign. After checking your typing, press the return key.

Because the library owns many books about job applications, the computer will list the short entries for these titles. Notice that some of them are reference books. The location symbol "Ref" will be on the third line when the title is a reference book. Let's try a new procedure to stop this search so that you will be ready to practice another subject search with me. Refer to command number nine on the information sheet. Hold down the control key and press the letter "P" (as in Patricia). The computer should display, "Titlequery in process. What do you want to do?" Now type the abbreviation for function f-u-n-c and press the return key. The computer should now display "Inquiry title?" and is ready for a new search.

Let's review the two procedures that stop the computer:

The first one freezes the screen. You must press the control key and at the same time type the letter "S". To start your search again, press the space bar.

The second procedure stops a search in progress so that you or the next

Young: Addendum

person can do a new search. You must press the control key and at the same time type the letter "P". When the screen displays "What do you want to do? " type f-u-n-c, the abbreviation for the word function, and press the return key. The computer will display title question mark which means a new search can be entered.

Our last search is for books about a person. Even though proper names are not listed in the <u>Library of Congress Subject Headings</u>, they can be used as headings. For example, you can locate either biographies or literary criticism of the author Kate Chopin by entering her name in the computer as a subject heading. This will be very similar to the author search. The only difference is that we will now type an equal sign (the subject symbol) instead of an ampersand (the author symbol). Try it with me.

Speak slowly when spelling name

Refer to command number ten on the information sheet. Type an equal sign, type c-h-o-p-i-n, type a comma, press the space bar, type k-a-t-e. Now type the dollar sign. [Pause] Check your typing. Press the return key.

When this tape was recorded, the computer displayed one title about Kate Chopin. The title of the book was <u>Edith Wharton and Kate Chopin, a Reference Guide</u>. Remember that you always receive a long, detailed entry when there is only one book about your subject. If the computer is displaying a long entry for you, notice that there are two subject headings assigned to this book. One is the name Wharton, Edith and the other name is Chopin, Kate. When this tape is over, you might want to do a second subject search for books about Edith Wharton.

We should also repeat this subject search without a space after the comma just as we did in the author search.

Pause

See command number eleven on your answer sheet and then try the second Chopin search. Type an equal sign, c-h-o-p-i-n, comma (do not press the space bar), k-a-t-e, type the dollar sign. Check your typing. Press the return key. You should find at least one other book about Kate Chopin under this search.

Young: Addendum

Pause
Start music

When you have finished your search be courteous to the next person by always leaving the screen ready for a new search. The word "title" followed by a question mark should be the last word on the screen. If your search is still in progress, remember that you can stop it by pressing the control key and typing the letter "P". When the screen displays "What do you want to do?", you should type f-u-n-c and press the return key.

You will learn to use the online catalog through practice. As soon as this program ends, try some new searches. If you forgot some of the procedures, refer to the printed instructions by each terminal.

The UCF Library also owns a great deal of information that is not listed in the computer catalog. We subscribe to over 200 periodical indexes that will lead you to information in magazines, journals, newspapers, conference proceedings and government documents.

.Don't hesitate to ask for help at the Reference Desk on the second floor. The librarian will be glad to help you use the online catalog and will also guide you to specialized reference books, periodical indexes and other useful sources.

Good luck w th your searching!

Now, please rewind the audiotape when finished.

Thank you.

Audiotape Script
(Audiotape to be used with CLSI terminal)
by
Judy Young

UCF Library
November 1984

Young: Addendum

ONLINE CATALOG AUDIOTAPE EVALUATION

Please check one answer on questions 1-4

1. The length of the tape is:
    _____ too long
    _____ too short
    _____ appropriate

2. Background music would:
    _____ improve the tape
    _____ not improve the tape

3. The instructions on the tape are spoken:
    _____ too fast
    _____ too slow
    _____ just right

4   Which would you prefer?
    _____ one voice through the tape
    _____ alternating female/male voices

5. Comments/Suggestions for improving the tape (Continue on back if necessary)

Please check one answer in each group:

    Status: Student_____   Career Service_____   A&P_____   Faculty_____

If a student, what class?   FR_____   SOPH_____   JR_____   SR_____   GRAD_____

    Your computer skills are:
        _____ good
        _____ average
        _____ inadequate
        _____ nonexistent

    Your typing skills are:
        _____ good
        _____ average
        _____ inadequate
        _____ nonexistant

Before listening to the audiotape, your competency in using UCF Library online catalog was:
        _____ good
        _____ average
        _____ inadequate

After listening to the audiotape, your competency in using the UCF Library online catalog is:
        _____ good
        _____ average
        _____ inadequate

How do you perceive your library skills?

        _____ good
        _____ average
        _____ inadequate

During the past year how often have you used the services of the UCF Library?

        _____ more than once a week
        _____ more than once a month
        _____ more than once
        _____ never

                    Your Name_____
                                    (Optional)

8/31/84

Young: Addendum

INFORMATION SHEET TO BE USED WITH THE AUDIOTAPE ENTITLED
"INTRODUCTION TO UCF LIBRARY'S ONLINE COMPUTER CATALOG"

Before you start the audiotape, make sure that "Title?" is the last word on the computer screen. If this message is not on the screen, ask a librarian for help.

COMMAND NUMBER	YOU WILL ENTER OR TYPE THIS COMMAND	YOU ARE TELLING THE COMPUTER TO
1	,slaughterhouse five$ [RETURN]	Do a title search
2	vonsfiv99Ø [RETURN]	Do a title ID search
3	,silent spring$ [RETURN]	Do a title search
4	carsspr99Ø [RETURN] (you may not need to type this)	Do a title ID search
5	&toffler, alvin$ [RETURN]	Do an author search (with a space after the comma)
6	&toffler,alvin$ [RETURN]	Do an author search (without a space after the comma)
7	[CTRL] s (press the space bar)	Freeze the screen Continue the search
8	=applications for positions$ [RETURN]	Do a subject search
9	[CTRL] p [RETURN] func [RETURN]	Stop the search in progress (so that another search can be entered)
10	-chopin, kate$ [RETURN]	Do a personal name subject search (with a space after the comma)
11	=chopin,kate$ [RETURN]	Do a personal name subject search (without a space after the comma)

Young: Addendum

Online Catalog Guides:

Discussion Group Handouts
and Sample Materials from
the LOEX Clearinghouse Collection

ALIS

USER'S

MANUAL

Arizona State University Libraries

ALIS Online Catalog Comment Form

Your Comments Please . . .

Thank you for using the ASU Libraries' Online Catalog, ALIS!
Please take a moment to answer these few questions about the catalog.
Your comments will help us to improve the catalog and to develop
additional instructional aids.

1. What type of search(es) did you conduct?

___ AUTHOR   ___ TITLE   ___ SUBJECT
___ KEYWORD AUTHOR ___ KEYWORD TITLE ___ KEYWORD SUBJECT ___ COMBINATION

2. To what degree were the following helpful?

	very helpful	helpful	not helpful	did not use
ALIS BOOKMARK				
ALIS USER'S MANUAL				
ONLINE HELP SCREENS				
LIBRARY STAFF				

Comments: _____

_____

3. To what degree did you find the ALIS system easy/difficult to use?

___ very easy ___ easy ___ difficult ___ very difficult

4. ANY PROBLEMS, OBSERVATIONS, COMMENTS??? _____

_____
_____
_____
_____
_____

Status: Student_____ Faculty_____ Library Staff_____ Other_____ DATE_____

Please deposit this form in the ALIS COMMENT form box

Arizona State University Libraries

What is ALIS?

The Automated Library Information System or **ALIS** is the online integrated
library system providing bibliographic and circulation information for items
owned by the ASU Libraries. By online, we mean that the user communicates
directly with the computer that stores the Libraries' database.

By using ALIS, you can

> Perform an author search
> Perform a title search
> Perform a subject search
> Perform keyword searches
> Perform a combined search for authors, titles, and/or subjects
> Find location and media information for an item
> Find out if an item is charged out and when it is due back
> Find out how many copies of an item are owned by the Libraries

What Library Records are in ALIS?

> Science and technology materials (G-GN,Q,R,S,T)
> Social science and humanities materials acquired or added to the database
>   after 1975
> Paper copy, U.S. government documents added to the database beginning in
>   1984 (title access only) and some older government documents that
>   have circulated
> Records for Roman alphabet monographs in classifications
>   BF,D,E,F,G,H,J,K,L (except ASU theses), M (Hayden collection only),
>   NA, P and PN
> Some brief records for pre-1975 social science and humanities materials,
>   Architecture Library materials, and music scores
> ASU West Library holdings
> Law Library materials acquired since 1981
> Catalogued records for the Arizona collections and Arizona Historical
>   Foundation

What is not in ALIS?

> Some social science and humanities materials listed in the card catalog
> Most government documents (Arizona, United Nations, United States)
> Individual holdings records of serials/journals (consult Public Serials
>   List [PSL])
> Articles in magazines, newspapers, journals, and other serials
> Individual poems, short stories, and other works in collections
> Many items from the Libraries' specialized collections--manuscripts,
>   photographs, archives, maps, East Asian Language Collection

Using ALIS

In addition to using the brief instructions on the ALIS bookmarks, you may
learn how to use ALIS from a series of online "HELP" screens containing
instructions for performing searches and operating the terminal. Also, there
is an ALIS User's Manual which provides more in-depth directions, explanations,
and additional examples for using ALIS.

Arizona State University Libraries

TIPS FROM ALIS

1. ALIS instructions are on the BOOKMARK, the ONLINE HELP SCREENS, and in the ALIS USER'S MANUAL.

2. ENTER = SEND (F1).

3. "LOCKED" means the system is PROCESSING your request.

4. A CARET (∧) appears under words the system cannot process or where COMMANDS or OPERATORS have been INCORRECTLY entered or OMITTED.

5. When the system says "There are no books which match your request," try the search one more time or change your strategy.

6. Report a terminal DOWN or displaying "LOCKED" for more than three minutes to the Information or Reference Desks.

7. COMBINED searches require EXTRA TIME. Be patient!

8. Use LIBRARY OF CONGRESS SUBJECT HEADINGS (LCSH) for subject (S) or keyword subject (KS) searching. Copies of this list are in the Reference Area.

9. In exact order LCSH subject searches (S), include commas when they are a part of the subject heading. For example, enter

     S ART, MODERN

Enter headings with subdivisions with a "space, DASH, DASH, space" (--)

     S CHILDREN'S LITERATURE, ENGLISH -- STORIES, PLOTS, ETC

THIS TERMINAL
IS DOWN

USE ANOTHER
TERMINAL
OR COM CAT

Arizona State University Libraries

ALIS Online Catalog Database Error Report Form

You found an error??

Thank you for using the ASU Libraries' Online Catalog, ALIS!
Please take a moment to report errors you found in spelling, birth/death dates,
or call numbers. **Use the ALIS COMMENT FORM to report other problems.**

SEARCH ENTERED: (Write exactly what you typed)

AUTHOR _____

KEYWORD AUTHOR _____

TITLE _____

KEYWORD TITLE _____

SUBJECT _____

KEYWORD SUBJECT _____

COMBINATION _____

SCREEN(S) WHERE THE ERROR APPEARS:

_____ Number of Author, Title, Subject Matches Screen

_____ "Number of Book ID's Found" Screen

_____ "Item Status Screen"

_____ "Bibliographical Record Screen"

_____ Other (please specify) _____

PLEASE DESCRIBE THE PROBLEM: _____
_____
_____
_____
_____

Status: Student_____ Faculty_____ Library Staff_____ Other_____

DATE _____

Please deposit this form in the ALIS COMMENT form box

Arizona State University Libraries

(ak´ses) n.

ARIZONA STATE UNIVERSITY LIBRARIES   **FALL 1985**

ac·cess (ak´ ses) *n.* 1. A means of approaching or nearing.

INTRODUCING ALIS

If you have visited the Hayden or branch libraries' reference areas during the past month you have, no doubt, noticed the new computer terminals which have been installed. These terminals provide access to the Libraries' online catalog and signal a significant step in the Libraries' continuing efforts to improve the quality and delivery of library services. The implementation of the online catalog places ASU Libraries among an elite group of major research libraries which employ state of the art library technology to provide a computerized, interactive catalog for public use. Though the online catalog, called **ALIS** (Automated Library Information System), is now operational, like most online catalogs it is still in a developmental stage and will continue to evolve and incorporate changes and enhancements which reflect new technological developments.

ONLINE CATALOGS

There is no simple definition of an online catalog, however, most computerized catalogs are primarily finding tools which can tell the user whether or not the library has cataloged an item and where in the library a particular item can be located. Additionally, computer software must permit the interaction of the user with the library's online database which may serve to support a variety of library functions, of which the online catalog is only one. One important criterion must also be met before a library's online system can qualify as a full-fledged online public access catalog (OPAC); it must be useable with little or no assistance from library staff for most transactions. Sometimes this last criterion is expressed as requiring an online catalog to be "user friendly". The ALIS system meets these requirements for an online catalog in addition to providing levels of information and search strategies impossible to achieve outside the online environment.

THE ALIS DATABASE

The foundation of any automated library system is the database upon which the various components of the system depend. ASU is fortunate in that bibliographic information

(continued inside)

Transfer to the computer of information on the books still listed in the Libraries' Card Catalog is currently underway, and is expected to be completed within five years.

ALIS is "user friendly" and provides prompts and lists of available options from most screens.

Arizona State University Libraries

for a significant portion of the Libraries' holdings already existed on computer tapes as a result of automated cataloging procedures instituted over a decade ago. In preparation for the opening of the Daniel E. Noble Science and Engineering Library several years ago, and that library's need for its own catalog, information on all science and technology books was entered into the Libraries' growing database. The database has continued to increase by the addition of new library materials and the steady incorporation of information on books listed in the Libraries' card catalog. This database has been the basis for generating the Libraries' COM (Computer Output Microfiche) Catalog and now forms the foundation of bibliographic information upon which the ALIS online catalog is constructed.

WHAT'S IN ALIS/WHAT'S NOT

The online catalog can be used to access most science and technology materials as well as materials in the social sciences and humanities which have been added to the Libraries' collections since 1975. Additionally, ALIS contains brief information on approximately 10,000 government documents and information on most Law Library materials acquired since 1981. Holdings of the ASU West Library can also be found in ALIS. Records of circulating materials which are still listed in the Libraries' main card catalog are added to the online catalog as they are returned. The transfer of the remainder of the records in the card catalog to the Libraries' online database is currently underway in a systematic fashion and is expected to be completed within five years. Of course, all new materials cataloged for the Libraries are added to the database in three week "updates," making ALIS the single place to consult for the most current library holdings.

What is not in ALIS? ALIS does not contain information on individual articles found in newspapers, magazines, or journals. Many of the Libraries' specialized collections such as maps, patents, photographs, manuscripts, and most government documents are not included in ALIS but continue to be accessed through separate indexes or finding tools.

Because the online catalog is a new tool still undergoing development, the Libraries will continue to produce and provide periodic supplements to the current 1975-1985 cumulation of the COM Catalog.

USING THE ONLINE CATALOG

Currently, the majority of ALIS online catalog terminals available for public use are located in the reference areas of the Hayden and branch libraries. Use of the online catalog requires no previous knowledge of computers or experience with online retrieval systems, as the system prompts users through a series of instructions and available options displayed on each screen. With a little practice, most cataloging searches can be done more efficiently than was previously possible through the COM or card catalogs.

SPECIAL FEATURES

ALIS departs from traditional card or COM catalogs in several significant ways. It provides current information on the availability of each item in the database by indicating whether an item you have located in the catalog is checked out ("charged") or whether it is on the shelf, and allows you to perform keyword searches and even combined searches using Boolean operators.

KEYWORD SEARCHING

The keyword search capability of ALIS makes it possible to locate materials in the catalog by searching individual words in titles, subject headings or authors names, regardless of the order in which these words appear in the complete title, subject heading or name. In effect, this makes every significant word in a title or subject heading, and each individual part of a personal or corporate author's name an access point in the catalog. Keyword searching can be useful when you have only partial or incomplete information on a particular item for which you are looking. Keyword searching can also be used to increase retrieval in the subject index or be used when you are unsure of the precise construction of subject headings. Terminology too new or specific to be reflected in subject headings may be searched as keywords in titles to uncover potentially relevant materials when exact titles of individual works are unknown. The increased research potential afforded by keyword searching is a significant benefit of the ALIS catalog.

COMBINED SEARCHING

The ALIS system also allows you to perform combined searches using the Boolean operators AND, OR, and ANDNOT. This feature of the catalog is useful for increasing precision of retrieval (AND, ANDNOT) and increasing recall (OR). Effective use of this capability will require some rudimentary knowledge of Boolean logic and careful attention to system protocol when doing more complex searches. Because of this and the fact that combined searches require significantly increased computer processing time, it is recommended that alternative search strategies first be considered.

TRUNCATION

ALIS also provides a rather sophisticated system for truncating (shortening) title words, subject terms or authors' names to retrieve all words, terms or names which begin with that shortened version of the word. This is accomplished by entering as many of the letters in a term as you wish, followed by either an "at" symbol (@) or a question mark (?). The two truncation symbols allow for different truncation strategies and can only be used in keyword searches. Using truncation effectively can often provide an alternative search strategy to doing more complex and time consuming combined searches.

AN INVITATION

As is apparent from this brief discussion of the Libraries' online catalog, ALIS is a powerful and sophisticated library research tool. It can be used at a very basic level to perform the functions traditionally provided by the card and COM catalogs as well as be used to explore new and creative approaches to library research which are unique to online catalog systems such as ALIS. The ASU Libraries' commitment to an online catalog presents new challenges and new opportunities to researchers in all fields, and surely

(continued on back page)

Arizona State University Libraries

(continued)

will change the way we think about and conduct library research in the years ahead.

LEARNING MORE ABOUT ALIS

ALIS training sessions for faculty will be offered. Until the schedule is announced, you are encouraged to visit the Hayden, Noble, Music or Architecture library to take ALIS for a "test drive". Assistance in using the catalog is provided in the form of online help screens and a printed "bookmark" summarizing the command options and procedures for using ALIS. The "bookmark", reproduced on the **inside** page, and a copy of a more comprehensive ALIS User's Manual are available near the ALIS terminals.

Additionally, during the introduction of the online catalog, volunteers from throughout the library staff will also be available to assist ALIS users in the Hayden and Noble reference areas.

Harvey Sager
Library Instructional Services

PROFS TO PROFS

All members of the Libraries' professional staff will be accessible through the University's PROFS system in the near future. Individual accounts are being established for each professional librarian enabling the librarians to send and receive messages to faculty and other members of the University community who also have PROFS accounts.

Faculty members will now have a quick way to forward requests via PROFS for materials they would like to have added to the Libraries; the libraries' subject specialists will be able to communicate more quickly with some faculty departments concerning library tours and bibliographic instruction programs, new acquisitions, and new services offered. User ID's for library staff members may be obtained by consulting the PROFS directory.

Maxine Reneker
Associate University Librarian for Public Services

ARIZONA STATE UNIVERSITY VIGOROUSLY PURSUES AFFIRMATIVE ACTION AND EQUAL OPPORTUNITY IN ITS EMPLOYMENT, ACTIVITIES AND PROGRAMS

(ak´ses) n.

Published by the ASU Libraries
Volume 6, Number 1
Harvey Sager, Editor

The editor welcomes your suggestions for topics you would like to see addressed in future issues of *(ak´ses)n.*

101148
Arizona State University
University Libraries
Tempe, AZ 85287

Non-Profit
Organization
U.S. Postage Paid
Permit No. 1
Tempe, Arizona

Arizona State University Libraries

WELCOME TO ALIS*

*The ASU Libraries' Online Catalog

ALIS (**A**utomated **L**ibrary **I**nformation **S**ystem) is the database which provides bibliographic and circulation information for many of the materials owned by the ASU Libraries.

ALIS CONTAINS RECORDS FOR
Science and technology materials
Social science and humanities materials added to the database after 1975
Most Law Library materials acquired since 1981

ALIS DOES NOT CONTAIN RECORDS FOR
Most materials listed on the card catalog
Individual articles in journals
Most government documents
Manuscripts, maps, and specialized collections

HOW TO USE ALIS
You can begin a search from most screens. Press the TAB key to move the CURSOR (blinking underline) to SEARCH LINE 1, or, if this is not possible, enter "Q" and press SEND (F1) to return to the WELCOME screen.

To Search
1. Type the search code
2. Press the space bar
3. Enter your search request

   CODE
   A   for author
        A DODGSON CHARLES LUTWIDGE
   KA   for keyword(s) in author's name
        KA DODGSON
   T   for title
        T ALICE IN WONDERLAND
   KT   for keyword(s) in title
        KT WONDERLAND
   S   for first word of Library of Congress
        Subject Heading
        S CATS
   KS   for keyword(s) anywhere in subject heading
        KS CHILDREN'S STORIES
4. Press SEND (F1)

You may combine searches (for example, author AND title; author OR author's pseudonym; or author ANDNOT a subject). You need to use Boolean operators (AND, OR, ANDNOT) and parentheses.

(KA DODGSON) AND (KT ALICE)
(KA DODGSON LUTWIDGE) OR (KA CARROLL LEWIS)
(KS CATS) ANDNOT (KS FICTION)
(KT ALICE) AND ((KA CARROLL) OR (KA DODGSON))

TRUNCATION
Words may be "truncated" or shortened to retrieve all terms that begin with the letters entered. In Author (A) or Title (T) searches, ALIS automatically treats the last word or initial entered as if it is truncated.

In keyword searches, the truncation symbol @ retrieves names or words beginning with the letters before the @.

   KA CAR@ LEWIS
   retrieves CAROL, CARROLL, CARROLLTON, etc.

In keyword searches, the truncation symbol ? produces an alphabetical list of names or words beginning with the letters before the ? from which you may select relevant matches

   KS ILLUSTRA?
   retrieves ILLUSTRATED, ILLUSTRATION, etc.

TYPING ERRORS
Correct typing errors by backspacing until you reach the error, then type over it. Press the PAGE/CLEAR/LINE to erase any letters to the right of the cursor.

```
((ITEM STATUS)) FOR: ARIZONA STATE UNIVERSITY LIBRARIES
                    MONOGRAPH

Dodgson, Charles Lutwidge, 1832-1898
The annotated Alice: Alice's adventures in Wonderland & Through the looking
New York, C.N. Potter
         TOTAL COPIES 1

   LOCATION          STATUS      DUE DATE  MEDIA
              COPY STATUS FOR:  HAYDEN
1)SPECIAL COLLECTIONS   SHELF     06-17-83 MONOGRAPH, NON-CIRC
   CALL #: PR4611 .A7

B-BIBLIOGRAPHIC INFO              O-OTHER BRANCH COPIES
L-OTHER LIBRARY COPIES           F FIRST   H-HELP
R RETURN TO PREVIOUS STEP        Q QUIT TO WELCOME SCREEN
   ENTER COMMAND AND PRESS SEND:
```

FINDING MATERIALS IN THE LIBRARIES
Use the call number on the left of the Item Status Screen (Call #: PR 4611 .A7) combined with the location (Special Collections) and branch (Hayden) to locate materials. Status and media designations also may be necessary to locate materials.

SELECTED LOCATIONS

HAYDEN LIBRARY	LEVEL	NOBLE SCIENCE & ENGINEERING LIBRARY	LEVEL
Arizona Historical		Current Periodicals/	
Foundation	4	Microforms	1
Arizona Collection	4	General Stacks	
Chicano Collection	4	G-GC, Q-QC	2
Curriculum	4	QD-TX	3
General Stacks		Map Collection	2
A-H	3	Reference	1
J-Z	4	Reserve	1
Government		Solar Energy	1
Documents	3		
Microforms	2		
Reference	1		
Reserve			
Lower Level			
Serials (Periodicals)	2		
Special Collections	2		

The ALIS "bookmark"

Arizona State University Libraries

Kennedy Library, Cal Poly

FINDING PERIODICALS

1. Start with a TITLE? prompt on the screen. .... **Title?**

   If the screen says: Type:
   CIRCONLINE in process. 14:28
   What do you want to do?   **func <cr>**

2. Type an exclamation point. .... **!**

3. Type the full name of the periodical or magazine you are looking for.

   Capitals, punctuation, and leading articles (A, AN, or The at the beginning of the title) may be omitted, but the spacing, spelling and sequence of words must be exact.

4. Type a dollar sign ($) after the title .. **$**

5. Example: .... **!Time$**

6. Press the return key and information about the item will be displayed on the screen.

7. If we do not own the item the terminal will respond .... **NOT ON FILE**

8. If we do own the item, the display will include its call number and the holdings we have that are bound or on microfilm.

9. See a Reference Librarian for help Using Poly Cat.

FINDING BOOKS BY TITLE

1. Start with a TITLE? prompt on the screen. .... **Title?**

2. Type an exclamation point .... **!**

3. Type in the title up to 29 characters.

   Only type in the first 29 characters of the title. Capitals, punctuation, and leading articles (A, AN, or The at the beginning of the title) may be omitted, but the spacing, spelling and sequence of words must be exact.

4. Type a dollar sign ($) after the title
   Example: .... **!Animal Farm$**

5. Press the **RETURN** key and items will begin to display on the screen.

Sample Title Search

Title?   !Animal Farm$

ANIFARM980
PR6029 R8 A5 1954   Call Number
Orwell, George   Author
Animal farm   Title
BRO2189490

(You can disregard the stuff after the main part of the entry)

KEY	PUB	PUBYR	CST
ANIFARM98	HARCO	1954	$20.00
MC	ED	L.A.D.	V
B		1/27/84	N

Stop scrolling with the **ctrl** and **P** keys.
Restart the display by typing-**cont** <return>
Begin another search by typing-**func** <return>

FINDING BOOKS BY AUTHOR

1. Start with a TITLE? prompt on the screen .... **Title?**

2. Type an ampersand .... **&**

3. Type the author's last name, leave a space, and type the first name or initial.

   Capitals, punctuation, and leading articles (A, AN, or The at the beginning of the title) may be omitted, but the spacing, spelling and sequence of words must be exact.

4. Type a dollar sign ($) after the title
   Example: .... **&Orwell George$**

5. Press the **RETURN** key and items will begin to display on the screen.

SAMPLE AUTHOR SEARCH

TITLE?   &Orwell George$ <return>

ANIFARM980
PR6029 R8 A5 1954   Call Number
Orwell, George   Author
Animal farm   Title
BRO189490

BRIPAMP980
DA300 078 v.2   Call Number
Orwell, George   Author
British pamphleteers   Title
49-18576
BRO0324300

Books by G.Orwell continue to come up.....

Stop scrolling with the **ctrl** and **P** keys.
Restart the display by typing-**cont** <return>
Begin another search by typing-**func** <return>

Kennedy Library, Cal Poly

LS/2000

A computerized catalog of materials in C-MU Libraries

books
journals
government documents
technical reports
musical scores
records

Prepared by
Peggy Seiden, Pat Sullivan

PROMPTS / MOVING AROUND

STARTING A SEARCH / OTHER SEARCHES

SEARCH CHOICE / AUTHOR SEARCH

TITLE SEARCH / SUBJECT SEARCH

SHORTCUTS / LOCATION CODES

Carnegie-Mellon University Libraries

Searching LS/2000

TO START A SEARCH:

Hit **NEW SEARCH** or type **/ES** and hit the RETURN key. You will see the main menu.

You have 5 searching options (Author, Title, Corporate/Conference Name, Other and Key Word.)

To Use Main Menu:

Enter the key word you want to search with and hit RETURN or type the number of the search you want and hit RETURN.

For search definitions type **?** and hit RETURN.

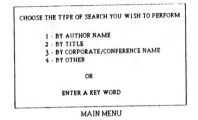

```
┌─────────────────────────────────────────────────┐
│ CHOOSE THE TYPE OF SEARCH YOU WISH TO PERFORM    │
│                                                   │
│        1 - BY AUTHOR NAME                         │
│        2 - BY TITLE                               │
│        3 - BY CORPORATE/CONFERENCE NAME           │
│        4 - BY OTHER                               │
│                                                   │
│                     OR                            │
│                                                   │
│        ENTER A KEY WORD                           │
│                                                   │
└─────────────────────────────────────────────────┘
                 MAIN MENU
```

To Use Other Searches:

Type 4 and hit RETURN.

You will see the Other Searches Menu which gives you 9 additional search options.

Type the number of the search you want and hit RETURN, or Type **/ES** and hit RETURN to go back to the main menu.

For search definitions type **?** and hit RETURN.

```
┌─────────────────────────────────────────────────┐
│ CHOOSE THE TYPE OF SEARCH YOU WISH TO PERFORM    │
│                                                   │
│     1 - BY CALL NUMBER                            │
│     2 - BY LC SUBJECT HEADING                     │
│     3 - BY MUSIC PUB NUMBER                       │
│     4 - BY SUPT DOC NO.                           │
│     5 - BY REPORT NUMBER                          │
│     6 - BY SERIES                                 │
│     7 - BY LANGUAGE                               │
│     8 - BY PERIODICAL TITLE                       │
│     9 - BY AUTHOR/RELATOR (FINE/RARE BOOKS)       │
│     (END)                                         │
└─────────────────────────────────────────────────┘
                OTHER SEARCHES
```

STARTING A SEARCH / OTHER SEARCHES

SEARCH CHOICE / AUTHOR SEARCH

TITLE SEARCH / SUBJECT SEARCH

SHORTCUTS / LOCATION CODES

Carnegie-Mellon University Libraries

Responding to LS/2000 Prompts

LS/2000 will ask you to enter various types of information at different points in the search. Below are the prompts you will encounter in LS/2000 and the correct response.

LS/2000 PROMPT	WHERE IT OCCURS	YOU RESPOND WITH
CHOICE:	Main or Other Searches menu	Type the number beside the search you want and hit RETURN. OR Enter a keyword and hit RETURN.
CHOICE: R	List of terms, titles, names	Type the REF number of your choice and hit RETURN.
CHOICE: R1/	Only 1 term, name or title	Hit RETURN.
(MORE)	List of terms, titles names exceeds 1 screen	Hit RETURN to see the rest of the list. Type /B and hit RETURN to go back a screen.

Moving Around In LS/2000

When using LS/2000 remember to:

- Wait for the cursor before you type in any response.

- Hit RETURN after you type in a response or command.

- Enter the exact spelling and punctuation. (NOTE: Like the card catalog there is one exception, initial articles of titles must be omitted.)

IF YOU WANT TO	TYPE COMMAND AND HIT RETURN	OR HIT FUNCTION KEY
Delete letters		DEL
Start or End a search	/ES	NEW SEARCH
Backup 1 step in search	^	PREV STEP
Go Back 1 screen in a list of titles, key words, names	/B	BACK
Go Forward 1 screen in a list of titles, key words, names when MORE is on bottom of screen	/F	FORWARD
To Find Responses appropriate at this level	?	QUICK HELP
Enter a Comment about the catalog	/CM	COMMENT
Print a screen of text	/P	PRINT

PROMPTS / MOVING AROUND

STARTING A SEARCH / OTHER SEARCHES

SEARCH CHOICE / AUTHOR SEARCH

TITLE SEARCH / SUBJECT SEARCH

SHORTCUTS / LOCATION CODES

Carnegie-Mellon University Libraries

Choosing a Search

STEP 1: Decide which method will produce the information quickly.

STEP 2: Be ready to try another search if yours doesn't work.

IF YOU KNOW	AND WANT TO FIND	WE RECOMMEND
Title	The book	TITLE SEARCH [Menu choice 2 or /TI]
Author	All books	AUTHOR SEARCH [Menu choice 1 or /AU]
Subject	Some books	KEY WORD SEARCH [Menu choice (enter a Key Word) or /KW] or LC SUBJECT HEADINGS SEARCH [Menu choice 4 on first menu, then 2 on the second menu or /SU]
Corporate Name or Conference Name	Works by a group (eg. the Robotics Institute) or conference reports	CORPORATE/CONFERENCE SEARCH [Menu choice 3]

How to do an Author Search

STEP #	YOU ENTER	LS/2000 RESPONDS WITH
1	At the main menu type 1 and hit RETURN.	A screen formatted like this: ENTER AUTHOR NAME: LAST NAME FIRST NAME MIDDLE NAME
2	Do you know how to spell the author's last name? If yes: Type the last name and hit RETURN. Enter the first initial and hit RETURN. If no: Type as much of the last name of which you are sure and hit RETURN twice.	A list of the author (or authors) that match(es) what you typed.
3	Enter the REF # found beside the author's name to see a list of titles by that author and hit RETURN.	A list of short titles by the author and the call numbers for those works.

NOTE: If LS/2000 responds with "NO MATCH TO THIS ENTRY, RETURN TO CONTINUE."

- Check the spelling.

- Hit RETURN to reenter.

SEARCH CHOICE / AUTHOR SEARCH

TITLE SEARCH / SUBJECT SEARCH

SHORTCUTS / LOCATION CODES

Carnegie-Mellon University Libraries

How to Do a Title Search

STEP #	YOU ENTER	LS/2000 RESPONDS WITH
1	At the main menu type **2** and hit RETURN.	A screen that prompts you to type the title.
2	Type as much of the title as you are sure of and hit RETURN. Omit initial articles such as *the, an or a*.	A list of the title(s) that match(es) what you typed.
3	Enter the **REF #** found beside the title you wish to see and hit RETURN.	The detailed catalog record for the work you have found.

NOTE: If LS/2000 responds with "NO MATCH TO THIS ENTRY, RETURN TO CONTINUE."

- Check the spelling and punctuation.

- Hit RETURN to reenter.

How to do a Subject Search

STEP #	YOU ENTER:	LS/2000 RESPONDS WITH
1	At the main menu enter one key word you want to look up and hit RETURN.	A list of terms or phrases which begin with the term you entered.
2	Select the **REF #** found beside the key word and hit RETURN.	A display showing where the key word appears in the catalog records: author's surname, title, subject heading, series, publisher or corporate/conference name.
3	Enter the **REF #** found beside the field you want to look at and hit RETURN.	Search procedures will vary depending upon which field you wish to search.

NOTE: If LS/2000 responds with "NO MATCH TO THIS ENTRY, RETURN TO CONTINUE."

- Check that you have entered only one word.

- Check the spelling.

- Hit RETURN to reenter.

TITLE SEARCH / SUBJECT SEARCH

SHORTCUTS / LOCATION CODES

Carnegie-Mellon University Libraries

LS/2000 Search Commands

Commands that Start Searches

TO START	TYPE COMMAND AND HIT RETURN	OR HIT FUNCTION KEY
New search or abort a search	/ES	NEW SEARCH
Author search	/AU	
Title search	/TI	
Key word search	/KW	
LC Subject Heading search	/SU	
To display list of Other searches	/OS	

NOTE: You can append = and your search term as a shortcut.

For Example: /AU=Cyert, Richard will bring up a list of library holdings written by Cyert.

Location Codes

The location codes are made up of the name of the library, the floor number, the section of the library, and, where applicable, the subsection of the library. The list below includes the most common location codes.

EXAMPLE: In the following code, HL4 indicates that the work is located on the fourth floor of Hunt Library. -FA limits the location to the Fine Arts collection. /INDEX further limits the location of the work to the Fine Arts Index Area.

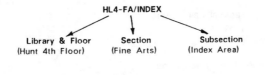

HL4-FA/INDEX

Library & Floor (Hunt 4th Floor) — Section (Fine Arts) — Subsection (Index Area)

LIBRARIES

E&S Engineering and Science Library, Wean Hall
HL Hunt Library
    [LL(Lower Level); 1; 2; 3; 4]
MI Mellon Institute Library

SECTION

-AV	Audiovisual Services
-BK	Book Stacks
-CIRC DESK	Circulation Desk
-COMP	Computer Science
-GOVTDOC	Government Documents
-JOUR	Journals
-MUS	Music Area
-NEWBK	New Books

SECTION (Continued)

-REF	Reference
-RESV AREA	Reserve Area
-SPEC	Special Collections
-TECH REPT	Technical Reports

SUBSECTION

/ARCH	Archives
/BIOG	Biography
/FA	Fine Arts
/FB	Fine Book Room
/FICT	Fiction
/INDEX	Index Section
/MICRO	Microforms
/OFC	Office
/OVRSZ	Oversize

SHORTCUTS / LOCATION CODES

Carnegie-Mellon University Libraries

LS/2000

A Service

CMU Libraries

LS/2000, an integrated library system, is a computerized catalog that provides the CMU community with online access to the materials in all branches of the University Library system --- Hunt, Engineering & Science and Mellon Institute.

Currently, this online catalog represents the majority of the libraries' holdings for books. Online access to journals, technical reports, government documents, musical scores and sound recordings is planned for the near future. Bibliographic records will be added as the collection grows.

At present, terminals for public searching are located on the first and fourth floors of Hunt Library, and at the Engineering & Science Library and Mellon Institute Library. Printers are also available at these locations. More public terminals will be added in the future.

Using the terminals in the libraries, you can search LS/2000 for a specific work or for a list of works on a particular topic or by a particular author. Traditional, as well as new approaches, are provided to access this information. Some of them are:

- Searching for author, title or subject

- Searching by a keyword, in the title, subject heading or name

- Searching by Dewey Decimal call number

- Searching for series title

- Limiting by publication date or language

Once the desired record is found, the screen will display location, call number and availability of that particular item.

If you wish to learn more about LS/2000, you can obtain a brochure describing the system and the various types of searches at all LS/2000 terminals. In addition, introductory sessions are offered throughout the term. These classes teach basic searching techniques and cover some more advanced skills.

For more information, or to learn when the next session is scheduled, inquire at the Hunt Reference Desk (x2442)

July 1984
rev. 2/86

Carnegie-Mellon University Libraries

PERSONAL NAME SEARCH

Use the Personal Name search to find:

•Authors and editors of books
•Artists, composers, performers
•A person as the subject of a book

At the Main Menu, select Personal Name and hit RETURN.

Type the full last name and hit RETURN. For common names, it is good to include both last and first names. For unusual names, the last name may be enough. Hit RETURN when you are finished.

TITLE SEARCH

Use Title Search when you know the title, or most of the title, of a book, journal, or musical work.

At the Main Menu, select Title Search and hit RETURN.

Omit all initial articles such as "a", "an", and "the". Type the first few words of the title and hit RETURN. It is not necessary to type the full title.

KEYWORD SEARCH

At the Main Menu, enter one word relevant to your search and hit RETURN.

The system responds with a list of terms. Choose the one that best represents your subject area by typing the Ref # (R #) of that term and hitting RETURN.

The system then displays what part(s) of a record your term occurs in. Select an R # and hit RETURN. For many keyword searches, "Subjects and Titles" is the best choice.

FOR ALL SEARCHES

LS/2000 will respond with a list of titles that match the search statement you entered. To view the full record for one title, type the R # beside that title and hit RETURN.

If LS/2000 responds with "No Match of This Entry, Return to Continue":
•Check your spelling and punctuation
•Use truncation (see **Search Hints**), especially if what you type in is more than 60 characters long.

SEARCH HINTS

•**Correcting Mistakes:** Use the CLEAR DELETE key to backspace and correct typos.

•**Punctuation:** Always enter punctuation as it appears in a title or in an author's name.

•**Initial Articles:** Always omit initial articles (A, An, The) in titles.

•**Acronyms:** You can search on acronyms such as "IEEE" and "ICPSR"

•**Truncation:** You can avoid problems and expand your search results by truncating, or shortening, your search statement. For example, typing "comput" as a keyword retrieves many variations such as computer, computers, computing, computation, and so forth. You can shorten multi-word searches, like titles and author names, the same way, by omitting one or more words at the end of a title, or by using a last name and first initial only.

SEE OTHER SIDE FOR GENERAL INFORMATION

WHAT IS LS/2000?

LS/2000 is an online catalog for the three Carnegie Mellon University Libraries. It includes books and collections of other media. Some periodical titles are also listed in LS/2000. Please consult a librarian if you can't locate an item.

LS/2000 is a menu-driven system. You can use the catalog by making choices at each screen or by using the Quick Search Commands.

GETTING STARTED

To start a search, press the NEW SEARCH function key or type /ES to get to the Main Menu.

Pick the kind of search you want to do, type <u>EITHER</u> the number <u>OR</u> a single keyword, and hit RETURN.

Three common search types are described on the reverse of this guide.

FUNCTION KEYS

The keys at the upper left of the keyboard will perform functions, such as returning you to the main menu or the previous screen, or allowing you to send comments about the system to library staff. The function keys are:

New Search: Returns to Main Menu
Previous Step: Returns to prior step
Next Item: Goes to next item on record
Print: Prints full screen

Use the SHIFT KEY with the function keys for these choices:

SHIFT Forward: Goes forward one screen in a list
SHIFT Back: Goes backward one screen in a list
SHIFT Comment: Use to send a comment to library staff
Info: Use to find information about library events, policies and services.

INFORMATION FUNCTION

Press SHIFT and the function key INFO, or type /IF to get information on:

- Announcements
- Library Hours
- Library Publications
- Services
- Policies

QUICK SEARCH COMMANDS

Use these codes to shortcut menu screens. You can type them at most points in a search.

/PN = Personal Name
/TI = Title
/KW = Keyword search
/AT = Author-title key search
/ES = Start new search

**TERMINALS VARY.
IF YOU NEED HELP,
ASK A REFERENCE LIBRARIAN.**

Carnegie-Mellon University Libraries

Library User Guide #3

USING THE **LUIS ONLINE CATALOG** TO FIND BOOKS AND MATERIALS

WHAT IS LUIS?

LUIS stands for Library User Information Service. It is Central State University Library's online computer catalog which enables you to search by TITLE, AUTHOR or SUBJECT (materials cataloged 1978 to date) for bibliographic, location and holdings information for most books, periodicals and other materials received by the Library. LUIS terminals are located on the 1st floor across from the Information Desk and also on the other Library floors near the Information Desks.

WHAT CAN LUIS TELL YOU?

LUIS provides the major bibliographical facts about books, journals and other materials. These include author, title, place of publication, publisher, date, number of volumes, call number, library location, and the number of copies held. Step-by-step instructions for using LUIS are provided on the terminal screen.

COMMANDS

This guide briefly lists the basic commands for the LUIS online catalog. For introductory searching instructions, TYPE:

e   press ENTER to view GENERAL INTRODUCTION to LUIS
a, t, or s press ENTER to view more detailed AUTHOR, TITLE or SUBJECT searching instructions.

All searches in LUIS begin with one of three search commands followed by a search term. These commands are:

Command	To Search	Note	Example	Press
a =	author	(last name, first name)	a = orwell g	(Enter key)
t =	title	(Ignore ''A,'' ''An'' or ''The'' when it begins a title)	t = sun also rises t = newsweek	(Enter)
s =	subject	(Use Library of Congress Subject Headings)	s = television ad	(Enter)

Central State University Library

TRUNCATION

A search term may be truncated—or **shortened**—by typing only as much of a name or phrase as is necessary to identify the wanted item. This is not an abbreviation, but a portion of the complete term. An unusual or lengthy search term will get fewer items while a commonly used or truncated term will retrieve a larger number of items.

For example, "t = scientific" matches over 200 computer records. But "t = scientific am" matches less than 15 records in the computer. Truncation — or shortening a term — can be used to avoid spelling and typing errors — or when the first name of an author or a full title is unknown.

When you are typing, if an error does occur, press the BACKSPACE ARROW. If the computer becomes "stuck," press the RESET key.

SUBJECT HEADINGS

One of the most common ways to search the online catalog is by a SUBJECT. When you are searching for a subject on the online catalog, using SUBJECT HEADINGS correctly can give you a thorough idea of which books the library has on a given subject. Often, books are listed under obvious headings such as "OKLAHOMA" or "PSYCHOLOGY." However, determining the appropriate subject headings for some topics can be difficult.

For example, books on endangered species are listed under the subject heading, "RARE ANIMALS." Books on World War I are listed under "EUROPEAN WAR, 1916-1918" and books on Blacks are found under the subject heading, "AFRO-AMERICANS." The best way to deal with this problem is to use the **LIBRARY OF CONGRESS SUBJECT HEADINGS.** This two volume set of red books and an updated microfiche list are located near the 1st floor online catalog. Using this LIBRARY OF CONGRESS LIST can save you a lot of time and help to avoid frustration when you are using the Computer catalog.

To practice, think of a term that fits your subject and look it up alphabetically in the LIBRARY OF CONGRESS SUBJECT HEADINGS. If you look up "BRAVERY", for instance, you will find:

        BRAVERY
        see COURAGE

"see" references lead you from a term not being used to the one that is being used.

When you look under COURAGE, you will find:

        Courage   (BJ1533.C8)
                sa Fear
                    Fortitude
                    Heroes
                    Morale
                    Timidity
            x   Bravery
                    Heroism
                xx Conduct of Life
                    Ethics
                    Fear
                    Heroes
        --Juvenile literature
        --Quotations, maxims, etc.
        Courage in Art
                xx Art

"sa" or "see also" references are suggesting related terms which might be useful to you.
"x" references are not used in the catalog.
"xx" references list general terms which might also be helpful.

Central State University Library

SUB-HEADINGS OF SUBJECTS

Subject Headings will often have subdivisions or sub-headings to help define the subject more specifically. Some examples are:

Types of material	GEOLOGY--DICTIONARIES GEOLOGY--EXAMINATIONS, QUESTIONS, ETC.
Geographical place names	GEOLOGY--UNITED STATES GEOLOGY--YOSEMITE VALLEY GEOLOGY--ZAMBIA
Specific aspects of subject	GEOLOGY--ECONOMIC GEOLOGY--STRATIGRAPHIC GEOLOGY--STRUCTURAL
Addition of Dates	UNITED STATES--HISTORY--CIVIL WAR, 1861-1865 UNITED STATES--HISTORY--20th CENTURY
Combinations of above	GREAT BRITAIN--HISTORY--TUDORS, 1485-1603 GREAT BRITAIN--HISTORY--HENRY VII, 1485-1509 BRITAIN--HISTORY--ELIZABETH, 1558-1603--FICTION

NOTE: When using SUB-HEADINGS, always type **2** dashes between the main heading and the sub-heading. An example is:

UNITED STATES--HISTORY

Read the Library of Congress **Subject Headings** preface for a complete explanation of the symbols and the arrangement used. If you have any trouble finding subject headings, be sure to ask for help at the Information Desk.

LUIS ONLINE CATALOG: SAMPLE SEARCH

A sample SUBJECT SEARCH on "Courage" is tried on the Online catalog. Type "s" (for Subject) = courage and press the enter key. The computer screen lists two subject choices. Number 1 is "courage." Number 2 is "courage" with a sub-heading "fiction." Type a Number 1 for some general books on courage and press the enter key. A list of 4 titles appears. To read more about title number 3 — "Profiles in Courage," type a number 3 and press enter. This screen appears:

OTHER COMMANDS WHICH MAY APPEAR DURING A SEARCH

Several abbreviated COMMANDS may appear at the bottom of the computer screen during a search. A list of these commands and their meaning follows:

Type of Display	Command	Function
Index	I	This command enables a person to return to an index or **list of books** if viewing a guide or bibliographic display screen. If followed by a number (e.g., 18), it will restore a segment of an index display beginning with the line number specified.
Guide	g	This command enables a person to return to a guide display or **list of subjects** from an index or bibliographic display. In a subject search, typing g followed by a line number will result in display of the guide beginning with that number.
More	m	A general command to display **more** of any subject guide, index or bibliographic record that does not fit on one screen, or from a complete or last screen of a bibliographic record to display the next bibliographic record.
Help	h	This command provides special instruction to **help** continue the search or interpret information displayed on a screen.

Central State University Library

The LUIS Online Catalog

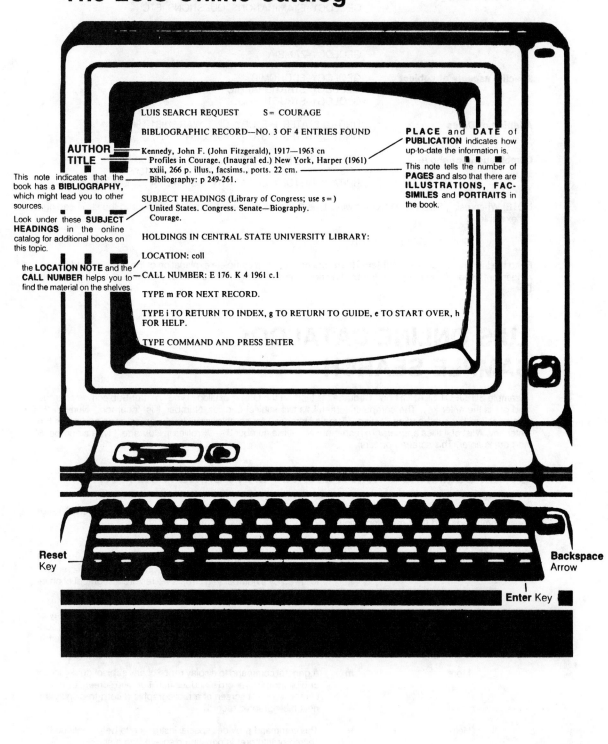

LUIS SEARCH REQUEST   S = COURAGE

BIBLIOGRAPHIC RECORD—NO. 3 OF 4 ENTRIES FOUND

AUTHOR —— Kennedy, John F. (John Fitzgerald), 1917—1963 cn
TITLE —— Profiles in Courage. (Inaugral ed.) New York, Harper (1961)
xxiii, 266 p. illus., facsims., ports. 22 cm. ——
—— Bibliography: p 249-261.

This note indicates that the book has a **BIBLIOGRAPHY**, which might lead you to other sources.

SUBJECT HEADINGS (Library of Congress; use s =)
United States. Congress. Senate—Biography.
Courage.

Look under these **SUBJECT HEADINGS** in the online catalog for additional books on this topic.

HOLDINGS IN CENTRAL STATE UNIVERSITY LIBRARY:

LOCATION: coll

the **LOCATION NOTE** and the **CALL NUMBER** helps you to find the material on the shelves.
—— CALL NUMBER: E 176. K 4 1961 c.1

TYPE m FOR NEXT RECORD.

TYPE i TO RETURN TO INDEX, g TO RETURN TO GUIDE, e TO START OVER, h FOR HELP.

TYPE COMMAND AND PRESS ENTER

PLACE and **DATE** of **PUBLICATION** indicates how up-to-date the information is.

This note tells the number of **PAGES** and also that there are **ILLUSTRATIONS, FAC-SIMILES** and **PORTRAITS** in the book.

Reset Key

Backspace Arrow

Enter Key

Central State University Library

LOCATING THE BOOKS AND OTHER MATERIAL

Check the abbreviation in the LOCATION area on the online catalog screen. If the abbreviation **"coll."** appears, this indicates that the book is in the COLLECTION on the 2nd or 4th floor of the library. **"Ref."** in the Holdings area indicates a REFERENCE book on the 1st floor. **"Per"** is a PERIODICAL or journal on the 3rd floor. For other abbreviations of library locations, check the note on the computer terminal — or ask at the Information Desk.

Next, write down the LETTERS and all of the NUMBERS after the word CALL NUMBER on the online screen for the books that interest you. Look up the **first** LETTER on the LIBRARY LOCATOR SIGN that is located across from the first floor Information Desk on the wall. The LOCATOR tells which floor in the library has the book.

CALL NUMBERS

The Central State University Library uses a LIBRARY OF CONGRESS CLASSIFICATION NUMBER such as:

BD
482
.A82

Books with LC Call Numbers are shelved alphabetically by the **letter(s)** on the first line,

A   AC   B   BD   BF   C

then in order by the **number** on the second line,

B	B	B	BA	BD	BD
6	82	5673	3	290	4176

then in order by the third line. **The number on the third line is always arranged as if it were a decimal.** In the example below, the call number ending .A82 comes before the one ending .A9 because .82 is smaller than .9.

Alphabetical	BD	BD	BD	BD
Numerical Order	482	482	482	482
Alphabetical & Decimal Order	A82	.A9	.C589	.C6

Occasionally, call numbers will have additional information, e.g., "cassette," "microfilm," "storage." Ask at the Information Desk for help in locating these materials.

By Bonnie King

April, '84

Central State University Library

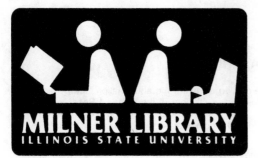

BRIEF GUIDE TO LCS

LCS (Library Computer System) is an on-line system for locating books and periodicals at Milner Library, Illinois State University and at 27 other Illinois colleges and universities. To search for materials at ISU use the instructions below. If you do not find what you want ask for help at the nearest service desk.

INITIATING A SEARCH

you may search for an item by author, author/title or call number as follows:

EXAMPLE: PS3537.T3234G8
John Steinbeck's **Grapes of Wrath**

if you know:	type command:	followed by:		press the return key:
Author and title	ATS/	4 letters (author's last name)	5 letters (first word of title)	always press the return key
		EXAMPLE: ATS/STEIGRAPE (RETURN KEY) (◄┘)		
title only	TLS/	4 letters (first word)	5 letters (second word)	always press the return key
		EXAMPLE: TLS/GRAPWRATH (RETURN KEY) (◄┘)		
author's name	AUT/	6 letters (author's last name)	3 letters (author's first name)	always press the return key
		EXAMPLE: AUT/STEINBJOH (RETURN KEY) (◄┘)		
call number of specific item	DSC/	complete call number of specific item		always press the return key
		EXAMPLE: DSC/PS3537.T3234G8 (RETURN KEY) (◄┘)		
call number in shelf area	SPS/	call number (whole or part)		always press the return key
		EXAMPLE: SPS/PS3537.T3 (RETURN KEY) (◄┘)		

1

Milner Library, Illinois State University

SPECIAL RULES IN INITIATING A SEARCH

- **TO CORRECT ERRORS:** Use the **BACKSPACE** Key on the keyboard.

- **FOR WORDS AND NAMES WITH FEWER THAN THE REQUIRED LETTERS:** Fill in with blanks using the space bar on the keyboard.

    EXAMPLE: Thomas Day
    AUT/DAY ___ ___ ___ THO
    (Press the space bar three times after Y, type THO and press the return key)

    EXAMPLE: **The Sun Also Rises**
    TLS/SUN ___ ALSO ___
    (Press the space bar once after N and once after O and press the return key)

    EXAMPLE: Lu, Min-Jen, **Taiwan's Economic Development**
    ATS/LU ___ ___ TAIWA
    (Press the space bar twice after U, type TAIWA and press the return key)

- **TREAT HYPHENATED WORDS AS ONE WORD.**

    EXAMPLE: **Non-book materials in libraries** by Richard Fothergill
    ENTER: TLS/NONBMATER

- **CERTAIN ENGLISH AND FOREIGN LANGUAGE WORDS ARE NOT USED WHEN CONSTRUCTING SEARCHES.** These words which are listed on the terminal in Milner are as follows:

A	DEM	GREAT BRITAIN.	LA	SENATE.	UNITED STATES
ALLA	DEN	GT. BRIT.	LAS	SOBRE	UNITED STATES.
ALLO	DEPARTMENT	GT.BRIT.	LE	STUDIES	UNTER
AMERICAN	DEPT.	GUIDE	LES	STUDY	US
AN	DER	HISTORY	LOS	SUR	U. S.
AND	DES	HOUSE	NA	SYMPOSIUM	U.S.
ANNUAL	DI	HOUSE.	NATIONAL	THE	V
AT	DIE	HOW	NEW	TO	VON
BULLETIN	DO	I	O	UBER	W
BY	DU	IL	OF	UEBER	WITH
CONFERENCE	EL	ILLINOIS	ON	UM	Y
CONGRESS	EN	ILLINOIS.	OS	UN	YEAR BOOK
CONGRESS.	ET	IM	PO	U. N.	YEARBOOK
DA	FOR	IN	PRO	U.N.	ZA
DAS	FROM	INTERNATIONAL	PROCEEDINGS	UND	ZU
DE	FUER	INTRODUCTION	REPORT	UNE	ZUM
DEL	FUR	IZ	REPORTS	UNITED NATIONS	ZUR
DELLA	GREAT BRITAIN	JOURNAL	SENATE	UNITED NATIONS.	

- **IF YOU ARE UNSUCCESSFUL IN LOCATING MATERIAL USING AUTHOR/TITLE COMMAND** (ATS/) try the title only command (TLS/). Some LCS records do not have an author.

2

Milner Library, Illinois State University

INTERPRETING THE SCREEN

- **NO MATCHING SEARCH CODES:** Indicates no book by that author and/or title in the file.

- **SAMPLE OF A SINGLE RECORD**

(A) BF632.5.U4

(B) ULRICH, ROGER ELWOOD, 1931-

(C) CONTROL OF HUMAN BEHAVIORS

(D) Glenview, ILL

(R) 66-14832

(E) 478471   **(F)** 1966   **(G)** 5   **(S)** Added: 801029

(H)	**(I)**	**(J)**	**(K)**	**(L)**			**(P)**
01	001	001	16-4W	STX			
02	002	001	16-4W	STX	CHGD	820129/830129	NO
03	003	001	16-4W	STX			
04	001	002	16-4W	STX	**(M)** **(N)**	**(O)** **(P)** **(Q)**	
05	002	002	16-4W	STX	CHGD	820811/820908 IS Reserve	

(A)	Call Number		**(K)**	Loan Period*
(B)	Author		**(L)**	Location Code*
(C)	Title		**(M)**	Circulation Code*
(D)	Place of Publication		**(N)**	Date Charged Out
(E)	LCS Title Number		**(O)**	Date Due
(F)	Year of Publication		**(P)**	Campus Code
(G)	Total Number of Copies		**(Q)**	Borrower Code
(H)	Line Number		**(R)**	Library of Congress Card Number
(I)	Volume Number		**(S)**	Date This Record Added to LCS
(J)	Copy Number			

*A list of loan periods, location codes and circulation codes and their meanings is posted near the terminals.

- **SAMPLE OF MULTIPLE MATCHES:** Results when more than one record matches the searching code.

```
Page 1              2 Matches            0 Skipped (all displayed in 1)
01  DONAHUE, PHIL.          DONAHUE, MY OWN STORY$ NEW YORK      1979
02  DONAHUE, PHIL.          DONAHUE, MY OWN STORY$ NEW YORK      1979
```

- **IF YOU GET MULTIPLE MATCHES:** Do a detailed search by line number(s) to see the complete record for each title.
  1. Type Dsl/
  2. Followed by: Line Number(s)
  3. Then Remember to: Press Return Key (⏎)
  4. Examples:
     Line #:1 | Lines #:1, 2
     Type: dsl/1 | Type: dsl/1/2

- **IF YOU GET MORE THAN TEN MATCHES:** LCS displays only 10 matches at a time. To see all of the matches, you must ask for additional pages of matches.

To See:	Type	Then Remember to:	Repeat the sequence
2nd group of 10 matches	pg 2	Press Return Key (⏎)	pg 2, pg 3, pg + until you have
3rd group of 10 matches	pg 3	Press Return Key (⏎)	found your book. Then use dsl/
4th group of 10 matches	pg+	Press Return Key (⏎)	to display detailed information

3

Milner Library, Illinois State University

PERIODICALS AND SERIALS

If you are looking for a periodical or serial title, use the title command (TLS/), title code and add/ SER before you press the return key.

> **EXAMPLE:** **NEW SCIENTIST** (periodical) (NEW is included in the non-significant word list on the terminal. (See page 2)
> **TYPE:** TLS/SCIE/SER (Press return key)

- **SAMPLE OF MULTIPLE PERIODICAL MATCHES:** Results when more than one record matches the searching code.

Page 1	4 Matches	0 Skipped (all displayed in 1)
01	LOS ANGELES COUNTY MUSEUM OF NAT	BULLETIN SCIENCE
02		SCIENCES
03		SCIENTIA MILANO :ETC.:
04		NEW SCIENTIST.

> **TYPE:** DSL/4 (Return)

- **SAMPLE OF A SINGLE PERIODICAL RECORD**

Ⓐ			**Ⓑ**	**Ⓒ**
Q 1 .N52			NEW SCIENTIST	LONDON

NOLC			529781 **Ⓓ**	2 **Ⓔ**	ADDED: 811009 **Ⓕ**	SER **Ⓖ**	PER **Ⓗ**

Ⓙ	**Ⓚ**	**Ⓛ**	**Ⓜ**	
01	STX	001	NOCIR **S**	UNBOUND ISSUES
02	STX	001	NOCIR **S** **Ⓘ**	v.45- 1970-
03	STX	001	2W-1D S	14-44 1962-1969
04	STX	001	NOCIR **S**	MICROFILM V.1-12 1956-1961 **Ⓘ**
05	STX	001	NOCIR	94 1982
06	STX	001	NOCIR	93 1982
07	STX	001	NOCIR	92 1981
08	STX	001	NOCIR **Ⓝ**	91 1981 **Ⓞ**

PAGE 1 MORE ON NEXT PAGE. ENTER PD2

Ⓐ	call number	**Ⓘ**	summary indicator (s) and summary statement
Ⓑ	title	**Ⓙ**	line number
Ⓒ	place of publication	**Ⓚ**	location code
Ⓓ	title number	**Ⓛ**	copy number
Ⓔ	number of copies	**Ⓜ**	loan information (circulation information)
Ⓕ	date record was added to data base	**Ⓝ**	volume, edition, part number
Ⓖ	serial indicator	**Ⓞ**	year or years
Ⓗ	periodical indicator		

SEARCHING FOR AN ITEM AT ANOTHER CAMPUS

To search for an item at one of these campuses, type in the general search command and search code followed by a slash (/) and the campus code. To search for Kurt Vonnegut's **Player Piano** at the University of Illinois:

> **EXAMPLE:** Vonnegut, Kurt, **Player Piano**
> **TYPE:** ATS/VONNPLAYE/UC

- **CODES FOR LCS LIBRARIES**

AR	Aurora College	IW	Illinois Wesleyan University
CC	University of Illinois at Chicago	JU	Judson College
CS	Chicago State	KK	Kankakee Community College
CT	Catholic Theological Union	LF	Lake Forest College
DP	De Paul University	MC	Library of the Health Sciences
EA	Eastern Illinois University		University of Illinois at Chicago
EL	Elmhurst College	ML	Millikin University
GS	Governors State University	NC	North Central College
IS	Illinois State University	NO	Northern Illinois University
IT	Illinois Institute of Technology	NU	Northeastern Illinois University

SC	Southern Illinois University—Carbondale
SE	Southern Illinois University—Edwardsville
SM	Southern Illinois University—Medical Center
SS	Sangamon State University
SX	St. Xavier College
TC	Triton College
UC	University of Illinois—Urbana-Champaign
WE	Western Illinois University

LCS 6/12/85

4

USER MANUAL FOR LEONARDO

WHO (OR WHAT) IS LEONARDO?

KEYBOARD

AUTHOR SEARCH

TITLE SEARCH

CALL NUMBER SEARCH

BROWSING BY CALL NUMBER

SUBJECT SEARCH

FINDING THE RIGHT SUBJECT HEADING

HOLDINGS SEARCH

COMMANDS

Carrier Library, James Madison University

LEONARDO* IS AN ONLINE CATALOG WHICH CURRENTLY PROVIDES AUTHOR, TITLE, SUBJECT, AND CALL NUMBER ACCESS
TO OVER HALF THE ITEMS IN CARRIER LIBRARY. ALL CURRENTLY RECEIVED BOOKS ARE IN LEONARDO, AS WELL AS
MOST BOOKS ADDED SINCE 1973. LEONARDO ALSO INCLUDES MATERIALS IN EML (EDUCATIONAL MEDIA LABORATORIES),
THE MUSIC LIBRARY, AND THE JUVENILE COLLECTION, BUT NOT THE DEWEY DECIMAL COLLECTION NOR GOVERNMENT
DOCUMENTS. SOME FEATURES OF LEONARDO NOT AVAILABLE IN THE CARD CATALOG INCLUDE:

    1.   CIRCULATION INFORMATION -- YOU CAN FIND OUT IF A BOOK IS AVAILABLE, CHECKED OUT (PLUS
         THE DUE DATE AND WHETHER IT HAS BEEN RECALLED), ON RESERVE, MISSING, OR AT THE BINDERY.

    2.   BROWSING CAPABILITY -- YOU CAN FIND A LIST OF BOOKS IN CALL NUMBER ORDER AS THEY WOULD
         APPEAR ON THE SHELVES.

*LEONARDO IS AN IMPLEMENTATION OF THE VIRGINIA TECH LIBRARY SYSTEM WHICH DISPLAYS HOLDINGS OF THE
 JMU LIBRARIES.

WHO (OR WHAT) IS LEONARDO?

KEYBOARD

AUTHOR SEARCH

TITLE SEARCH

CALL NUMBER SEARCH

BROWSING BY CALL NUMBER

SUBJECT SEARCH

FINDING THE RIGHT SUBJECT HEADING

HOLDINGS SEARCH

COMMANDS

Carrier Library, James Madison University

THE FOLLOWING KEYS PERFORM SPECIAL FUNCTIONS:

1. RETURN KEY. THIS KEY MUST BE PRESSED AFTER EACH COMMAND
   IN ORDER TO SEND THE MESSAGE TO THE COMPUTER.

2. BACKSPACE KEY. PRESS THIS KEY TO CORRECT A TYPING ERROR.

3. SLASH (/) KEY. THIS IS THE SLASH USED IN SEARCH COMMANDS.
   SEE FOLLOWING SECTIONS OF THIS MANUAL FOR INSTRUCTIONS ON
   PERFORMING SEARCHES.

4. PERIOD, COMMA, COLON, AND OTHER PUNCTUATION. YOU NEED NOT
   USE THESE KEYS BECAUSE PUNCTUATION IS NOT USED IN LEONARDO.

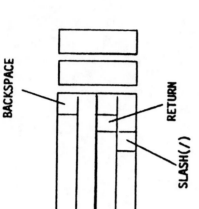

KEYBOARD

AUTHOR SEARCH

TITLE SEARCH

CALL NUMBER SEARCH

BROWSING BY CALL NUMBER

SUBJECT SEARCH

FINDING THE RIGHT SUBJECT HEADING

HOLDINGS SEARCH

COMMANDS

Carrier Library, James Madison University

THE COMMAND FOR AN AUTHOR SEARCH IS: A/

    ENTER: A/ AND THE AUTHOR'S LAST NAME.   INCLUDE THE AUTHOR'S FIRST NAME OR
                INITIAL IF KNOWN.

    EXAMPLE: A/HEMINGWAY△ or △A/HEMINGWAY△ERNEST
    PRESS: RETURN KEY

         TIPS: 1. DO NOT SPACE AFTER THE SLASH (/).
                2. IF YOU USE THE FIRST NAME OR INITIAL, BE SURE TO PUT A SPACE AFTER
                    THE LAST NAME.

         NOTE: △ = SPACE

AUTHOR SEARCH

TITLE SEARCH

CALL NUMBER SEARCH

BROWSING BY CALL NUMBER

SUBJECT SEARCH

FINDING THE RIGHT SUBJECT HEADING

HOLDINGS SEARCH

COMMANDS

Carrier Library, James Madison University

THE COMMAND FOR A TITLE SEARCH IS: T/

ENTER: T/ AND THE TITLE
EXAMPLE: T/SUN△ALSO△RISES
PRESS: RETURN KEY

TIPS: 1. DO NOT SPACE AFTER THE SLASH (/).

        2. OMIT ANY LEADING ARTICLES SUCH AS: THE, A, AN, LA, L', DIE.

        3. BE SURE TO SPACE BETWEEN WORDS.

NOTE: △ = SPACE

TITLE SEARCH

CALL NUMBER SEARCH

BROWSING BY CALL NUMBER

SUBJECT SEARCH

FINDING THE RIGHT SUBJECT HEADING

HOLDINGS SEARCH

COMMANDS

Carrier Library, James Madison University

THE COMMAND FOR A CALL NUMBER SEARCH IS: C/

    ENTER: C/ AND THE COMPLETE CALL NUMBER

    EXAMPLE: C/HV3006 △ A4 △ D478 △ 1983

    PRESS: <u>RETURN KEY</u>

        TIPS: 1. DO NOT SPACE AFTER THE SLASH (/).

                2. BE SURE TO PUT A SPACE BEFORE EACH PART OF THE CALL NUMBER THAT
                    BEGINS WITH A LETTER AND ALSO BEFORE EACH DATE.

        NOTE: △ = SPACE

CALL NUMBER SEARCH

BROWSING BY CALL NUMBER

SUBJECT SEARCH

FINDING THE RIGHT SUBJECT HEADING

HOLDINGS SEARCH

COMMANDS

Carrier Library, James Madison University

TO RETRIEVE A LIST OF BOOKS AS THEY WOULD APPEAR ON THE SHELVES, USE THE COMMAND FOR A CALL NUMBER SEARCH: C/

ENTER: C/ AND A PORTION OF THE CALL NUMBER

EXAMPLE: C/BF575△S75   (LEAVING OFF THE LAST PORTION OF THE CALL NUMBER
                           BF575 S75 P3)

PRESS: RETURN KEY

TIPS: 1. DO NOT SPACE AFTER THE SLASH (/).

        2. BE SURE TO PUT A SPACE BEFORE EACH PART OF THE CALL NUMBER THAT
            BEGINS WITH A LETTER AND ALSO BEFORE EACH DATE.

        3. TO RETRIEVE MORE ITEMS, ENTER A SHORTER PORTION OF THE CALL
            NUMBER, FOR EXAMPLE, C/BF575, AND PRESS THE RETURN KEY.

NOTE: △ = SPACE

BROWSING BY CALL NUMBER

SUBJECT SEARCH

FINDING THE RIGHT SUBJECT HEADING

HOLDINGS SEARCH

COMMANDS

Carrier Library, James Madison University

SUBJECT SEARCH

THE COMMAND FOR A SUBJECT SEARCH IS: S/

ENTER: S/ AND THE SUBJECT TERM FOUND IN LIBRARY OF CONGRESS SUBJECT HEADINGS

EXAMPLE: S/SOCIAL WORK WITH YOUTH

PRESS: RETURN KEY

TIPS: 1. DO NOT SPACE AFTER THE SLASH (/)

        2. BEFORE ENTERING YOUR SUBJECT, MAKE SURE THE SUBJECT IS ONE LISTED
            IN LIBRARY OF CONGRESS SUBJECT HEADINGS (LCSH), THE BIG RED BOOKS
            LOCATED NEAR THE TERMINAL. IF THE TERM YOU HAVE CHOSEN IS NOT ONE
            THE COMPUTER WILL RECOGNIZE, LCSH WILL REFER YOU TO THE CORRECT
            SUBJECT TERM TO USE.

        3. PERSONAL NAMES, PLACE NAMES AND ORGANIZATION NAMES MAY BE USED
            AS SUBJECTS EVEN THOUGH THEY ARE NOT LISTED IN LCSH.

        4. IF YOU ARE UNSURE OF YOUR SUBJECT TERM, ASK A LIBRARIAN TO HELP YOU.

FINDING THE RIGHT SUBJECT HEADING

HOLDINGS SEARCH

COMMANDS

Carrier Library, James Madison University

THE KEY TO SEARCHING LEONARDO EFFECTIVELY BY SUBJECT IS TO USE THE RIGHT SUBJECT HEADING FOR YOUR TOPIC. THE LIBRARY OF CONGRESS SUBJECT HEADINGS, TWO RED BOOKS NEAR YOUR TERMINAL, WILL DIRECT YOU TO TERMS THAT THE COMPUTER WILL RECOGNIZE AS VALID SUBJECT HEADINGS. THESE BOOKS WILL ALSO REFER YOU TO OTHER HEADINGS THAT MAY BE RELEVANT TO YOUR TOPIC AND WILL LIST SUB-HEADINGS THAT DIVIDE SUBJECT HEADINGS INTO SPECIFIC PARTS.

BELOW IS AN EXAMPLE FROM THE LIBRARY OF CONGRESS SUBJECT HEADINGS:

STEP 1. LOOK UP A WORD OR PHRASE AS IT OCCURS TO YOU. IF IT IS FOLLOWED BY A "SEE" REFERENCE, TURN TO THAT WORD OR PHRASE.

STEP 2. IF IT IS PRINTED IN BOLD FACE TYPE, THAT WORD OR PHRASE CAN BE SEARCHED AS A SUBJECT HEADING.

STEP 3. WORDS OR PHRASES FOLLOWING "SA" OR "XX" ARE RELATED SUBJECT HEADINGS THAT CAN BE SEARCHED IN A SUBJECT SEARCH.

STEP 4. WORDS FOLLOWING "X" ARE SYNONYMOUS TERMS THAT ARE NOT USED AS SUBJECT HEADINGS.

STEP 5. SUBDIVISIONS OF THE MAIN HEADING ARE GIVEN FOLLOWING A DASH. IN LEONARDO THE EXAMPLE WILL APPEAR AS: EUTHANASIA--SOCIAL ASPECTS.

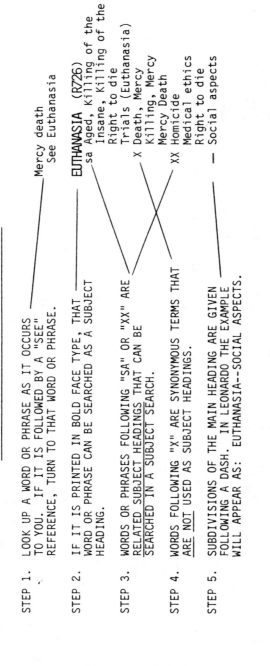

Mercy death
    See Euthanasia

EUTHANASIA (R726)
sa Aged, Killing of the
    Insane, Killing of the
    Right to die
    Trials (Euthanasia)
x   Death, Mercy
    Killing, Mercy
    Mercy Death
xx Homicide
    Medical ethics
    Right to die
—   Social aspects

FINDING THE RIGHT SUBJECT HEADING

HOLDINGS SEARCH

COMMANDS

THE COMMAND FOR A HOLDINGS SEARCH IS: H/

ENTER: H/ AND THE COMPLETE CALL NUMBER OF THE ITEM

EXAMPLE: H/HA202△A35

PRESS: RETURN KEY

TIPS: 1.   DO NOT SPACE AFTER THE SLASH (/).

        2.   BE SURE TO PUT A SPACE BEFORE EACH PART OF THE CALL NUMBER THAT
             BEGINS WITH A LETTER AND ALSO BEFORE EACH DATE.

        3.   THE HOLDINGS SCREEN TELLS YOU IF THE ITEM IS IN ANOTHER LOCATION
             BESIDES THE GENERAL COLLECTION. IT ALSO TELLS YOU WHICH EDITIONS
             OF A BOOK THE LIBRARY OWNS AND WHETHER THERE IS MORE THAN ONE COPY.
             IF YOU NEED MORE INFORMATION ABOUT THE HOLDINGS SCREEN, ENTER HELP
             AND PRESS RETURN KEY.

        4.   IF THE SCREEN TELLS YOU "NO HOLDINGS", THAT MEANS THE BOOK IS
             PROBABLY IN THE GENERAL COLLECTION.

        5.   THIS PART OF THE SYSTEM IS INCOMPLETE: YOU MAY WISH TO CONSULT THE
             LIBRARIAN FOR HELP.

NOTE: △ = SPACE

HOLDINGS SEARCH

COMMANDS

Carrier Library, James Madison University

COMMANDS USED IN LEONARDO:

A/ = AUTHOR SEARCH. ENTER A/ AND AUTHOR'S NAME, LAST NAME FIRST.

C/ = CALL NUMBER SEARCH. ENTER C/ AND COMPLETE CALL NUMBER.

C = CIRCULATION. THE COMPUTER WILL TELL YOU WHEN TO ENTER C AND WILL GIVE YOU CIRCULATION INFORMATION ABOUT A PARTICULAR ITEM.

CA = CARD. TO SEE A SCREEN THAT LOOKS LIKE A CARD IN THE CARD CATALOG COMPLETE WITH PUBLICATION INFORMATION, ENTER CA AFTER YOU HAVE MADE A SUCCESSFUL AUTHOR, TITLE OR CALL NUMBER SEARCH.

H = HOLDINGS SEARCH. ENTER H/ AND THE COMPLETE CALL NUMBER. HOLDINGS REFER TO WHAT THE LIBRARY OWNS OR "HOLDS".

NS = NEXT SCREEN. ENTER NS, THEN PUSH RETURN, WHEN YOU WANT TO ADVANCE TO THE NEXT SCREEN WITHIN A SEARCH.

PS = PREVIOUS SCREEN. ENTER PS, THEN PUSH RETURN, WHEN YOU WANT TO RETURN TO THE PREVIOUS SCREEN WITHIN A SEARCH.

S/ = SUBJECT SEARCH. ENTER S/ AND A SUBJECT TERM FROM LIBRARY OF CONGRESS SUBJECT HEADINGS.

S = SPECIAL STATUS, WHICH INDICATES AN ITEM IS NOT CURRENTLY AVAILABLE FOR CIRCULATION. THE COMPUTER WILL TELL YOU WHEN TO ENTER S AND WILL GIVE YOU THE REASON FOR THE ITEM'S UNAVAILABILITY.

T/ = TITLE SEARCH. ENTER T/ AND THE TITLE OF THE BOOK.

COMMANDS

Carrier Library, James Madison University

FOCUS ON

DIAL ACCESS
TO THE
ONLINE CATALOG DATABASE

THE ONLINE CATALOG DATABASE

Lansing Community College and Lansing Public Library have entered their collections (books, magazines, and audio-visual materials) into a combined database which now may be accessed via microcomputers equipped with modems located off campus or out of the libraries. These instructions describe how to access and interpret the system. LCC does not provide a user support phone number for owner's equipment use assistance. If you wish to borrow materials from either of these collections, please contact the appropriate library for lending regulations and hours of operation: Lansing Community College Library, phone (517) 483-1657; Lansing Public Library, phone (517) 374-4600.

► CONNECTION INFORMATION

1. Access hours are normally 7:30 A.M. through 10 P.M. Monday through Friday and 7:30 A.M. to 6 P.M. on Saturday.

2. There is one telephone line, 300 baud.

3. <u>Dial (517) 483-1772</u>.

   Listen for a high-pitched tone on your telephone and then attach it to your accoustical coupler. You are on-line to the combined data-base of Lansing Community College and Lansing Public Library. After dialing, if a busy signal is heard, the dial-up connection is in use. Wait a few moments and dial the number again.

   When a / slash or //// slashes appear, touch your return key twice and the cursor will appear to the left of your screen.

4. At this point, the online catalog database may be accessed using the standard search keys: author, title, or subject. Consult the follow-ing instructions for specific information.

LIBRARY INFORMATION SERVICES

Library Information Services, Lansing Community College

HOW TO USE THE COMPUTER CATALOG

➡️ Whenever the screen displays the question TITLE? you may use any one of the three methods shown below to search for books, magazines, or audio-visual materials.

TO SEARCH BY: T I T L E .

   1. Type a period .

                                              EXAMPLES:

   2. Type EXACT title of book or   .Future without shock$
       magazine spacing between each   .Newsweek$
       word, followed directly by a $.   .Careers in word processing
                                             .Megatrends$

   3. Hit the RETURN key.

TO SEARCH BY: A U T H O R ,

   1. Type a comma ,

                                              EXAMPLES:

   2. Type author's last name, followed   ,Lundborg, Louis$
       by a space; type author's first   ,Lundborg, L$
       name or initial and a $,Jung, Carl$
                                              ,Chaucer$

   3. Hit the RETURN key.

TO SEARCH BY: S U B J E C T ;

   1. Type a semicolon ;

   2. Type your subject, followed   EXAMPLES:
       directly by a $.
                                             ;adult education$
                                             ;word processing$
   3. Hit the RETURN key.   ;computers$

                HEX and OCTAL CODES for LCC/LPL Catalog Database Commands

HEX	OCTAL	COMMAND	HEX	OCTAL	COMMAND
18	30	CTRL-P	2E	56	PERIOD (.) FOR TITLE SEARCHES
7F	177	SHIFT-RUB	2C	44	COMMA (,) FOR AUTHOR SEARCHES
0D	15	RETURN	2F	57	SLASH (/) FOR CALL # SEARCHES
1E	36	CTRL-N	3B	73	SEMICOLON (;) FOR SUBJECT SEARCHES
24	44	DOLLAR SIGN ($) FOR TRUNCATION			

Library Information Services, Lansing Community College

INTERPRETING THE SCREEN DISPLAY

```
      ┌BERATPM990 ──────────────────── 1
  *   │ E 860 .B47 ──────────────── 2a)
   ╲  │ Bernstein, Carl, 1944- ──────────── 3
      │ All the President's men ──────────── 4
      └New York, Simon and Schuster (1974)──────── 5
 6 ── DESCRIPT:    349 p.  ports.  24 cm.
      SUBJECT1:    Bernstein, Carl, 1944-
      SUBJECT2:    Woodward, Bob
      SUBJECT3:    The Washington Post
      SUBJECT4:    Watergate Affair, 1972-
      Addauthor1:  Woodward, Bob, joint author
      O:           0972066

          KEY        PUB              PUBYR      CST
      BERATPM99                                  $8.95

      MC   ED    L.A.D.               V
                 6/14/82              N                8
  7 ┌ASL    3 1382 00136 6330    ON SHELF      19    10  9
    └LPL  364.132 B54a
 2b) ╲    ? 3  1329 00062 9325    ON SHELF      59    6
```

1. **ID** - Title identifier number. Type in this number to see an entire record. No symbols are needed when typing the ID.

2. **CALL NUMBER** - Copy this down because books are arranged on the shelves in call number order.

   a) **LCC CALL NUMBER** - Always appears on second line of display (a Library of Congress classification).

   b) **LPL CALL NUMBER** - Appears next to their location symbol at the bottom of a fully displayed record i.e. 364.132 B54a (a Dewey Decimal classification).

3. **AUTHOR**

4. **TITLE**

5. **PUBLISHER**

6. **DESCRIPTION** - Includes a brief physical description of the item.

7. **LOCATION** - ASL = ARTS & SCIENCES LIBRARY, LANSING COMMUNITY COLLEGE
   OCL = OLD CENTRAL LIBRARY, LANSING COMMUNITY COLLEGE
   VTL = VOCATIONAL TECHNICAL LIBRARY, LANSING COMMUNITY COLLEGE
   LPL = LANSING PUBLIC LIBRARY
   LPJ = LANSING PUBLIC LIBRARY JOLLY CEDAR BRANCH

8. **BAR CODE** - Computer number for checkout purposes.

9. **STATUS** - Tells availability of item. Due date appears if checked out.

   *Short information may display when there are several hits for your search. To see the full record for any item, just type the ID (the title identifier number) after getting back to the INQUIRY.

NOTE: Lansing Public Library is still adding its collection to the data base. If you find a record which says "no items", has no LCCNOTE or LCC call number, the book belongs to Lansing Public Library.

ADDITIONAL INFORMATION

The message Not on File appears when:
- the title, author, or subject is not in the database, or
- the search was typed incorrectly, or
- your inquiry is not searchable by that particular method. Try another.

To STOP a scrolling display:
- press **CONTROL** and **P** keys simultaneously to stop the scroll.
  A prompt will appear on the screen, "What do you want to do?"

     type CONT to continue the scrolling or

     type FUNC to change functions (INQUIRY Title? will appear)

<u>HOW TO USE THE COMPUTER CATALOG</u>

➡ Whenever the screen displays the question <u>TITLE</u>? you may use any one of the three methods shown below to search for books, magazines, or audio-visual materials.

TO SEARCH BY: <u>T I T L E .</u>

    1. Type a period .

    2. Type EXACT title of book or
       magazine spacing between each
       word, followed directly by a $.

    3. Hit the RETURN key.

EXAMPLES:

.Future without shock$
.Newsweek$
.Careers in word processing
.Megatrends$

TO SEARCH BY: <u>A U T H O R ,</u>

    1. Type a comma ,

    2. Type author's last name, followed
       by a space; type author's first
       name or initial and a $

    3. Hit the RETURN key.

EXAMPLES:

,Lundborg, Louis$
,Lundborg, L$
,Jung, Carl$
,Chaucer$

TO SEARCH BY: <u>S U B J E C T;</u>

    1. Type a semicolon ;

    2. Type your subject, followed
       directly by a $.

    3. Hit the RETURN key.

EXAMPLES:

;adult education$
;word processing$
;computers$

<u>HEX</u> and <u>OCTAL CODES</u> for <u>LCC/LPL Catalog Database</u> Commands

HEX	OCTAL	COMMAND	HEX	OCTAL	COMMAND
18	30	CTRL-P	2E	56	PERIOD (.) FOR TITLE SEARCHES
7F	177	SHIFT-RUB	2C	44	COMMA (,) FOR AUTHOR SEARCHES
0D	15	RETURN	2F	57	SLASH (/) FOR CALL # SEARCHES
1E	36	CTRL-N	3B	73	SEMICOLON (;) FOR SUBJECT SEARCHES
24	44	DOLLAR SIGN ($) FOR TRUNCATION			

Library Information Services, Lansing Community College

The LSU Libraries, Louisiana State University and Agricultural and Mechanical College

All searches in **LOLA** begin with one of three commands. Key in

        a = to find an author
        t = to find a title
        s = to find a subject

Press the **ENTER** key after every command.

Type **a**= followed by the **AUTHOR'S** last name or the name of the institution, organization, or society serving as the author. Press the **ENTER** key.

      Examples: **a**=long hu* **(ENTER)**
                      a=unesco **(ENTER)**
                      a=louisiana state univ* **(ENTER)**

     *TIP: Type only the first few letters when uncertain about spelling, etc. **LOLA** allows truncation.

Type **t**= followed by the first word(s) of the **TITLE**. Press the **ENTER** key.

      Examples: **t**=louisiana enterpris **(ENTER)**
                      t=1984 **(ENTER)**

   TIP: Omit beginning articles such as a, an, the, la, or der.

Type **s**= followed by the appropriate **LIBRARY OF CONGRESS SUBJECT HEADING**. See the *Library of Congress Subject Headings* **(LCSH)** lists located near the terminals in the reference areas.

      Examples: **s**=jazz mus **(ENTER)**
                      s=cookery, amer **(ENTER)**
                      s=music—united states **(ENTER)**

   TIP: Type **SUBJECT HEADINGS** exactly as they appear in the **LCSH**.

   INDEX . . . When your search results in multiple entries, **LOLA** displays a list of author/title combinations. This listing is called an **INDEX** screen.

   GUIDE . . . If your search results in more authors, titles, or subject headings than can be displayed on one screen, **LOLA** displays a **GUIDE** screen. A **GUIDE** groups the index into sections.

   For complete information on any item from an **INDEX** or a **GUIDE** screen, type the number to the left of the item and press **ENTER**.

   HELP . . . Type **h** at any point during the search and press **ENTER** for further instructions.

- Capitalization is not necessary.
- To correct mistakes, backspace using the ⬧ key and type over the error.
- When typing numbers, do not substitute the letter o for the number 0 or the letter l for the number 1.
- If you press a key and nothing happens, press the **RESET** key.
- If your search is unsuccessful, try the Card Catalog or ask a staff member for assistance.

The LSU Libraries, Louisiana State University and Agricultural and Mechanical College

LCS

Online Catalog Searching Guide

ATS/	AUTHOR-TITLE SEARCH
	ats/dickens hard times—
TLS/	TITLE SEARCH
book:	*tls/heart is a lonely hunter—*
serial:	*tls/journal of anatomy—/ser*
AUT/	AUTHOR SEARCH
	aut/hemingway, ernest
	aut/symposium on blood
SUB/	SUBJECT SEARCH
	sub/halley's comet
	sub/bridges, suspension
SER/	BOOK IN SERIES
	ser/manchester monographs
SPS/	CALL NUMBER SEARCHES
DSC/	browse: *sps/mt55b22m3*
	specific title: *dsc/mt55b22m3*
	specific journal volume: *dsc/qm1j86,v=144*
	specific journal year: *dsc/qm1j86,y=1986*

Follow the prompts at the end of each screen display to complete your search.

LCS Telephone Center: 292-3900

LIBRARY LOCATION CODES

Following is a list of the LCS three-letter codes for specific library locations. Please ask library staff about any code not on this list or type HELP followed by the code (e.g., HELP edu).

AGI Agriculture Library, 45 Ag. Admin., 2120 Fyffe Rd.
AGO Agronomy Dept. Library, 333 Kottman Hall, 2021 Coffey Rd.
ARV University Archives, 204 Converse Hall, 2121 Tuttle Park Place
BOS Biological Sciences Library, 200 B & Z, 1735 Neil Ave.
BSL Black Studies Library, 210 Main Library, 1858 Neil Ave. Mall
BUS Business Library, 110 Page Hall, 1810 College Rd.
CGA Communication & Graphic Arts, 147 Journalism Bldg., 242 W. 18th Ave.
CHE Chemistry Library, 310 McPherson Laboratory, 140 W. 18th Ave.
CHI Children's Hospital Library, 216B Children's Hospital, 700 Children's Drive
CLA Classics, German, Linguistics & Romance Languages Reading Room, 300S Main Library, 1858 Neil Ave. Mall
CRL Center for Research Libraries, order from interlibrary Loan, 103 Main Library, 1858 Neil Ave. Mall
CTE Center for Teaching Excellence, 1 Lord Hall, 124 W. 17th Ave.
EAS East Asian Studies Reading Room, 320N Main Library, 1858 Neil Ave. Mall
EDU Education/Psychology Library, 060 Arps Hall, 1945 N. High St.
EES East European and Slavic Studies Reading Room, 300NE Main Library, 1858 Neil Ave. Mall
ENR Engineering/Architecture Library, 112 Caldwell Laboratory, 2024 Neil Ave.
ENX c/o Physics Library, 1011 Smith Laboratory, 174 W. 18th Ave.
ETC English, Theatre & Communications, 200N Main Library, 1858 Neil Ave. Mall
FIN Fine Arts Library, 166 Sullivant Hall, 1813 N. High St.
GEO Geology Library, 180 Orton Hall, 155 S. Oval Drive
HEA Health Sciences Library, 376 W. 10th Ave.
HIL Hilandar Research Library, 227 Main Library, 1858 Neil Ave. Mall
HIS History, Political Science & Philosophy, 200S Main Library, 1858 Neil Ave. Mall
HOM Home Economics Library, 325 Campbell Hall, 1787 Neil Ave.
JDC Jewish Studies Reading Room, 320SE Main Library, 1858 Neil Ave. Mall
JOU Journalism Library, 100 Journalism Building, 242 W. 18th Ave.

LAT Latin American Studies Reading Room, 300NW Main Library, 1858 Neil Ave. Mall
LAZ Lazenby Hall c/o Biological Sciences Library, 200 B & Z, 1735 Neil Ave.
LLX Law Library, 219 Law Building, 1659 N. High Street
LL- Other codes used for areas within the Law Library
MAI Main Library Stacks, c/o Circulation Desk, 1858 Neil Ave. Mall
MAP Map Collection, 200 Main Library, 1858 Neil Ave. Mall
MAT Mathematics Library, 10 Math Bldg., 231 W. 18th Ave.
MEJ Middle East Studies Reading Room, 320SW Main Library, 1858 Neil Ave. Mall
MET Materials Engineering Library, 197 Watts Hall, 2041 College Rd.
MIC Microforms & Periodicals Room, Info. Svc. Dept., First Floor, Main Library, 1858 Neil Ave. Mall
MUS Music/Dance Library, 186 Sullivant Hall, 1813 N. High St.
OHI State Library of Ohio, 1114 Ohio Depts. Bldg., 65 S. Front St.
OH-OSU OSU Collection. Ask at RAR. for information call the State Library (462-6948)
PER Perkins Observatory c/o Physics Library, 1011 Smith Laboratory, 174 W. 18th Ave.
PHA Pharmacy Library, 207 Lloyd M. Parks Hall, 500 W. 12th Ave.
PHY Physics Library, 1011 Smith Laboratory, 174 W. 18th Ave.
RAR Rare Books & Manuscripts, 327 Main Library, 1858 Neil Ave. Mall
REF Reference Room, Info. Svc. Dept., First Floor, Main Library, 1858 Neil Ave. Mall
SOC Social Work Library, 400 Stillman Hall, 1947 College Road
STO Stone Lab. c/o Biological Sciences Library, 200 B & Z, 1735 Neil Ave.
STX in Storage, c/o Circulation Desk, Main Library, 1858 Neil Ave. Mall
TOP Topaz Library, 114 Fry Hall, 338 W. 10th Ave.
TRI Lawrence & Lee Theatre Research Institute Library, 1432 Lincoln Tower, 1800 Cannon Drive
UND Undergraduate Library, 205 Sullivant Hall, 1813 N. High St.
VET Veterinary Medicine Library, 229 Sisson Hall, 1900 Coffey Rd.
WCL West Campus storage. Request at any Circulation Desk.
WMN Women's Studies Library, 220 Main Library, 1858 Neil Ave. Mall

Comments, questions, and suggestions related to LCS are welcome. Please submit items to a library suggestion box or contact the Automation Office, 106 Main Library, 1858 Neil Avenue Mall, 292-6151.

SEARCH STEPS — Note: commands to be typed are given in **bold-face type**: variables are given in *italic type*. See search examples on front panel.

LOOKING FOR:	BEST LCS SEARCH(ES) TO START:	NEXT STEP(S):
Book(s)		
by author and title	**ats**/*author's last name title—*	**dsl**/*line number* [for availability & location]
by title	**tls**/*title—* or **tbl**/*line number* [for full catalog information]
by author	**aut**/*author name (phonebook style)* → or **dsl**/*line number*
by book series title	**ser**/*collective series title*	**tbl**/*line number*
by subject	**sub**/*topic or subject headings*	**dsl**/*line number* or **dsl**/*line number*
		tbl/*line number* **tbl**/*line number*
Journal, Magazine, or Other Serial		
by title	**tls**/*title of journal—***/ser** → **dsl**/*line number,***v**=*volume*
		,y=*year*
		,l=*library location code*
		,cur [for current issues]
by organization	**aut**/*issuing organization name*	**dsl**/*line number*
Conference Proceedings		
by conference name	**aut**/*complete name of conference* → **dsl**/*line number*
by organization	**aut**/*sponsoring organization name* or
by subject	**sub**/*topic—***congresses**	**tbl**/*line number*
Call Number		
to browse	**sps**/*call number* [whole or partial] → **dsl**/*line number*
for specific item	**dsc**/*call number* [complete; for journals, add qualifiers such as, **v**= shown in Journal search, above.]

ABOUT LCS

LCS (Library Control System) is a computerized catalog and circulation system which includes books, documents and journals in the Ohio State University Libraries - Columbus Campus (OSU), OSU Law Library (LL), the State Library of Ohio (SL), the Ohio Historical Society (HS), and the Center for Research Libraries (CL) in Chicago.

For all OSU library materials, LCS provides access by author, title, and call number. For most materials acquired since 1972, LCS also provides subject access.

For some information needs, sources other than LCS or the card catalogs should be used (e.g., periodical indexes, directories, etc.).
Assistance in using LCS is available:
• enter HELP directly on LCS
• attend an LCS workshop (offered each quarter)
• ask library staff

KEYBOARD HINTS

HELP LOC CAT

Page turning keys

ENTER Directional Keys

Print Reset Alt

• ENTER each search.

• CORRECT TYPING ERRORS by moving cursor with directional keys, then retype.

• If keyboard or printer locks, press ALT and RESET keys.

• PRINT key works only when a printer is attached.

SEARCHING HINTS

• OMIT ARTICLES (a, an, the, and foreign equivalents) at the beginning of a title.

• ADD A HYPHEN after all title (TLS/ or ATS/) searches.

• FOLLOW PROMPTS at the bottom of each LCS display.

• TYPE in all lower-case letters.

• CAN'T FIND IT? ASK LIBRARY STAFF FOR ASSISTANCE!

• Call 292-3900 to locate, check-out, or renew materials.

NVP & M-B
6/87

The Ohio State University Libraries

For additional information on LCS, ask
for these brochures:

LCS Search Guide

LCS Practice Searches

Search LCS from Home

Searching for Conference Proceedings on LCS

For assistance in using LCS, feel free to ask library
staff, or attend an LCS workshop. Workshops are
offered each quarter; schedules are available in all
OSU Libraries.

The Ohio State University

LIBRARIES

LCS and the Card Catalog

A User's Guide to Catalog Choices

The card catalogs of The Ohio State University
Libraries *are not current*; no cards have been added
since 1982. The Library Control System (LCS)
now serves as the catalog of the OSU Libraries.

LCS also serves as the circulation system for the
OSU Libraries, and the catalog and circulation
system of the State Library of Ohio.

For all OSU library materials, LCS provides access
by *author, title,* and *call number.* For most
materials acquired since 1972, LCS also provides
subject access.

It is usually preferable to *check LCS first,* then
use the card catalogs. For some needs, sources
other than LCS or the card catalogs should be used
(e.g., periodical indexes).

This brochure highlights some features of LCS and
the card catalogs. If you have additional questions,
or cannot find what you're looking for in either
catalog, *please ask library staff for
assistance.*

NVP & M-B   6/87

Why Use LCS?

- LCS lists all OSU library materials. It is the only source of information for books and other materials acquired by the OSU Libraries since 1982.

- LCS lists volumes of periodicals and journals owned by the OSU Libraries.

- LCS indicates circulation status (available, checked out, etc.).

- LCS lists items on order or in processing for the OSU Libraries.

- LCS allows searching by call number for specific items or shelf browsing.

- LCS includes books and government publications available from the State Library of Ohio in downtown Columbus.

- Using a terminal with a printer attached, you may obtain copies of bibliographic records or lists of titles.

What's not in LCS?

- LCS does not provide subject access or full catalog records for most items acquired by the OSU Libraries before 1972.

- LCS is not an index to articles in periodicals, magazines, journals or other serials.

- LCS is not an index to some uncataloged materials, e.g., maps, some government documents, and manuscripts.

Why use card catalogs?

- The card catalogs provide full catalog records for OSU materials acquired before 1982, allowing searches by author or title, and by:

  subject

  editor or secondary author(s)

  series (collective title or a set of books)

- The Main Library card catalog, on the first floor, is a listing of materials in all OSU Libraries on the Columbus campus added before 1982.

- Specialized card catalogs are available for languages in non-Roman disciplines. Consult librarians in Language and Area Studies, 3rd Floor, Main Library for details.

What's not in the card catalogs?

- Items acquired by the OSU Libraries since 1982 are not included in the card catalogs.

- Many items which are listed in LCS, the online catalog, are not included in the card catalogs (e.g., ERIC documents, items on order, State Library of Ohio books, etc.)

- Like LCS, the card catalogs do not include many uncataloged items (e.g., maps) and do not index articles in periodicals.

The Ohio State University Libraries

LIAS at a Glance

An Introductory Guide to Searching the Online Catalog

IF YOU WANT:	INPUT:	SEE PAGE
To Start	⏎ ⏎ ⏎	3
To Search	SEARCH	5
	TITLE	10
	AUTHOR	10
	SUBJECT	10
	FIND	10
To See Next Screen	NEXT	7
To See Previous Screen	PREV	7
Availability Information	STATUS	8
To Return to an Earlier Display	BACK	9
To Retrieve a Record by Call No. or Item No.	CALL	9
To Obtain a Summary of Your Account	PATRON SUMMARY	9
To Tailor Search to a Specific Library	LIBRARY	11
To Identify Items Shelved in the Same Area	SHELF	12
To Expand from a Selected Record	BRIDGE	13
To Report a Mistake	OOPS	14
Help at Any Point	HELP	4
A Brief Description of LIAS	HELP LIAS	2

Pennsylvania State University Libraries

How to Use This Guide

This guide introduces you to LIAS, the **L**ibrary **I**nformation **A**ccess **S**ystem developed by The Pennsylvania State University. LIAS is an online library catalog — instead of consulting drawers of index cards, you can now use a computer terminal to determine the library's holdings.

LIAS contains information about the books, serials (journals, magazines, etc.), music scores, theses, and sound recordings owned by the University Libraries. Other items — government documents, microforms, maps, and archives — may also be included. For a detailed list of materials available in your library, type HELP LIAS and press *.

1
When you see this symbol ☐, press the key or type the command indicated.

2
User input (i.e., what you type into the system) is italicized.

3
☐ sends your message to the computer.

*NOTE: The symbol on the key varies according to the terminal you use:
☐ = RETURN = ENTER = NEW LINE

Getting Started

Press the ☐ key *three times*.

Once you have initiated your session, LIAS will respond with the following display:

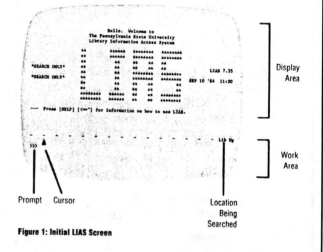

Figure 1: Initial LIAS Screen

Points to Remember

Begin your session by pressing ⬅ *three times*.

Wait for the >>> prompt to appear on the screen before you type any information.

The request you type will appear at the bottom of the screen at the >>> prompt.

Some terminals are equipped with function keys that allow you to enter a command by simply pressing the key. The function keys on terminals in the University Libraries are on the top row and are labeled.

Press the ⬅ key after you finish typing your request. This sends your message to the LIAS computer.

To correct an error while entering your request, use the BACKSPACE or DEL key to move the cursor to the error, and then retype the information.

Requests can be entered in lower or upper case letters.

A new search can begin anytime.

If you have problems, press or type HELP ⬅ or consult a library staff member at a public service desk.

Basic Commands

SEARCH

Purpose: To find an item in LIAS. You do not need to know whether your desired term is a title, author, subject, or series.

User Input: SEARCH *term(s)* ⬅ *

Examples:

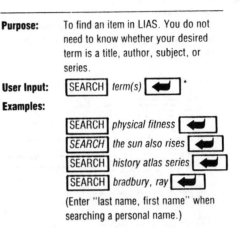

SEARCH *physical fitness* ⬅

SEARCH *the sun also rises* ⬅

SEARCH *history atlas series* ⬅

SEARCH *bradbury, ray* ⬅

(Enter "last name, first name" when searching a personal name.)

LIAS Response:
A list of entries that match or resemble the term you are searching. An entry represents the heading that would appear at the top of cards in a card catalog.

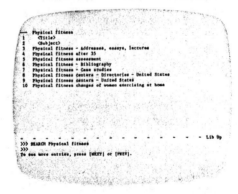

Figure 2: Entry Screen

(Notice that the term "physical fitness" has been used as both a title and a subject.)

*NOTE: In some locations, LIAS is set on an automatic search option. This means you do not have to precede your request with SEARCH .

To select an entry, press the appropriate number key.

Example: 2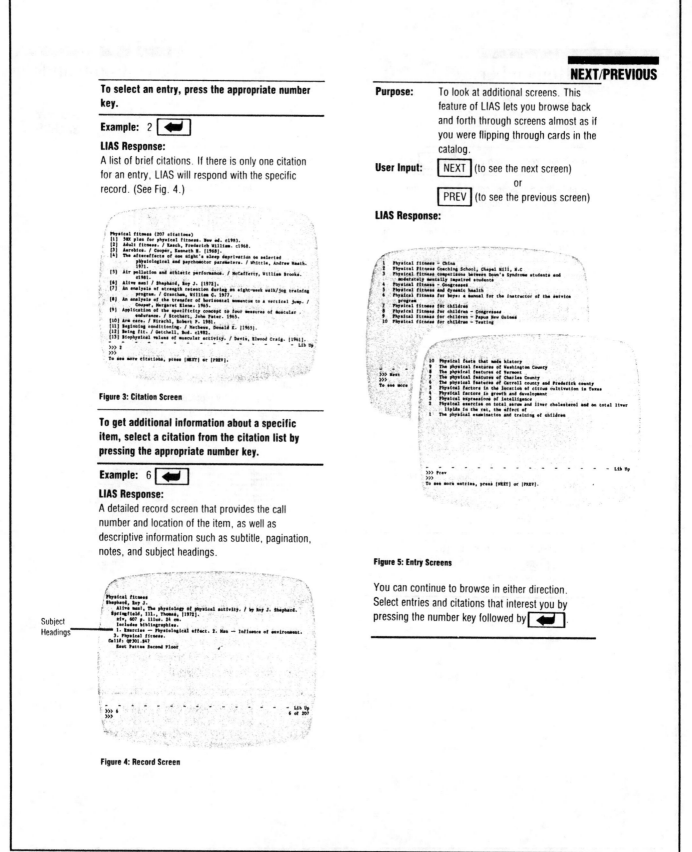

LIAS Response:

A list of brief citations. If there is only one citation for an entry, LIAS will respond with the specific record. (See Fig. 4.)

Figure 3: Citation Screen

To get additional information about a specific item, select a citation from the citation list by pressing the appropriate number key.

Example: 6

LIAS Response:

A detailed record screen that provides the call number and location of the item, as well as descriptive information such as subtitle, pagination, notes, and subject headings.

Subject
Headings

Figure 4: Record Screen

Purpose: To look at additional screens. This feature of LIAS lets you browse back and forth through screens almost as if you were flipping through cards in the catalog.

User Input: NEXT (to see the next screen)

or

PREV (to see the previous screen)

LIAS Response:

Figure 5: Entry Screens

You can continue to browse in either direction. Select entries and citations that interest you by pressing the number key followed by .

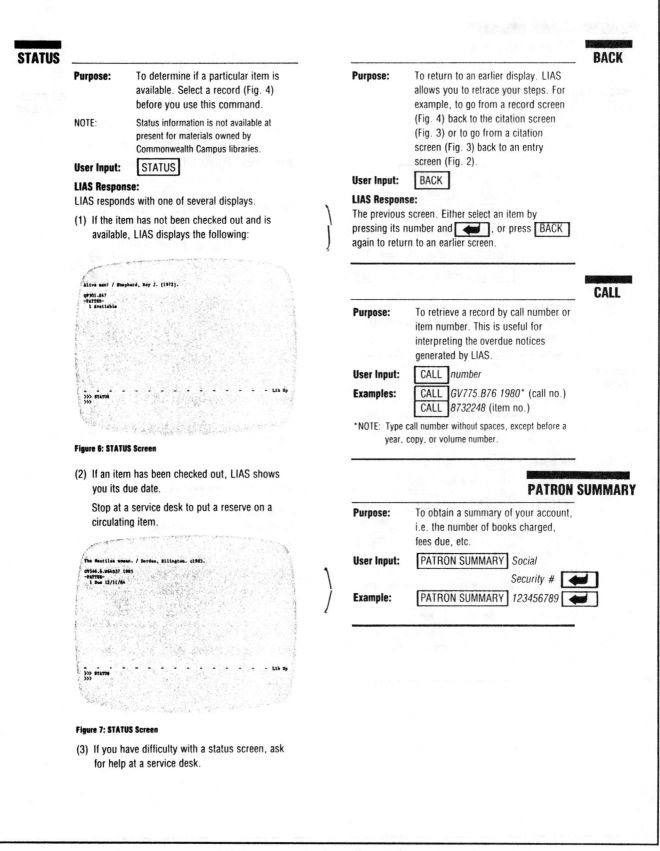

STATUS

Purpose: To determine if a particular item is available. Select a record (Fig. 4) before you use this command.

NOTE: Status information is not available at present for materials owned by Commonwealth Campus libraries.

User Input: STATUS

LIAS Response:
LIAS responds with one of several displays.

(1) If the item has not been checked out and is available, LIAS displays the following:

Figure 6: STATUS Screen

(2) If an item has been checked out, LIAS shows you its due date.

Stop at a service desk to put a reserve on a circulating item.

Figure 7: STATUS Screen

(3) If you have difficulty with a status screen, ask for help at a service desk.

BACK

Purpose: To return to an earlier display. LIAS allows you to retrace your steps. For example, to go from a record screen (Fig. 4) back to the citation screen (Fig. 3) or to go from a citation screen (Fig. 3) back to an entry screen (Fig. 2).

User Input: BACK

LIAS Response:
The previous screen. Either select an item by pressing its number and ⬅, or press BACK again to return to an earlier screen.

CALL

Purpose: To retrieve a record by call number or item number. This is useful for interpreting the overdue notices generated by LIAS.

User Input: CALL *number*

Examples: CALL *GV775.B76 1980** (call no.)
CALL *8732248* (item no.)

*NOTE: Type call number without spaces, except before a year, copy, or volume number.

PATRON SUMMARY

Purpose: To obtain a summary of your account, i.e. the number of books charged, fees due, etc.

User Input: PATRON SUMMARY *Social Security #* ⬅

Example: PATRON SUMMARY *123456789* ⬅

Refined Commands

AUTHOR/TITLE/SUBJECT

Purpose: To restrict your search to a specific type of entry — author, title, or subject.

User Input: [AUTHOR] *terms*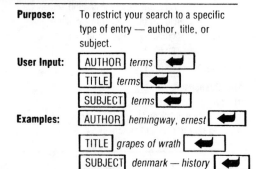
[TITLE] *terms*
[SUBJECT] *terms*

Examples: [AUTHOR] *hemingway, ernest*
[TITLE] *grapes of wrath*
[SUBJECT] *denmark — history*

LIAS Response:
A list of entries matching or resembling the term(s) you are searching.

FIND

Purpose: To find items in LIAS when you know the title *and* author, or to find serials (journals, magazines, newspapers) when the title is known.

User Input: [FIND] *serial title*
[FIND] *title/author*

Examples: [FIND] *newsweek*
[FIND] *journal of adhesion*
[FIND] *megatrends/naisbett*

LIAS Response:
LIAS responds with either a citation screen (fig. 3) or record screen (fig. 4). Select an entry by pressing the appropriate number key and ⏎.

CAUTION: If [FIND] does not retrieve the record you want, type your terms again using the [SEARCH] command.

LIBRARY

Purpose: To tailor your search to a particular library or group of libraries.

User Input: [LIBRARY] *location code* ⏎
Note: [HELP] [LIBRARY] provides a list of location codes.

Examples: [LIBRARY] *aa* (Altoona Campus) ⏎
[LIBRARY] *rf, mp* (Reference and Maps) ⏎
[LIBRARY] *all* (All Libraries) ⏎

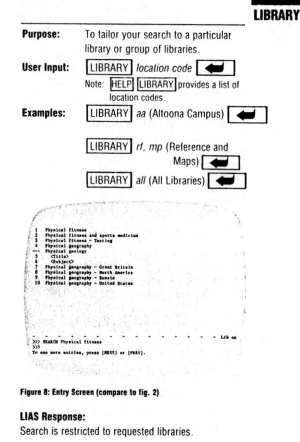

Figure 8: Entry Screen (compare to fig. 2)

LIAS Response:
Search is restricted to requested libraries.

CAUTION: Each LIAS terminal is automatically set to search the records of the library, or group of libraries, where it is located. This "default" location is indicated in the lower right edge of the screen's display area. If you use the [LIBRARY] command, make sure you reset your terminal to its default condition either by pressing ⏎ twice or by entering [LIBRARY] and the correct code for your location.

Purpose: To browse through items by call number as if you were looking at the items on the shelves. Select a record (Fig. 4) before using this command.

User Input: SHELF

LIAS Response:

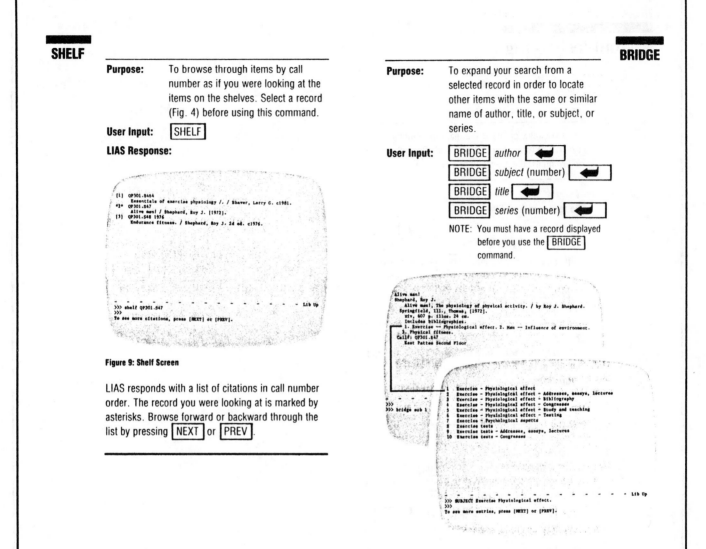

[1] QP301.8464
    Essentials of exercise physiology /. / Shaver, Larry G. c1981.
2 QP301.547
    Alive man! / Shephard, Roy J. [1972].
[3] QP301.548 1976
    Endurance fitness. / Shephard, Roy J. 2d ed. c1976.

>>> shelf QP301.547   - - Lib Up
>>>
To see more citations, press [NEXT] or [PREV].

Figure 9: Shelf Screen

LIAS responds with a list of citations in call number order. The record you were looking at is marked by asterisks. Browse forward or backward through the list by pressing NEXT or PREV .

Purpose: To expand your search from a selected record in order to locate other items with the same or similar name of author, title, or subject, or series.

User Input: BRIDGE *author*

BRIDGE *subject* (number) ⬅

BRIDGE *title* ⬅

BRIDGE *series* (number) ⬅

NOTE: You must have a record displayed before you use the BRIDGE command.

Alive man!
Shephard, Roy J.
    Alive man!, The physiology of physical activity. / by Roy J. Shephard.
Springfield, Ill., Thomas, [1972].
    xiv, 607 p. illus. 24 cm.
    Includes bibliographies.
    1. Exercise -- Physiological effect. 2. Man -- Influence of environment.
    3. Physical fitness.
Call#: QP301.547
    East Pattee Second Floor

 1 Exercise - Physiological effect
 2 Exercise - Physiological effect - Addresses, essays, lectures
 3 Exercise - Physiological effect - Bibliography
 4 Exercise - Physiological effect - Congresses
 5 Exercise - Physiological effect - Study and teaching
 6 Exercise - Physiological effect - Testing
 7 Exercise - Psychological aspects
 8 Exercise tests
 9 Exercise tests - Addresses, essays, lectures
10 Exercise tests - Congresses

>>>
>>> bridge sub 1

                                                    - Lib Up
>>> SUBJECT Exercise Physiological effect.
>>>
To see more entries, press [NEXT] or [PREV].

Figure 10: Bridge Screens

LIAS Response:
A list of entries that match or resemble the specified item. Select the entry that interests you and press

⬅

Troubleshooting

Here are a few problems that patrons commonly experience when they first use LIAS. Consult the following list if you encounter a problem.

1
No response from LIAS

Make sure you have pressed the [⬅] key after typing your command.

If you have pressed the [⬅] key and there is still no response, notify the nearest staff member.

Consult the COM and card catalogs until LIAS is working again.

2
LIAS responds with "Invalid command" or "Invalid input," or beeps.

Double check your request:
   Have you included a command?
   Have you spelled it correctly?

3
Mistakes on LIAS records

Notify the system about mistakes (e.g., spelling errors) on a record by typing [OOPS], followed by a short explanation of the problem.

A record must be on the screen before [OOPS] can be used.

Example:
User Input: [OOPS] *spelling error in title* [⬅]

LIAS Response:
"Thanks for the info."

4
The screen is blank

Check the terminal's contrast dial to make sure it is adjusted properly.

Hit [⬅] twice. If there is no response, notify a staff member.

Penn State is an affirmative action, equal opportunity university

U.Ed. 86-100

Pennsylvania State University Libraries

LIAS: REMOTE ACCESS GUIDE

Library Information Access System (LIAS), the Pennsylvania State University's online catalog, is available not only in the library, but also from remote terminals on- or off-campus. This includes terminals available in offices, homes, apartments, or dormitories.

Two types of access methods can be used to reach LIAS from remote terminals. The first is direct dial service. The second is via terminals which are hardwired into the Computation Center at University Park.

DIRECT DIAL ACCESS

NECESSARY HARDWARE

• Asynchronous terminal

• One of three modems:

    a. Bell 103 compatible (300 baud)

    b. Bell 212 compatible (1200 baud)

    c. Vadic 34XX compatible (1200 baud)

INSTRUCTIONS FOR USE

STEP 1: Set terminal to FULL DUPLEX, no parity, 8 bits.

STEP 2: Dial (814)865-LIAS

STEP 3: At tone, connect telephone to modem. Press [RETURN] once.

STEP 4: At SELECTION prompt, press [RETURN] once.

STEP 5: You are now connected to the system switch at Pattee Library. The system responds with A. If LIAS is busy or B. If LIAS is available.

    A. SYSTEM: **Busy, wait?###**

            (### = number of users waiting)

       USER: If you wish to wait, Press [y] and [RETURN]

           If you do not wish to wait, Disconnect and hang up.

    B. SYSTEM: **We are P.S.U.** (Beep)

STEP 6: Press [RETURN] three times

STEP 7: LIAS will respond: **Welcome . . .**
                    >>>

STEP 8: Make terminal adjustments. See flip side for instructions.

STEP 9: Begin searching (Consult LIAS: An Introductory Guide to Searching the Online Catalog, available at any PSU library).

STEP 10: To exit from LIAS, simply disconnect telephone from modem.

COMPUTATION CENTER ACCESS

NECESSARY HARDWARE

• Terminal hardwired into the University Park Computation Center Data Switch.

INSTRUCTIONS FOR USE

STEP 1: Set terminal to FULL DUPLEX, no parity, 2400 baud. Follow usual procedures for accessing the Computation Center Data Switch.

STEP 2: Enter: LIAS

STEP 3: System responds: **CONNECTED** Press [RETURN] once.

STEP 4: At SELECTION prompt, press [RETURN] once.

STEP 5: You are now connected to the system switch at Pattee Library. The system responds with A. If LIAS is busy or B. If LIAS is available:

    A. SYSTEM: **Busy, wait?###**

            (### = number of users waiting)

       USER: If you wish to wait, Press [y] and [RETURN]

           If you do not wish to wait, Disconnect.

    B. SYSTEM: **We are P.S.U.** (Beep)

STEP 6: Press [RETURN] twice

STEP 7: LIAS will respond: **Welcome . . .**
                    >>>

STEP 8: Make terminal adjustments. See flip side for instructions.

STEP 9: Begin searching (Consult LIAS: An Introductory Guide to Searching the Online Catalog, available at any PSU library).

STEP 10: Follow usual disconnect procedures.

Pennsylvania State University Libraries

TERMINAL ADJUSTMENT

LIAS assumes you are using a standard hard copy terminal, with a display that is 80 characters wide and 24 lines long. If you are not using a hard copy device, you can improve the readability of the screen display and enhance the functional characteristics of your terminal by specifying the type of terminal you are using. Owners of microcomputers should consult their microcomputer manuals to identify the terminals emulated by their computer. Input:

terminal model number

example: **terminal dec vt52**

Not all terminals are supported by LIAS. For a list of supported terminals and more information, input:

help terminal type

To modify the width and length of display, input:

terminal w=xx   (where xx = no. of characters on lines)
terminal l=xx

For more instructions on changing the width and length of display, input:

help terminal width
help terminal length

LIBRARY OPTION

The library you are searching is indicated at the bottom right hand corner of the screen by **lib** followed by a two letter code, e.g. **lib up**.

To change the library(ies) being searched, input:

lib xx or **lib xx, yy**   (where xx and yy = library codes)

For a list of library codes, input:

help library codes

《 LIAS WILL AUTOMATICALLY DISCONNECT YOU AFTER 3 MINUTES OF INACTIVITY. 》

AVAILABILITY

* LIAS is currently available: **7 days a week**
                                8 a.m. – midnight

COST

* The only charge incurred by the user is the communications charge. This appears on your monthly telephone bill.

* There is no need to open an account with the library to use LIAS.

ASSISTANCE

* For assistance call (814)865-2112 during the following hours: 9 a.m. – 10 p.m., Monday – Thursday
                                                                9 a.m. – 9 p.m., Friday & Saturday
                                                                Noon – 10 p.m., Sunday

* Only general information is available evenings and weekends.

Pennsylvania State University Libraries

STANFORD UNIVERSITY LIBRARIES

J. Henry Meyer Memorial Library

<u>SEARCHING SOCRATES BY SUBJECT</u>

Socrates is the Stanford online catalog. In addition to all Meyer Library materials, Socrates lists materials acquired by Green Library and its branches (e.g., Art; Biology) since 1973 and by coordinate libraries (e.g., Hoover; Law) since 1977.

Step 1 = Consult the <u>Library of Congress Subject Headings</u> list for the appropriate subject heading(s) for your topic.

Popular music
See Music, Popular (Songs, etc.)

> For explanation of
> <u>Library of Congress
> Subject Headings</u> see
> reverse side.

Step 2 = Use the <u>Subject Phrase (SP)</u> index in Socrates; ignore all punctuation except the double hyphen (--) to separate subdivisions:

Example in GUIDED mode:

Type of search: sp
Subject Phrase: music popular songs etc--united states

Example in COMMAND mode:

find sp music popular songs etc--united states

Socrates will retrieve subject headings <u>beginning with</u> the exact phrase you have typed. If you type a period at the end of the phrase, Socrates searches only for that exact heading (without additional words or subdivisions). For example, the search "find sp rock music." will retrieve general books about rock music, but not those listed under the heading "rock music--united states."

> REMINDER: *These same Library of Congress subject headings should be searched in the Green card catalog if you want to locate items not included in Socrates.*

OTHER TYPES OF SUBJECT SEARCHES:

<u>Subject Word (S)</u> = Searches all words in all subject headings, titles, and organization names. (Be careful to avoid common words in this index!) Use only if you have a distinctive keyword or cannot find a Library of Congress Subject heading.

<u>Subject Name (SN)</u> = Searches for items <u>about</u> people and <u>about</u> their works. *(Note: Personal names are not included in the SP index.)*

<u>Subject Name/Subject Word (SNS)</u> = Combines the features of SN and S indexes, e.g.,

fin sns kennedy, john f/assassination
fin sns wagner/lohengrin
fin sns shakespeare/characters

> *For more information about subject indexes, type HELP followed by the abbreviation for an index (e.g., s, sn, sp, etc.) or HELP SUBJECT.*
>
> *Type HELP GLOSSARY for a list of all available HELP messages.*

Meyer Library, Stanford University

USING LIBRARY OF CONGRESS SUBJECT HEADINGS

To translate YOUR TOPIC into the subject heading language used in Socrates and most Stanford card catalogs, consult the LIBRARY OF CONGRESS SUBJECT HEADINGS list (2 vol. set located near Socrates terminals).

EXAMPLE

If you want books about popular music, the subject headings list will refer you from "popular music," which is not used as a heading, to "Music, Popular (songs, etc.)."

Music, Polish-American
　See Polish-American music

Music, Polynesian
　x Songs, Polynesian

Music, Popular (Songs, etc.) (Indirect)
　ss Bluegrass music
　　Country music
　　Gospel music
　　Rock music
　　Salsa
　x Popular music
　　Popular songs
　　Songs, Popular
　　Soul music
　xx Songs
　　Vocal music
　— Recording
　　See Music, Popular (Songs, etc.)—Writing and publishing
　— Writing and publishing (MT67)
　　x Music, Popular (Songs, etc.)—Recording
　　　Songwriting
　　xx Authorship
　　　Composition (Music)
　　　Music printing
　— Arizona
　　ss Chicken scratch music
　— Jamaica
　　ss Reggae music
　— Mexico (M1683.18-1683.2)
　　x Música norteña
　　　Norteno music
　— Texas (M1630.18-1630.2)
　　x Música norteña
　　　Norteno music
　— Trinidad
　　ss Calypso (Songs, etc.)
　　　Steel band music
　— United States
　　ss Blues (Songs, etc.)
　　　Cowboys—Songs and music

Regular typeface = not a subject heading. Use instead the recommended subject heading given after word "See."

Bold Face type = used as a subject heading.

Sa = see also these related terms, which are usually more specific than the bold face heading above. Use them to narrow your search.

X = terms not used as subject headings.

XX = these related terms are usually more general than the bold face heading above. Use them to broaden your search.

Many subject headings are followed by a number which indicates where books on the subject are most commonly shelved. These numbers may be useful for browsing.

Many subject headings are qualified by subdivisions which organize or limit the topic by time, geography or other subtopics. Not all possible subdivisions are listed for each subject; be sure to try others of interest that fit the pattern indicated here. (Examples: music—history and criticism—16th century)

Use the exact subject heading phrases, as found above, in searching Socrates with the SP (subject phrase) index:

　　　fin sp music, polynesian

　　　fin sp music, popular songs etc--united states

　　　(For More Information on Searching Socrates by Subject, see Reverse side)

12/86

Meyer Library, Stanford University

A Reference Guide to

#630

SOCRATES

The Online Library Catalog of Stanford University

1. General Information

Socrates contains bibliographic citations of materials acquired at Stanford libraries after 1972 (coordinate libraries after 1976), including all materials at Meyer Library, and all serials at Stanford.

In general, searching Socrates is a three-step process. First and optionally, you select the collection you want to search. (If you do not explicitly choose a collection, then CATALOG, a file that combines many of the collections, is selected for you automatically.) Second, based on search criteria you type, Socrates finds appropriate bibliographic citations for you. Third, you examine those citations, in either a full or condensed form.

Use of Socrates is free in the libraries and to University-funded accounts. Faculty, staff, and students may obtain a free Socrates account for personal use outside the library by asking for one at the Green Library Privileges desk and at branch libraries.

2. Service Schedule

Socrates is presently available all day everyday *except:*

Thursday	6 am - 7 am
Saturday and Sunday	5 am - 8 am

3. Getting Started

For patron terminals in the library, press the BEGIN key.

For other terminals, logon to the Forsythe Data Center computer (Gandalf class 20 or TELNET FORSYTHE), using your account. Then type the command:

SOCRATES to start a search session of the online catalog

Press the RETURN key at the end of each command to Socrates.

(On free Socrates accounts, Socrates is started for you automatically when you logon.)

Note: Most commands in Socrates can be abbreviated to 3 or more letters; for example, DIS for DISPLAY, or SEL for SELECT.

4. The Two Search Modes: GUIDED & COMMAND

At any point in your Socrates session, you may type either of the following commands to choose or change a search mode:

GUIDED places you in Guided mode, the easiest way to use Socrates for the new or inexperienced user. No previous computer-searching experience is needed; *just read and respond to the instructions the computer gives you.* This mode is automatically chosen for you.

COMMAND places you in Command mode, whose instructions are more terse than Guided mode. It is designed for the experienced user. Switch to Command mode anytime after you are comfortable with Guided mode.

5. The Search Procedure

A search in Socrates consists of 3 basic steps:

1) Choosing a File to Search (Optional)

For most searches, you will want to use the CATALOG file, which is selected automatically if you don't choose a file explicitly. But type the SELECT command if you want to look at a specific collection.

SELECT file identifies what data collection ("file") you want to search. The Stanford library files available include:

- CATALOG selected automatically; this is the easiest and most efficient file for simple searches and for rapid scanning of large amounts of material; it combines information from the bracketed files below:

  - BOOKS — monographic materials
  - SERIALS — publications issued in parts, e.g., periodicals, series, magazines, journals
  - SCORES — music scores
  - RECORDINGS — sound recordings
  - MAPS — partial map-collection information
  - FILMS — partial film-collection information
  - ARCHIVES — archival and manuscript collections

- TECHNICAL REPORTS — technical reports in science libraries

Other files may be available; type SELECT to see all your choices.

2) Specifying Search Criteria

To begin a search, type the command FIND. Socrates will show you a list of types of searches you can do:

Type	Meaning	Sample Search Value
A	AUTHOR, personal name	*J.D. Salinger*
O	ORGANIZATION, as author	*Smithsonian*
TP	TITLE, initial phrase	*Portrait of the Artist as*
T	TITLE, any words	*Portrait Artist*
S	SUBJECT, topical words	*Genetic Engineering*
SN	SUBJECT, personal name	*Martin Luther King*

Socrates first asks you which type or types of information you want to use in the search. Next Socrates asks for the "search values" (the values you want to be looked up) and then does the search.

Other search types (or "indexes") may be available for particular files. Type HELP ALL INDEXES for a complete list for the selected file.

5. The Search Procedure (continued)

3) Examining the Search Result

If you are searching in CATALOG, the citations in your search result will be shown to you summarized under headings (categories) that matched your search. SCAN the headings to select items of interest, and type the DISPLAY command to see the citations within the headings. (If you are searching in other files, you will see the individual citations right away, rather than headings to scan.)

SCAN h	to see the headings of your result, starting at heading number "h".
e.g., SCAN 4	
DISPLAY 6	to examine all brief citations for heading "h".
DISPLAY h	
DISPLAY h.c	to examine brief citations for heading "h", starting at citation number "c".
DISPLAY 6.2	
DISPLAY h.c FULL	to examine complete information for citation "c" of heading "h".
DISPLAY 6.2 FULL	

6. Getting Help

HELP type HELP when you aren't sure about the situation you are in, or when you want to learn more. Socrates will describe your current situation and your options.

OPTIONS tells you what you can do next, including the commands to use.

HELP GLOSSARY tells you the help topics that Socrates has information about.

HELP topic gives you help on a particular topic in the glossary; for example, HELP CONTENTS.

SHOW SEARCH tells you the search commands you have issued to obtain your current result.

SUGGEST if you'd like to make suggestions or comments on Socrates, or on the data you have retrieved. Use this command if you want to ask questions of library staff or request special library services.

call 723-1811 if you want a member of the library staff to help you use Socrates, or help you use the libraries' collections.

7. Getting Out

END to leave Socrates. (On free Socrates accounts, END includes LOGOFF.)

LOGOFF to disconnect from the Forsythe Data Center.

<attn> or <break> press this key to interrupt Socrates' typing or searching. Note though that Socrates will always pause after it has filled the screen with information.

No matter what you do, you can't damage Socrates or the data files. If you have serious problems, just turn your terminal off.

More information about Socrates appears on the back....

8. The Searching Commands

Several other commands besides FIND are useful in searching. Like FIND (and SELECT too), these commands may be typed in the full form shown below, or you may type as many pieces of the command as you want (for example, FIND or FIND TP), and let Socrates ask you for the remaining pieces of the command as necessary.

FIND type value   starts a new search for "value" by its "search type"; for example,
FIND AUTHOR WILLIAM SHAKESPEARE

AND type value   narrows an existing search; for example,
AND TITLE KING
[but see #10, Combining Types of Searches]

AND NOT type value   narrows an existing search; for example,
AND NOT TITLE RICHARD

OR type value   expands a search; for example,
OR AUTHOR FRANCIS BACON

BACKUP   returns to the search result prior to the latest AND, AND NOT or OR command.

RETRY IN file   executes the current search in another library file.

9. Search Values

Capitalization and punctuation are not significant in search values.

Personal Name Indexes

Type only as much of a name as you are certain of, e.g.:

William Shakespeare   Masters
C P Snow   Public, John Q

You can use initials for the first and middle names.

Initial-Phrase Searching

If you know the entire title, organization name or subject (or know how it begins), use the appropriate phrase index: TP, OP or SP, for Title initial Phrase, Organization initial Phrase and Subject initial Phrase. (Remember, type HELP ALL INDEXES for a complete list of indexes for the selected file.) If you type the complete phrase, end it with a period for more efficient searching. Here are some examples:

To find: the serial "Journal of American History"
try typing;   FIND TP JOURNAL OF AMERICAN HISTORY.
or: FIND TP JOURNAL OF AMERICAN
but not: FIND TITLE JOURNAL OF AMERICAN HISTORY

You should omit any articles that begin the phrase, but do not omit any within the value. Articles are "a", "an", "the" and their equivalents in foreign languages. For example,

To find: the book "The Sun in the East"
try typing;   FIND TP SUN IN THE EAST.
or: FIND TITLE SUN EAST
but not: FIND TP THE SUN IN THE EAST

9. Search Values (continued)

Word Indexes

For efficient searching, type the least common words in a title, subject, or organization, omitting very common words, if possible. Type only the words you expect to be present in all the citations you want to retrieve. You may type the words in any order.

To find: items by an organization whose name contains the words San Mateo County and Historical Association
try typing;   FIND ORGANIZATION SAN MATEO HISTORICAL
but not: FIND ORGANIZATION SAN MATEO COUNTY ASSOCIATION

To find: books about strikes and the economy
try typing;   FIND SUBJECT STRIKE# ECONOMY# [see below]
or: FIND SP STRIKE#
but not: FIND SUBJECT EFFECT OF STRIKES ON ECONOMY

Stem Searching

If several forms of a word have a common stem, you can include all those forms in one search value by using the # symbol:

To find: books about programs or programmers
try typing;   FIND SUBJECT PROGRAM#
or: FIND SUBJECT PROGRAM OR PROGRAMMERS

10. Combining Types of Searches in CATALOG

You may freely combine types of searches (indexes) except in the CATALOG file. In that file you cannot use AND to:

-combine name searches: FIND AUTHOR MASTERS AND JOHNSON
Instead: SELECT BOOKS
FIND AUTHOR MASTERS AND JOHNSON

-combine different indexes: FIND AUTHOR CARROLL
AND TITLE WONDERLAND
Instead: FIND AT CARROLL/WONDERLAND

11. Browsing in the Files

Socrates lets you browse through many of the indexes of the CATALOG file, just as you might skim through the card catalog from card to card, looking for items of interest. Browsing often shows you useful citations related to your subject of interest that you might not find with a regular search. Browsing can also help you when variant spellings of a search value might hide some citations from you.

BROWSE type value   to browse in the "type" index,
e.g. BROWSE AUTHOR POE   starting at the given "value"
BROWSE SUBJECT ART

You can type just BROWSE if you want Socrates to ask you for the search type and value.

As you scan the headings and citations, you can type the DISPLAY command to examine specific citations in more detail. To continue browsing from the point where you left off, type the SCAN command.

You can BROWSE the subject headings that you find in one citation in order to find other works that are closely related to it. Subject headings appear under "Topics:" in the full display of the citation.

12. Examining the Search Result

Use the SCAN command, described on the front of this card, to examine headings in the CATALOG file and to continue browsing after interrupting a BROWSE to display a citation (see 11).

Use the DISPLAY command, also described on the front, to examine individual citations. You will see them in brief or, by adding the word FULL to the DISPLAY command, in their full form.

A series of citations or headings can be examined by adding a range to the DISPLAY or SCAN command. For example:

SCAN 4-6   to scan headings 4 through 6
DISPLAY 4,5, 4.7   to see the brief citations of 4.5 and 4.7
DISPLAY FULL ALL   to see full citations for all the headings

The CONTINUOUS option can also be added to SCAN or DISPLAY to tell Socrates not to pause after filling the screen. Press the BREAK key when you want to stop the display.

13. Collecting Citations Into a Bibliography

After finding citations, you may want to "keep" them. Socrates allows you to do any one of the following with the results of a SCAN or DISPLAY command by adding a TO option to it:

• To send citations via electronic mail

You can send a copy of the citations to a mailbox on a mainframe host, such as LOTS, via electronic mail. Add the TO ACCOUNT option to any SCAN or DISPLAY command. No more than 2,000 lines of citations may be mailed in one command. For example:

DISPLAY 1/5 FULL TO ACCOUNT

Socrates then asks for the names of the account and computer where the citations should be sent. For help answering that, type HELP.

• To put citations in a file on a personal computer

If you are using Socrates on a personal computer (such as an IBM PC or a 512K Macintosh) via Samson, you can save the citations in a file on the PC. To tell Socrates to save the citations, add the TO FILE option to the SCAN or DISPLAY command. For example:

DISPLAY ALL TO FILE

Socrates will ask for the file name, including the disk drive. If Socrates does not already know what type of PC you are using, it will ask you for that too. For help answering these questions, type HELP.

• To place citations in your "active file"

This feature, not available on patron terminals in the library or on free Socrates accounts, places the citations into the WYLBUR text editor's active file. To use it, add the option TO ACTIVE to the SCAN or DISPLAY command:

DISPLAY 7.1 FULL TO ACTIVE

The citations will be appended to your active file.

(8/29/86)

Meyer Library, Stanford University

Welcome to TOMUS

TOMUS offers access to the Penfield Library Collection
through Title, Author and Subject Indexes.

BASIC COMMANDS	SCREEN DISPLAYS
type **START** ➤ press **RETURN**	WELCOME TO TOMUS The Online Multiple User System

FIND and **DISPLAY** are basic commands. Both can be abbreviated and used in the following ways:

FA = FIND AUTHOR	**D** = Display for Author, Title, Call Number
FS = FIND SUBJECT	**DB** = Display for Author and partial Title
FT = FIND TITLE	**DF** = Display for complete information

For TITLE searching, the commands will be: **FIND TITLE** or **FT**

Does Penfield Library own: *The Pilgrim Hawk?*

type **FT Pilgrim Hawk**

Your search: FT PILGRIM HAWK
ITEMS found: 1 AT SUNY OSWEGO

1. _____, _____, (author) 1901-
              The pilgrim hawk, a love story. (title) New York and
London, Harper and Brothers (publisher) [c1940] (copyright)

Oswego _____ (call number)

For AUTHOR searching, the command is **FIND AUTHOR** or **FA**

Does Penfield Library own books by Kurt Vonnegut?

type **FA Kurt Vonnegut**

Your search: FA KURT VONNEGUT
ITEMS found: _____ AT SUNY OSWEGO

type **DF 9**

Item 9

AUTHOR	Vonnegut, Kurt
TITLE	_____.
PUBLICATION	New York: Delacorte Press [c1965].
DESCRIPTION	XIV, 217 p. 22 cm.
NOTES	"A Seymour Lawrence book."
CALL NUMBER	Oswego _____

OVER ↵

Penfield Library, State University of New York at Oswego

BASIC COMMANDS	SCREEN DISPLAYS
type **DF 11**	CALL NUMBER Oswego _____

> Note: Call numbers can also show notations for Media (Media), Reference (Ref), Periodicals (Per), or Curriculum Materials (CMC), indicating special locations for these items.

> For SUBJECT SEARCHING, the command is **FIND SUBJECT** or **FS**
> To check whether your terms are correct, use the *Library of Congress List of Subject Headings* (red books on podiums by terminals).
>
> What do you find under the subject **Education**?

type **FS Education**

> Your search: FS EDUCATION
> ITEMS found: _____ at SUNY Oswego

> To narrow or broaden a subject area like Education, use the commands **AND; AND NOT** (narrows); **OR** (broadens).
> Example: Use **Education and Sports**

type **FS Education and Sports**

> Your search: FS EDUCATION AND SPORTS
> ITEMS found: _____ at SUNY Oswego
> Broadens? _____   Narrows? _____

type **FS Education and not Sports**

> Your search: FS EDUCATION AND NOT SPORTS
> ITEMS found: _____ at SUNY Oswego
> Broadens? _____   Narrows? _____

type **FS Education or Sports**

> Your search: FS EDUCATION OR SPORTS
> ITEMS found: _____ at SUNY Oswego
> Broadens? _____   Narrows? _____

> Beware of the goose-egg syndrome or getting 0's under ITEMS found at SUNY Oswego. When this happens for Subject Searching, checking the *Library of Congress List of Subject Headings* may be helpful.
> Try looking for: **Child beating; Child abuse; Cruelty to children.**

type **FS Child Beating**

> Your search: FS CHILD BEATING
> ITEMS found: _____ at SUNY Oswego

type **FS Child Abuse**

> Your search: FS CHILD ABUSE
> ITEMS found: _____ at SUNY Oswego

type **FS Cruelty to Children**

> Your search: FS CRUELTY TO CHILDREN
> ITEMS found: _____ at SUNY Oswego

> The TOMUS HELP screens are useful. To use them, type
> **HELP, HELP AUTHOR, HELP TITLE,** or **HELP SUBJECT.**
> To try more detailed searching, use the
> *TOMUS Online Catalog Guide.*

PENFIELD LIBRARY
SUNY COLLEGE AT OSWEGO
LIBRARY INSTRUCTION

ABR/JF
6-86/10-86/8-87

Penfield Library, State University of New York at Oswego

 Tarrant County Junior College • South Campus Library

USING THE COMPUTER CATALOG

The computer catalog is the guide to the book collection. It tells you what books all three TCJC campus libraries have and where they are located. It also tells you whether the libraries have a specific book by title and what books the libraries have by a certain author or about a particular subject. The catalog will not list magazine articles, short stories, plays or poems. Ask the librarian to show you how to find these materials.

The computer catalog is divided into three separate sections — author, title, and subject.

> TCJC has three catalogs:
> > The Title Catalog
> >
> > The Author Catalog
> >
> > The Subject Catalog
> To look at the Title Catalog type T and press the enter key
> To look at the Author Catalog type A and press the enter kay
> To look at the Subject catalog type S and press the enter key
> If you are finished please press the clear key
> Please ask for help if needed

**Menu
Screen**

If this is not what you see when you approach the screen, press the **CLEAR** key, and then the **ENTER** key. This can be repeated any time you want to return to the Menu Screen.

If you know the exact title you are looking for, type **T** and press **ENTER**; if you are looking for a particular author, type **A** and press **ENTER**. The catalog will give you specific instructions on how to type in the title or author.

Remember to always read the instructions at the top of each screen.

1

In most cases you will be looking for material about a particular subject. This is when you will use the subject portion of the catalog. For example, to find information on solar energy, you type **SOLAR ENERGY** and press **ENTER**. The following is an example and explanation of what you would see on the screen:

```
1  — — — — — — — — — — — — — —  SUBJECT CATALOG
2  — — —  TO SEE SIMILAR SUBJECTS, TYPE X AND PRESS THE ENTER KEY
3  — — —  TO SEE NEXT ITEM PRESS THE ENTER KEY
4  — — —  TO ENTER A NEW SUBJECT PRESS THE PA1 KEY
5  — — —  SUBJECT:      SOLAR ENERGY

6  — — —  TITLE:        SOLAR ENERGY: TECHNOLOGY AND APPLICATIONS
7  — — —  CALL NUMBER:  TJ810.W54 1977                    BOOK      0098745
                                                           |         |
         LOCATION:     SOUTH      AVAILABLE     LRC        |         |
                                                           11        10

         TITLE:        SOLAR ENERGY:  THE AWAKENING SCIENCE
         CALL NUMBER:  TJ810.B43                          BOOK      0017619
8  — — —  LOCATION:     SOUTH         CHECKED OUT    LRC
         LOCATION:     NORTHEAST     AVAILABLE      LRC
9  — — — — — — — — — — — — — — — — — — — — — — —  |
         TITLE:        SOLAR ENERGY DICTIONARY
         CALL NUMBER:  TJ810.H86 1982                     BOOK      0135917
         LOCATION:     SOUTH         AVAILABLE LRC    REFERENCE
                                                          |
                                                          |
                                                          12
```

1. You are in the **subject** portion of the catalog, not the author or title portion.

2. If you type **X** you will see other subject headings relating to solar energy.
    NOTE: Some subjects are listed under unusually "tricky" headings. If you do not find the subject you are looking for, check the subject heading list available near the computer catalogs. This list is a print-out of all the subject headings used in our catalog. Ask at the information desk if you need help.

3. To see more books about solar energy, press the **ENTER** key.

4. To look at a different subject, press the **PA1** key.

5. This is the subject heading. This indicates what the books you see listed are about. NOTE: This is **not** a title of a book.

6. The title as it appears in the book. Up to three titles are listed on each screen.

7. Library of Congress call number. Copy this down as you will use this number to find the book on the shelf.

8. This tells you which campus LRC the book is in and if it is available.

2

Tarrant County Junior College South Campus Library

INTER-CAMPUS LOAN: We can get a book for you from other TCJC libraries.
First, make a note of the book's title, call number and campus location.
Be sure the book is listed as "available" and not "checked out."
Next, fill out an inter-campus loan request card at the circulation desk.
Your book will be waiting for you at the circulation desk one or two days later
after 2 p.m.

9. This is the building location. Most material is in the Learning Resource Centers
    on all three campuses, but occasionally books will be elsewhere.

10. Disregard, for library use only.

11. Books that can be checked out are on the second floor.

12. Reference books are on the first floor. They can **not** be checked out.

Finding the book on the shelves

The call number gives you the location of a book in the library. In the Library of
Congress system the letters of the call number tell you the broad subject area of the
book. Books are grouped on the shelves alphabetically by these letters. After the
books are grouped alphabetically by the broad subject areas they are arranged
numerically by the smaller subject areas.

QA	tells the subject
76	further defines the subject
.L9	identifies the author
1966	the year the book was published

This book
would be found:

DA 213 .K15	GN 281 .G17	QA 75 .C52	QA 76 .L9 1966	QA 115 .E12	QB 115 .E3

Keep in mind that books about a subject may not all be shelved in the same area.
For instance, under the subject of COMPUTERS, you will find books about computers in general under the call number QA76; books on business applications of computers are in the business area, HF5548; and books on design or repair of computers
are in the electronics area, TK7885. You will have no way to know this unless you
use the catalog. It is also a good idea to browse in the area where you find a book of
interest.

3

Tarrant County Junior College South Campus Library

Error Codes and Messages

In addition to the instructions at the top of each screen, the computer will give you some information as to what is going on. It does this in the operator information area at the bottom of the screen.

Operator
Information
Area

The computer needs time to search the catalog files for the information you have requested. Any of these three messages are asking you to wait while the computer retrieves the information you requested.

X

X (r)

X SYSTEM

Please do not press any other key while these messages are displayed in the Operator Information Area.

If any of these messages are displayed in the **Operator Information Area**, you must press the **RESET** key before you can continue.

X ? +

X ⚥ NUM

X ⚥ # ?

If this message appears in the Operator Information Area, the catalog is out of order. Please use the microfiche catalog or ask the librarian for assistance.

532

The Microfiche Catalog

When all computer catalogs are being used and you do not have time to wait, use the microfiche catalog. The microfiche catalog has the same information as the on-line catalog and is divided by title, author, and subject. The biggest difference will be that the microfiche catalog cannot tell you if something is checked out.

*Compiled by Linda Jensen
June 1987*

4

Tarrant County Junior College South Campus Library

Tarrant County Junior College
South Campus

A Guide
to the
Library Catalog

5301 Campus Drive
Fort Worth, Texas 76119

PLEASE NOTE -- YOU NO LONGER
NEED TO HOLD DOWN THE "ALT" KEY
WHEN PRESSING "CLEAR" OR "P4"
AS SHOWN ON PAGES 1 - 2 & 5.

TARRANT COUNTY JUNIOR COLLEGE
SOUTH CAMPUS

SC: 9/83

Tarrant County Junior College South Campus Library

A GUIDED TOUR OF TCJC ON-LINE CATALOG

The TCJC On-Line Catalog is your guide to the holdings (books and non-print materials.) It tells you what books the TCJC Learning Resource Centers (LRC's) have and where they are located. It also tells you whether the Library has materials by a particular author or about a particular subject.

The on-line catalog is divided into three separate sections — author, title and subject.

The on-line catalog lists entries for books, periodicals and non-print materials such as filmstrips, motion pictures and sound recordings. Books may be used in the LRC, or checked out for your use at home. Periodicals and reference books may not be checked out but can be used in the LRC. Non-print materials are for classroom use by the faculty.

This guide will help you learn how to locate library materials using the on-line catalog. The catalog itself contains many user instructions. **Be sure to read carefully the instructions at the top of each screen.** If at any time you need further information, please do not hesitate to ask a library staff member for assistance.

Tarrant County Junior College South Campus Library

If this is not what you see when you approach the screen:
- Press the RESET key
- Hold down the ALT key while pressing the CLEAR key
  (NOTE: the ALT key must be held down when pressing the CLEAR or PA1 key)

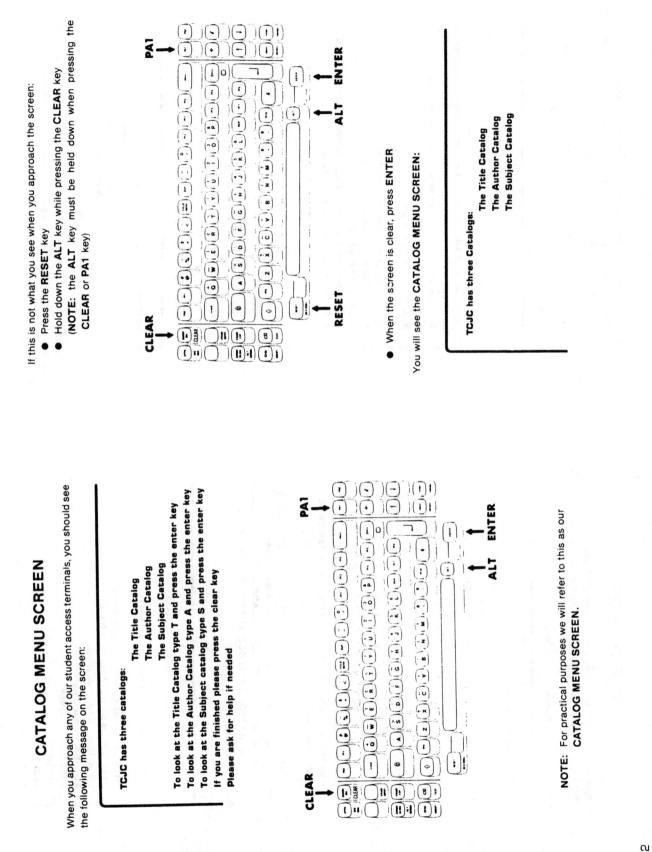

- When the screen is clear, press ENTER

You will see the CATALOG MENU SCREEN:

TCJC has three Catalogs:

      The Title Catalog
      The Author Catalog
      The Subject Catalog

CATALOG MENU SCREEN

When you approach any of our student access terminals, you should see the following message on the screen:

TCJC has three catalogs:

      The Title Catalog
      The Author Catalog
      The Subject Catalog

To look at the Title Catalog type T and press the enter key
To look at the Author Catalog type A and press the enter key
To look at the Subject catalog type S and press the enter key
If you are finished please press the clear key
Please ask for help if needed

NOTE: For practical purposes we will refer to this as our CATALOG MENU SCREEN.

Tarrant County Junior College South Campus Library

TITLE CATALOG

As implied by its three parts, there are three ways to locate most books in the catalog. If you know a book's title, look for it in the title catalog.

• Begin with the **Catalog Menu Screen:**

```
TCJC has three Catalogs:
                    The Title Catalog
                    The Author Catalog
                    The Subject Catalog
```

• Type T
• Press ENTER
This is what you see:

```
                    TITLE CATALOG

Type as much of the title as you know.
If a title begins with THE, A or An leave that word out.
For example to find THE AMERICANS, Type AMERICANS and
press the enter key
```

To look for any title you would look under the first word of the title, unless that word is THE, A or AN. In that case, look under the next word.
For example, to find the title AN APPROACH TO COMMUNITY MENTAL HEALTH,
• you type: **APPROACH TO COMMUNITY MENTAL HEALTH**
• Press ENTER

It prints:

```
                    TITLE CATALOG

To enter a new title press the enter key

TITLE: Approach to Community Mental Health
CALL NUMBER: RA790.C513    Book
LOCATION: South Available LRC
AUTHOR: Caplan, Gerald
PUBLISHER: Grune 1961
OTHER TITLE:
DESCRIPTION:
SUMMARY:
```

NOTE: the Title catalog displays only one item per screen and gives you the most complete information about that item (the author, publisher and date of publication, etc.)

If the title AN APPROACH TO COMMUNITY MENTAL HEALTH had not been in our collection, the catalog would have printed:

```
                    TITLE CATALOG

The title as entered is not in the catalog.
To choose a title listed below, type line number and press the
enter key.
To enter a title not listed below, press the enter key.
1 APPROACH TO KING LEAR
2 APPROACH TO KINGS
3 APPROACH TO LITERATURE
4 APPROACH TO MODERN PHYSICS
5 APPROACH TO MODERN POETRY
6 APPROACH TO PHYSICAL SCIENCE
7 APPROACH TO PHYSICAL SCIENCE: SUPPLEMENTARY CHAPTERS
8 APPROACH TO SHAKESPEARE
```

The on-line catalog prints the next eight titles that would appear alphabetically in the catalog after the title APPROACH TO COMMUNITY MENTAL HEALTH.

When finished with the Title Catalog you will:
• Hold down the **ALT** key while pressing the **CLEAR** key
• When the screen is clear, press **ENTER** key

You will again see the **Catalog Menu Screen:**

```
TCJC has three catalogs:
                    The Title Catalog
                    The Author Catalog
                    The Subject Catalog
```

You may now use any of the three sections of the catalog. If you are finished, please leave this message on the screen for the next user.

Tarrant County Junior College South Campus Library

AUTHOR CATALOG

If you are unsure of the Title but know the author's name, you would use the author catalog. The "author" in this case might be the person or organization responsible for originating the book. It could be a writer, editor, compiler, association, government agency, firm or other group. Additional authors of a book are called joint authors and an entry will usually be found in the author catalog for each of these also.

Begin with the **Catalog Menu Screen**

● Type **A**
● Press **ENTER**

It prints:

AUTHOR CATALOG

Type as much of the author's name as you know for example to find John Graves, Type Graves, John and press the enter key

---

● You type: Behrman, Daniel
          ↑ NOTE: be sure to include this space
● Press **ENTER**

This is what you see:

AUTHOR CATALOG

To enter a new author press the enter key
AUTHOR: **Behrman, Daniel**
TITLE: **New World of the oceans: Men and Oceanography**
CALL NUMBER: GC21.B45   Book   0017618
LOCATION: South   Available   LRC

TITLE: **Solar energy: the awakening science**
CALL NUMBER: TJ810.B43   Book   0017619
LOCATION: South   Available   LRC
LOCATION: Northeast   Available   LRC
LOCATION: Northwest   Available   LRC

The catalog will list up to three items per screen. If the LRC has more books by the same author, you will be instructed at the top of the screen to press ENTER to continue seeing books by your author.

(Reminder: read the instructions at the top of each screen carefully)

When finished with the **Author Catalog** you will again clear the screen and press **ENTER** so you will begin with the Catalog Menu Screen.

TCJC has three Catalogs:

The Title Catalog
The Author Catalog
The Subject Catalog

Tarrant County Junior College South Campus Library

SUBJECT CATALOG

The subject catalog lists books and other items the LRC has on a particular topic. When using the subject catalog, look first under the specific subject you have in mind rather than under a broader subject. For instance, look under "Racquetball" instead of "Sports", the name of an artist instead of "Art." "Algae" instead of "Botany," etc. If this approach does not locate material for you, then look under a broader term.

NOTE: Some subjects are listed under unusually "tricky" headings. If you do not find the subject you are looking for, don't assume the library does not have anything on your subject. Ask a staff member for assistance.

- Begin with the **Catalog Menu Screen**
- Type **S**
- Press **ENTER**

It prints:

SUBJECT CATALOG

Type as much of the subject as you know and press the enter key

- You type in the subject **RIOTS**
- Press **ENTER**

It prints:

You will see:

SUBJECT CATALOG

To see similar subjects, type X and press the enter key
To see next item press the enter key
To enter a new subject press the PA1 key

SUBJECT: RIOTS
TITLE: Disorders and Terrorism: Report of the task force
on disorders
CALL NUMBER: HV6477.A58   Book   0070051
LOCATION: Northeast Available LRC

TITLE: Riot protection check list for businesses
CALL NUMBER: HV8055.M739R   Book   0067634
LOCATION: Northeast Available LRC

TITLE: Store planning for riot survival
CALL NUMBER: HV8055.M739S   Book   0067637
LOCATION: Northeast Checked out LRC

Notice this message differs from those you have seen before.

Read the message at the top of the screen carefully.

If you want to see related subject headings for RIOTS
- You type **X**
- Press **ENTER**

It prints:

SUBJECT CATALOG

The following subjects are similar to the subject you entered.
To choose a subject listed below, type line number and press the enter key
To return to the subject entered press the enter key

Line number ____
1 Mobs
2 Crowds
3 Riot control

SUBJECT CATALOG

The subject as entered is not in the catalog.
To choose a subject listed below, type line number and press the enter key.
To enter a subject not listed below, press the enter key.

Line number
1   Faulkner, William
2   Faulkner, William - Addresses, essays, lectures
3   Faulkner, William - Bibliography
4   Faulkner, William - Characters - Indexes
5   Faulkner, William - Characters - Indians
6   Faulkner, William - Characters - Women

NOTE: By **not** typing in his whole name (Faulkner, William), the catalog calls up everything listed after Faulkner, W giving you a list of subject headings to choose from and maybe narrow down your search.

If you choose line number one (Faulkner, William)
● You type **1**
● Press **ENTER**
You will see:

SUBJECT CATALOG

To see next item press the enter key
To enter a new subject press the PA1 key

SUBJECT: Faulkner, William
TITLE: Achievement of William Faulkner
CALL NUMBER: PS3511.A86Z894 1996A   Book   0067103
LOCATION: South   Available   LRC

TITLE: Art of Faulkner's novels
CALL NUMBER: PS3511.A86Z974 1962   Book   0089920
LOCATION: Northeast   Available   LRC

TITLE: Dark prophets of hope, Dostoevsky, Sartre, Camus, Faulkner
CALL NUMBER: PN771.K38   Book   0055338
LOCATION: South   Available   LRC

Notice that up to three items are listed per screen and the instructions at the top of the screen tell you to see the next item press the enter key.

To return to the subject RIOTS
● You press the **ENTER** key
It prints:

SUBJECT CATALOG

To see next item press the enter key
To enter a new subject press the PA1 key

SUBJECT: RIOTS - HISTORY
TITLE: Riot makers: The technology of social demolition
CALL NUMBER: HV6477.M47   Book   0066440
LOCATION: Northeast   Available   LRC

Remember, subjects may be people as well as places, events, concepts, etc. When you are looking for something **about** a person, even if that person is an **author**, you must look in the subject catalog.

For example, books written by the author William Faulkner are found in the author catalog, but books **about him** (including books of criticism) are found in the subject catalog.

● Begin with the **Catalog Menu Screen**
● Type **S** and press **ENTER**
You will see:

SUBJECT CATALOG

Type as much of the subject as you know and press the enter key

● You type: **Faulkner, W**
● Press **ENTER** key
It prints:

10

Tarrant County Junior College South Campus Library

ERROR CODES AND MESSAGES

In addition to the instructions at the top of each screen the computer will give you some information as to what is going on. It does this in the **operator information area** at the bottom of the screen.

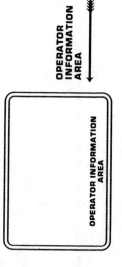

OPERATOR INFORMATION AREA

OPERATOR
INFORMATION
AREA

The computer needs time to search the catalog files for the information you have requested. Any of these three messages are asking you to wait while the computer retrieves the information you requested.

X   X   X SYSTEM

Please do not press any other key while these messages are displayed in the Operator Information Area.

If any of the following messages are displayed in the **Operator Information Area**, please press the **RESET** key before you continue.

X ? +   X ⚥ NUM   X ⚥ # ?

532

If this message appears in the Operator Information Area the on-line catalog is out of order. Please use the microfiche catalog or ask the librarian for assistance.

12

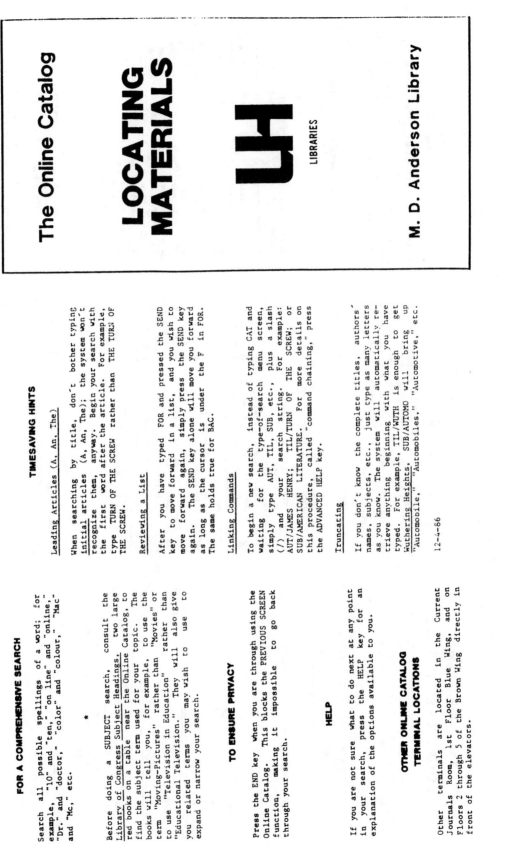

The Online Catalog

LOCATING MATERIALS

UH

LIBRARIES

M. D. Anderson Library

TIMESAVING HINTS

Leading Articles (A, An, The)

When searching by title, don't bother typing initial articles (A, An, The); the system won't recognize them, anyway. Begin your search with the first word after the article. For example, type TURN OF THE SCREW rather than THE TURN OF THE SCREW.

Reviewing a List

After you have typed FOR and pressed the SEND key to move forward in a list, and you wish to move forward again, simply press the SEND key again. The SEND key alone will move you forward as long as the cursor is under the F in FOR. The same holds true for BAC.

Linking Commands

To begin a new search, instead of typing CAT and waiting for the type-of-search menu screen, simply type AUT, TIL, SUB, etc., plus a slash (/) and your search string. For example: AUT/JAMES HENRY; TIL/TURN OF THE SCREW; or SUB/AMERICAN LITERATURE. For more details on this procedure, called "command chaining," press the ADVANCED HELP key.

Truncating

If you don't know the complete titles, authors' names, subjects, etc., just type as many letters as you know. The system will automatically retrieve anything beginning with what you have typed. For example, TIL/WUTH is enough to get Wuthering Heights, SUB/AUTOMO will bring up "Automobile," "Automobiles," "Automotive," etc.

12-4-86

FOR A COMPREHENSIVE SEARCH

Search all possible spellings of a word; for example, "10" and "ten," "on line" and "online," "Dr." and "doctor," "color" and "colour," "Mac" and "Mc," etc.

*

Before doing a SUBJECT search, consult the Library of Congress Subject Headings, two large red books on a table near the Online Catalog, to find the subject term used for your topic. The books will tell you, for example, to use the term "Moving-Pictures" rather than "Movies" or to use "Television in Education" rather than "Educational Television." They will also give you related terms you may wish to use to expand or narrow your search.

TO ENSURE PRIVACY

Press the END key when you are through using the Online Catalog. This blocks the PREVIOUS SCREEN function, making it impossible to go back through your search.

HELP

If you are not sure what to do next at any point in your search, press the HELP key for an explanation of the options available to you.

OTHER ONLINE CATALOG TERMINAL LOCATIONS

Other terminals are located in the Current Journals Room, 1st Floor Blue Wing, and on Floors 2 through 5 of the Brown Wing directly in front of the elevators.

M. D. Anderson Library, University of Houston

The Online Catalog
LOCATING MATERIALS

1

The Online Catalog provides access to books in the University of Houston Library. Remember, however, that the Online Catalog is NOT yet a complete list of the material the Library owns.

Check the CARD CATALOG for books not found in the Online Catalog.

Check the SERIALS LIST for magazines, journals, and newspapers.

If you have questions, ask for assistance at the Reference/Information Desk, 1 Red.

First check the Location code on the BRF screen to determine which of the nine University of Houston Libraries has your book:

University Park:

ANDERS /ANSTAK	M. D. Anderson Library
ARCH /ARSTAK	Architecture Branch Library
LAW /LASTAK	Law Library
MUSIC /MUSTAK	Music Branch Library
OPTOM /OPSTAK	Optometry Branch Library
PHARM /PHSTAK	Pharmacy Branch Library

Other Campuses:

DTOWN	UH Downtown
CLAKE	UH Clear Lake
VTORIA	UH Victoria

2

If the Location code for your book doesn't include "STAK" or is otherwise different from the codes in Section 1, this means that your book is in a special location within one of the Libraries. Here are the codes for the M. D. Anderson Library:

Code	Location	Floor & Wing
ANSTAK	Bookshelves	See Section 3
ANDOCR	Documents Reference Room	1 Red
ANHILL	Hill Room	8 Blue
ANILL	Interlibrary Loan Office	1 Red
ANINDX	Index Area	1 Red
ANINFO	Reference/Information Desk	1 Red
ANJRN	Current Journals Room	1 Blue
ANJUV	Juvenile Book Collection	3 Blue
ANMAP	Map Collection	2 Brown
ANMICR	Microform Collection	1 Blue
ANMED	Media Center	1 Blue
ANNEWS	Newspaper Collection	1 Blue
ANREF	Reference Collection	1 Red
ANRSRV	Reserves	1 Red
ANSPEC	Special Collections	8 Blue
ANSTAK	Bookshelves	See Section 3
ANTECR	Technical Reports	2 Red
ANTEXT	Textbook Collection	3 Blue
ANTHES	Thesis Collection	6 Blue
ANTXDC	Texas State Documents	2 Red
ANUSDC	U. S. Documents	2 Blue

*****

Questions? Ask for help at the Reference/Information Desk, 1 Red.

3

To find an ANSTAK book (a book on the regular shelves of the M. D. Anderson Library), locate the Call Number on the BRF screen. Match the FIRST LETTER with the Call Number Locations chart below and go to the floor and wing indicated.

CALL NUMBER LOCATIONS

First Letter of Call Number	Floor & Wing	First Letter of Call Number	Floor & Wing
A	5 Blue	N**	3 Blue
B	5 Blue	P	3 Brown
C	5 Brown	Q-QC	2 Red
D	5 Brown	QD-QM	2 Blue
E	4 Blue	QN-QR	2 Brown
F	4 Blue	R	2 Brown
G	4 Blue	S	2 Brown
H*	4 Brown	T	2 Brown
J	3 Blue	U	6 Blue
K	3 Blue	V	6 Blue
L	3 Blue	Z	6 Blue
M	3 Blue		

*HQ's on 6 Blue
**Most N's at Architecture & Art Library

EXAMPLES:

HD31.P3125	4 Brown***
LB874.B517	3 Blue
QA76.C3625	2 Red

***Color designations indicate the color of the signs in the respective wings.

M. D. Anderson Library, University of Houston

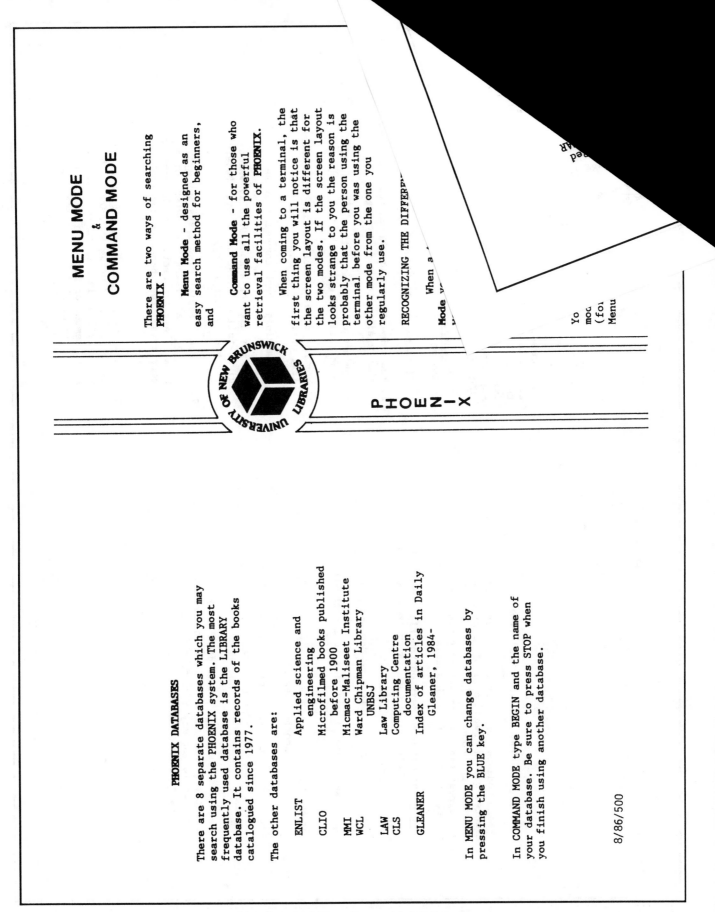

MENU MODE
& COMMAND MODE

There are two ways of searching **PHOENIX** -

Menu Mode - designed as an easy search method for beginners, and

Command Mode - for those who want to use all the powerful retrieval facilities of **PHOENIX**.

When coming to a terminal, the first thing you will notice is that the screen layout is different for the two modes. If the screen layout looks strange to you the reason is probably that the person using the terminal before you was using the other mode from the one you regularly use.

RECOGNIZING THE DIFFERE...

When a...

Mode ...

Yo
mo
(fo
Menu

PHOENIX DATABASES

There are 8 separate databases which you may search using the PHOENIX system. The most frequently used database is the LIBRARY database. It contains records of the books catalogued since 1977.

The other databases are:

ENLIST	Applied science and engineering
CLIO	Microfilmed books published before 1900
MMI	Micmac-Maliseet Institute
WCL	Ward Chipman Library UNBSJ
LAW	Law Library
CLS	Computing Centre documentation
GLEANER	Index of articles in Daily Gleaner, 1984-

In MENU MODE you can change databases by pressing the BLUE key.

In COMMAND MODE type BEGIN and the name of your database. Be sure to press STOP when you finish using another database.

8/86/500

University of New Brunswick Libraries

COMMAND MODE

To go to Command Mode press the [...] key. Then, when prompted, press the CLE[...] key.

To use Command Mode you have to know the commands to send to the computer. These are explained on the flip charts beside each terminal. Further detail is available in the lessons which you may obtain by pressing the key marked LESSN, or from the printed PHOENIX Users Manual.

Advantages of Command Mode include the following:

1. It is easier to combine search terms.

2. You can review your search terms and use them again without re-typing.

3. You may combine an author's name and book title in one search.

4. You may display sets earlier than the last one.

5. You may page back through your search.

6. You may ask for a Long Display which gives full publication details (useful for your bibliography).

7. The Long Display also lists Subject Headings describing the content of a book. These are useful search terms for retrieving other books on the same topic.

8. When searching subjects, search terms may be combined using AND, OR, or NOT (i.e. full Boolean searching - ask a staff member or consult flip chart beside terminal.)

MENU MODE

To go into Menu Mode press the beige key.

Menu Mode is very easy to use. You are presented with a "menu" or list of options on the screen and asked to choose one of them. As you progress through the system you are prompted with what to type or which special keys to press.

Note the coloured keys on the right-hand side of the keyboard. Beside each is an explanation of its function:

Red key - use to switch to Command Mode

Blue key - use if you wish to search another database

White key - use when you are ready to start another search

Brown key - use to display records and to continue display

Menu Mode is easy, but it does not have all the features that are available in Command Mode. After a while you may also find it slow. So - progress to Command Mode.

University of New Brunswick Libraries

COMMAND MODE

To locate materials by author, title or keyword, **PHOENIX COMMAND MODE** offer a more sophisticated, but easy-to-use search method to access information from the library's online catalogue.

Wait until the computer says **ENTER INPUT** before starting to type.

TO FIND A PERIODICAL TITLE

1. Type *b/p/* and the exact title of the periodical, including <u>any punctuation</u>.

   e.g. *b/p/maclean's*

2. Press the **GREEN ENTER** key. When the MORE...PRESS CLEAR message appears, press the **ORANGE CLEAR** key.

3. Type *c (for choose)* and the letter to the left of the title you want.

   e.g. *ca*

4. Press the **GREEN ENTER** key.

5. Type the letter *d (for display)*.

6. Press the **GREEN ENTER** key.

NOTE: Type *ca:d*
      Press ENTER
      Disregard steps 4,5,and 6

4

TO FIND BOOKS ON YOUR SUBJECT

Use the *s (search)* command (will retrieve books if the keywords occur in either the title or subject heading)

1. Type the letter *s* and a few words describing the subject.

   e.g. *s world disarmament**

2. Press the **GREEN ENTER** key.

3. When the computer tells you how many references are found with your keyword, type the letter *d (for display)*.

4. Press the **GREEN ENTER** key.

OR

Use the *s/s/ (search subject)* command (will retrieve books if the keywords occur in the subject heading only)

For best results, consult the Library of Congress Subject Headings (LCSH) <u>.</u>

1. Type *s/s/* and the appropriate LCSH.

   e.g. *s/s/ dyslexia*

2. Press the **GREEN ENTER** key.

3. Type *d (for display)*.

4. Press the **GREEN ENTER** key.

*Try searching *world and disarmament*. You will notice that the computer responds differently.

University of New Brunswick Libraries

2

TO FIND A BOOK WHEN YOU KNOW THE TITLE

Use the s /search/ command

1. Type the letter s (for search) and a few distinctive words in the title. Do not put in any punctuation.

   e.g. s lives girls women

2. Press the GREEN ENTER key.

3. When the computer tells you how many references have been found, type the letter d (for display).

4. Press the GREEN ENTER key.

NOTE: You can type dm (for medium display) or dl (for long display). There are many cases where essential information appears only in the medium and long display. (See display format at bottom of page).

OR

Use the b/t/ /browse title/ command

See page 1.

DISPLAY FORMATS

Set: 4, Item: 1204 of 1259, Record #: 256908

Location:	Main Library
Call#:	D811.5.R367
Author:	Reisman, Arnold.
Title:	Welcome tomorrow / Arnold and Ellen Reisman.
Imprint:	Cleveland, Ohio : North Coast Pub., c1982
Collation:	iv, 176 p. ; 18 cm. Paperback.
Subjects:	Reisman, Arnold, 1934 Aug. 2-
Subjects:	World War, 1939-1945 Personal narratives, Polish.
Other:	Reisman, Ellen.

TO FIND A BOOK WHEN YOU KNOW THE AUTHOR'S NAME

Use the s /search/ command

1. Type the letter s (for search) and the author's surname followed by a comma, then the first initial or name. Do not use a period after the initial.

   e.g. s drucker, p

2. Press the GREEN ENTER key.

3. When the computer tells you how many references have been found, type the letter d (for display).

4. Press the GREEN ENTER key.

OR

Should the search produce the message TOO MANY TERMS, then

Use the b/a/ /browse author/ command

1. Type b/a/ and the author's surname, followed by a comma, then his first initial or name.

   e.g. b/a/atwood,^m
                    space

2. Press the GREEN ENTER key. When the MORE...PRESS CLEAR message appears, press CLEAR.

3. Type c (for choose) and the letter to the left of the name you want.

   e.g. cb or cb-d

4. Press the GREEN ENTER key.

5. Type the letter d (for display).

6. Press the GREEN ENTER key.

University of New Brunswick Libraries

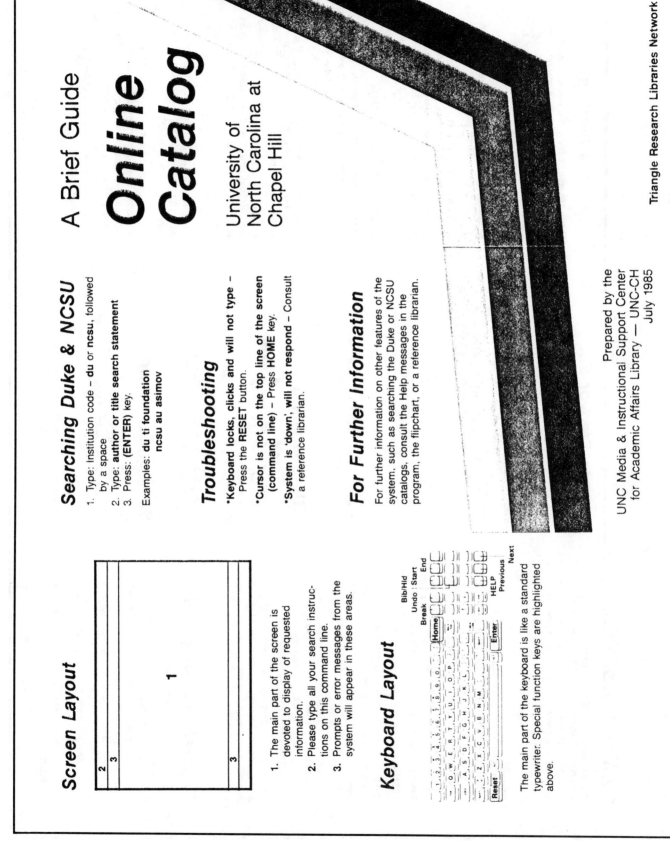

A Brief Guide

Online Catalog

University of
North Carolina at
Chapel Hill

Triangle Research Libraries Network

Prepared by the
UNC Media & Instructional Support Center
for Academic Affairs Library — UNC-CH
July 1985

Searching Duke & NCSU

1. Type: Institution code – **du** or **ncsu**, followed by a space
2. Type: **author or title search statement**
3. Press: **(ENTER)** key.

Examples: **du ti foundation**
        ncsu au asimov

Troubleshooting

***Keyboard locks, clicks and will not type** – Press the RESET button.

***Cursor is not on the top line of the screen** (command line) – Press **HOME** key.

***System is 'down'**, will not respond – Consult a reference librarian.

For Further Information

For further information on other features of the system, such as searching the Duke or NCSU catalogs, consult the Help messages in the program, the flipchart, or a reference librarian.

Screen Layout

1. The main part of the screen is devoted to display of requested information.
2. Please type all your search instructions on this command line.
3. Prompts or error messages from the system will appear in these areas.

Keyboard Layout

The main part of the keyboard is like a standard typewriter. Special function keys are highlighted above.

Davis Library, The University of North Carolina at Chapel Hill

Online Catalog

The online catalog of the University of North Carolina at Chapel Hill is part of the Triangle Research Libraries Network (TRLN) and is still under development. You can use the online catalog to search by author, title, or subject for the following records:

UNC-CH –

Academic Affairs Libraries– most items cataloged since 1975 and many previous items.

Health Sciences Library – most of the book collection.

Law Library – items cataloged since July 1985.

Duke – most items cataloged since July 1979.

NCSU – most of the university collection.

The system allows you to search the catalogs of any of the listed institutions. However, the system will automatically search the catalog of UNC-CH unless you specify otherwise.

Each institution maintains card catalogs which contain complete records of all university holdings, including those which are not yet a part of the system.

If you do not find an item you want in the online catalog, be sure to check the card catalog at that institution, or ask a reference librarian.

General Searching Rules

1. You may search only one title, author, or subject at a time.
2. You may do a series of searches within a session—just type a new search statement.
3. Capitalization is not necessary.
4. Type all numbers, abbreviations, acronyms and initialisms as they appear.
5. You may generally omit punctuation.
6. Leave spaces between all words.
7. There are no cross references in the system.

How to Start or End

Press the appropriate key – **START** or **END**. (see diagram) It is not necessary to press **START** or **END** between searches during a session.

START clears the system of any previous user's searches and provides an introductory screen.

END clears the system and completes your session at the terminal.

Author Searching

1. Type **au** *followed by a space*
2. Type: **the author's name** (last name first)
3. Press: **ENTER**

Example:
To search for works by Dan Rather, type:
au rather dan and press **ENTER**.

Title Searching

1. Type **ti** *followed by a space*
2. Type: **the title you want to search**, or the first part of the title. Do not use initial articles.
3. Press: **ENTER**

Example:
To search for *Foundation's Edge*, type:
ti foundations edge and press **ENTER**.

Subject Searching

1. Type **sub** *followed by a space*.
2. Type the Library of Congress. MESH. or Local subject heading you wish to search.
3. Press: **ENTER**.

Example:
To search for books on marketing type:
sub marketing and press **ENTER**.

Using the Indexes

There are author (**au**), title (**ti**), and subject (**sub**) indexes available to help you refine a search. These alphabetical listings may be useful when you are unsure of an author's full name, the exact title of a book, or the exact wording of a subject heading.

To search an index, type **in** before your author, title, or subject search statement.

Example:
To search the subject index for headings beginning with the word "Marketing", type: **in sub marketing** and press **ENTER**.

How to Get Help

There are several kinds of help available to you with the online catalog – help within the system, supplemental printed materials, and library personnel.

If you make an error during a search. the system will respond with appropriate explanations and suggestions.

For general information on the different features and functions of the system. such as searching the Duke and NCSU catalogs, you may request a list of available Help screens by typing **all** and pressing the **HELP** key.

You may also get help by typing the specific term you want explained (e.g., 'searching'), and then pressing **HELP**.

Several types of printed materials are also available. The flipchart. mounted beside the terminal, will answer many questions. The system manual is also available.

If you have further questions. consult a reference librarian.

Davis Library, The University of North Carolina at Chapel Hill

UT Library Online Catalog

User's Guide

Revised January 1987

What is the Online Catalog (UTCAT)?

A computerized file containing records for over 2.8 million items (mostly books and periodicals) in the UT Austin libraries. You can search the Online Catalog to get lists of items or information about a particular item, including its current status (checked out, etc.).

A supplement to the card catalog. The Online Catalog does not include all items in the UT libraries. It does include most items added to the collections since 1971 and many older items in the Perry-Castañeda Library (PCL), the Undergraduate Library, and the branch libraries. It includes very few items in the Humanities Research Center, the Tarlton Law Library, the Barker Texas History Center, or the Middle East, Asian, or South Asian Collections.

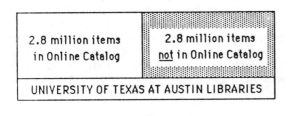

Still under development as we enhance the data file and work on new features. We want to know what you think of the Online Catalog system; to make a comment, press the **Comment** key.

Easy to use. Just follow instructions on each screen. You can't damage the system or erase data. For more help when searching or viewing results, press the **Help** key.

Important!

This guide is designed to be used with terminals in the libraries. Those using terminals or microcomputers in other locations may need to use different key combinations and special logon procedures. For more information, see the last page of this guide.

How the Online Catalog works

Always start by pressing the **Start** key. You can then do one of four different searches:

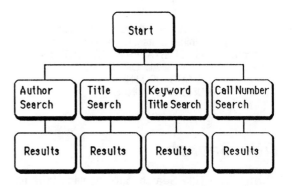

The computer always looks for records that *exactly* match what you type on the terminal. For best results, *experiment!* If your first search doesn't work, or for more complete searching, try several possibilities. Alternative spellings, abbreviations, or other variations will get different results.

After any search, you will see a Results screen, showing information about relevant items and their status. In Author, Title, and Call Number Searches, the computer opens the Online

---

University of Texas at Austin Library

Catalog file at the point where you told it to look; you can then page forward (but not back) through the file. In a Keyword Title Search, the computer retrieves a specific group of records that match your search request; you can then page forward through these records.

To finish your session at the terminal, press the **End** key.

Author Search

When: Use the Author Search when you want to find items by an author (which may be a person or an organization). If you know the exact title, use the Title Search.

How: Type as much of the name as you know.

For best results: At present, the Online Catalog records are not standardized like those in the card catalog. For most complete searching, try several forms of the name you want, including alternative spellings and abbreviations.

To find:	everything in the Online Catalog by Edgar Allan Poe
Search:	POE, EDGAR ALLAN
Then:	POE, EDGAR A
Then:	POE, E A
Then:	POE
(... etc.)	

To find:	everything in the Online Catalog by United States. Bureau of Mines.
Search:	UNITED STATES BUREAU OF MINES
Then:	U S BUREAU OF MINES
Then:	US BUR OF MINES
Then:	BUREAU OF MINES
(... etc.)	

Title Search

When: The Title Search is like looking up a title in the card catalog. Use it when you are sure you know the beginning of the title.

How: Type the first words of the title in exact order. Omit the first word if it is an article. You may leave off words at the end of the title.

To find:	The American Nation: A History
Search:	AMERICAN NATION

For best results: If your first search doesn't work, try variant forms of the words in the title or

try a Keyword Title Search. If you're not sure of the exact title you want to search, try a Keyword Title Search using likely words.

Conference proceedings: Often these publications can best be found by doing an Author Search under the name of the sponsoring group or the name of the conference itself.

Keyword Title Search

When: The Keyword Title Search is different from anything you can do with the card catalog. Use it when you know significant words in the title of a particular item you want to find, or that might be in titles you'd like to see. In effect, you can use the Keyword Title Search as a rough subject search.

How: Type any meaningful or significant words from the title in any order.

For best results: The Keyword Title Search retrieves a specific group of items that match your request. To be retrieved, a title must contain *all* the keywords you requested, spelled *exactly* as you typed them. For the most complete results, try several different searches on alternative spellings, abbreviations, or word combinations, as in this example:

To find items with the title words "integrated circuits," search INTEGRATED CIRCUITS. To find some related items, search INTEGRATED CIRCUIT, IC, etc.

If your first search gets too many items, *narrow* it by re-entering the search with an additional keyword. If your first search gets too few items, *broaden* it by re-entering the search with fewer keywords. Avoid very general keywords such as "business" or "energy," unless they are combined with more specific words.

Call Number Search

When: You can use the Call Number Search in two ways:

(1) To check the status of a specific item when you know its call number. Do this by typing the complete call number.

(2) To "browse" through listings of items on a certain subject, in the same way that you would browse through books on the shelf. Do this by typing the first line or two of a relevant call

University of Texas at Austin Library

number. Like browsing in the stacks, this will get you some--but not all--items on similar subjects.

How: Type the call number with a space after each part. Do not type the library name or a -q- or -f- (oversize book) symbol.

To find:	QC 370.5 C65 ENGIN	...**type this:** QC 370.5 C65

To find:	-q- 913.378 Ev15p MAIN	...**type this:** 913.378 EV15P

Using search results

Online Catalog search results give the title, author, call number, location, and current status of the item.

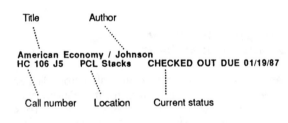

If the item is checked out, you may ask at the Circulation Desk to have it recalled for your use.

If the item is in a special location such as "PCL Reserves," you can often go to that location and use it.

If no current status is displayed, the item is not checked out and is probably on the shelf.

For best results: When in doubt about the meaning of an Online Catalog display, ask a library staff member. If you don't find what you want in the Online Catalog, try the card catalog or ask a library staff member for help.

Using the terminal

Use the keyboard like a typewriter. You may type UPPER CASE or lower case. The cursor, a lighted rectangle, always marks the space where your next character will appear. If you make a

mistake in typing, press the **Back Space** key until the cursor is over the incorrect character, then type over your mistake.

Arrows and dotted lines (-> _ _ _) on the screen indicate the places where you may type. If you move the cursor outside these areas, the keyboard may "lock up"; to release it, press **Reset**, then **Tab**.

When you have typed your search request, press the **Enter** key to send it to the computer. As soon as you press **Enter**, the message "INPUT INH," "X SYSTEM," or "X ⟨?⟩ " will appear on the bottom line of the screen. This means that the computer is working on your request.

Instructions at the bottom of each screen list your options at that point and tell how to move to other screens. From most points in the system, you can begin a new search by typing a single letter: **A**=author, **T**=title, **K**=keyword title, **C**=call number.

Special keys

Start returns you to the Start screen.

News gets you the latest information on changes and new features in the system.

Help gets you more information about what to do.

Tab moves the cursor to another area on the screen for typing.

Reset, then **Tab**, releases a locked keyboard.

Enter sends your request to the computer.

Comment lets you type a comment or suggestion about the Online Catalog and send it by computer to the system designers.

End finishes your session at the terminal.

How to handle problems

*You press **Enter**, the keyboard locks, and the message ""INPUT INH," "X SYSTEM," or "X ⟨?⟩ " appears at the bottom of the screen:* This is not a problem; it just means that the computer is working on your request.

University of Texas at Austin Library

You don't press Enter, but the keyboard locks and the message "INPUT INH" or the symbol ←☿→ appears at the bottom of the screen: Press Reset, then Tab, to release the keyboard.

No response for more than a minute: Did you remember to press the Enter key? If so, ask a library staff member for help.

Problems moving from one screen to another: Look at the bottom of the screen to see your current options. If all else fails, press the Start key.

Special note for users outside the library

UT students, faculty, and staff can now access the Online Catalog (UTCAT) from a variety of terminals and microcomputers, as outlined below. UTCAT is available during hours when library units are open. Printed guides telling how to access UTCAT are available in most General Libraries units.

If you have a question about the Online Catalog itself (how to construct a search, how to broaden or narrow a keyword search, how to interpret results, etc.), call the library at 471-3813. This number is available most of the hours the Perry-Castañeda Library is open.

Data Processing Division terminals

These terminals are hard-wired to the Data Processing IBM mainframe and are located in many administrative and departmental offices.

To access the Online Catalog, log on to the COM-PLETE system (COM41 or COM2) and type the command *UTCAT. You can search the Online Catalog just as you would in the library. To end your session and return to COM-PLETE, press the PF8 (END) key and follow the instructions on the screen.

If you are using a Data Processing Division terminal and have a computer system problem (trouble logging on/off, terminal not active, keys don't produce correct responses, etc.), call the Data Processing Division at 471-8800, Mon-Fri 8am-5pm.

Computation Center ASCII terminals or microcomputers (MICOM network)

ASCII terminals are located in the Computation Center's Public Terminal Facilities (the largest of which are in FAC 29 and TAY 101) as well as in some departmental offices. Microcomputers with modems and telecommunications software, such as KERMIT or MacKERMIT, can also be used to access UTCAT. Procedures and required key equivalents for this type of access are described in *Using UTCAT with ASCII Terminals and Microcomputers,* available at the Computation Center IBM Information Desk (WCH 7) and in most General Libraries units.

If you are using any terminal or microcomputer connected to the Computation Center and have a computer system problem (trouble logging on/off, terminal not active, keys don't produce correct responses, etc.), call the Computation Center at 471-3241, Mon-Fri 9am-5pm (Wed. 9am-4pm).

Computation Center Academic IBM 3081

Access to UTCAT is also available from TELEX-style terminals connected to the Computation Center's Academic IBM computer system. These terminals are located in the Computation Center's Public Terminal Facilities as well as in some departmental offices. Procedures for this type of access are described in *Using UTCAT from the Academic IBM 3081,* available at the Computation Center IBM Information Desk (WCH 7) and in most General Libraries units.

CHPC/DECnet (other UT system components)

Access to UTCAT from other UT System component institutions is being established through the DECnet system, connecting to the Cray "supercomputer" at the Center for High Performance Computing. Printed information will be available when this link is completed.

**The General Libraries
The University of Texas at Austin**

University of Texas at Austin Library

USING THE WSU DATABASE

1   Command Symbols

f
FIND - Use *f* to initiate a search in one file of the database (e.g., author, title, subject, series). Example: *f tik drugs*.

s
SELECT FOR DISPLAY - When a search produces more than 10 hits (items found), use *s* to display 10 titles at a time (e.g., *s*). Enter *s* <u>again</u> to display the <u>next</u> 10 items. Specific numbers may also be selected (e.g., *s* 21-30). If fewer than 10 items are found, they will display automatically. For full bibliographic and location/call number information on a title, <u>clear</u> the screen and select one item number at a time (e.g., *s* 3).

l
LOCATE - Use *L* to display library location, call number, and circulation status of one item at a time from a list of items. Use *L* with one item number (e.g., *L* 23).

r
RESTORE - Use *r* to display the contents of the prior screen after a Locate command. <u>Clear</u> the screen prior to typing *r*.

#
TRUNCATION - Use # to broaden a search. For example, *f tik impeach#* will find every title which contains any word beginning with the letters <u>impeach</u> (e.g., impeach, impeached, impeachment). Spacing <u>is</u> important: (e.g., *f suk insect#* will retrieve <u>more</u> items than *f suk insectic#*).

READ-ADAM - After selecting one item for display (e.g., *s* 4) or locating one item (e.g., *L* 3), type *read-adam* to display additional bibliographic information such as subjects, subject keywords, authors, notes, etc.

SORT - Items retrieved (hits) from a Find command may be sorted three ways, after <u>clearing</u> the screen:
    sortd   Use this command to sort the items found by publication date (e.g., *sortd*). Then use *s* to display the most recently published items first.
    sorta   Use this command to sort the items found into alphabetical order by author. Then use *s*.
    sortt   This command sorts a list of items found into alphabetical order by title.

b
BROWSE - Use *b* to scan a file as an aid in choosing a word for a search. Browsable files include author, title, series, and subject. For example, *b su chem*. To continue the browse, clear the screen, type *b*, and press RETURN again. Note: The *b* command only <u>shows</u> the file, it does <u>not</u> retrieve items.

Holland Library, Washington State University

2 | *suk* Subject Keyword (F2 key)

It is usually best when searching the SUBJECT file to use the SUK symbol.

EXAMPLES

1. Type *f suk* followed by a space.
2. Type one or more keywords defining your subject.   *f suk acoma indian#*
3. Press the RETURN key   *f suk palouse wheat*
4. If needed, use the *s* command to list items.   *f suk television*
   (See Box 1)   *violence child#*
5. Type *s* and an item number to get library   *s*
   (See Box 1) location and call number.   *s 3*

3 | *tik* Title Keyword (F1 key)

It is usually best when searching the TITLE file to use the TIK symbol.

EXAMPLES

1. Type *f tik* followed by a space.   *f tik gene manipulat#*
2. Type one or more keywords from the title.   *f tik insecticide#*
3. Press the RETURN key and proceed as in Box 2.   *f tik grande ronde*

4 | *au* Author (F3 key)

When searching the AUTHOR file, always use the AU symbol for individual
authors' names. Truncation is automatic.

EXAMPLES

1. Type *f au* followed by a space.
2. Type the author's surname followed by a space.   *f au scargill d*
3. Type the author's first initial or first name.   *f au hass robert*

   f au forth

4. Press the RETURN key and proceed as in Box 2.

NOTE: If you do not know the author's first initial, leave a space
after surname and type *#*.

Holland Library, Washington State University

5 | *su* Subject

Use the SU symbol to search the subject file with an official SUBJECT. This is particularly useful when the keywords in your subject are also keywords in other subjects.

EXAMPLES

1. Type *f su* followed by a space.

   f su law

2. Type the exact form of the subject heading you wish to search. You may need to consult a librarian to get the exact form.

   f su chemistry

   f su religion and science

3. Press the RETURN key and proceed as in Box 2.

6 | *ti* Title

You can also search the TITLE file by using the TI symbol and the exact form of a title. Unless your title is very short and non-distinctive (e.g., Time), it is usually wise to truncate (#).

EXAMPLES

1. Type *f ti* followed by a space.

   f ti time

2. Type the exact form of your title (or the first few words) followed by #.

   f ti moby dick #

   f ti algorithms for network #

3. Press the RETURN key and proceed as in Box 2.

7 | *at* Author-Title   (F4 key)

To search AUTHOR and TITLE files at once with a minimum of typing, use the AT symbol.

EXAMPLES

1. Type *f at* followed by a space.

   f at hem,sun

2. Type the first three letters of the author's surname, a comma, and then the first three letters of the first word of the title (ignoring initial articles). Do not leave a space after the comma.

   f at woo,to

   f at leh,bio

3. Press the RETURN key and proceed as in Box 2.

Holland Library, Washington State University

8   *auk*   <u>Au</u>thor <u>K</u>eyword

Use the AUK symbol to find works "AUTHORed" by a corporate body, i.e.,
a symposium or congress, government agency, company, foundation, etc.).
You <u>cannot</u> use AUK for individual authors' names.

<u>EXAMPLES</u>

1. Type *f auk* followed by a space.   *f auk columbia law*

2. Type one or more keywords from   *f auk washington state*
   the body's name.   *budget*

3. Press RETURN key and proceed as   *f auk sympos# geophys#*
   in Box 2.

9   *sek*   <u>Se</u>ries <u>K</u>eyword

When searching for works in a SERIES, it is usually best to use the SEK
symbol.

<u>EXAMPLES</u>

1. Type *f sek* followed by a space.   *f sek oxford studies history*

2. Type one or more keywords from the   *f sek science religion*
   name of the series.   *f sek california university*

3. Press RETURN key and proceed as in   *archaeology 9*
   Box 2.

NOTE: When searching for a particular title in a series, it is helpful to
include the <u>number</u> for that title.

10 | pbk Publisher Keyword

When searching for works by a publisher, use the PBK symbol. Use one or two keywords from the name.

EXAMPLES

1. Type *f pbk* followed by a space.

2. Type one or more keywords from the publisher's name.

3. Press RETURN key and proceed as in Box 2.

f pbk prentice hall

f pbk university california

f pbk doubleday

11 | se Series

You can also search the SERIES file by using the SE symbol and the <u>exact</u> form of the series title. Unless your title is short, it is usually wise to truncate (#).

EXAMPLES

1. Type *f se* followed by a space.

2. Type the exact form of the series title (or the first few words) followed by #.

3. Press the RETURN key and proceed as in box 2.

f se international agricult#

f se washington state council

f se sage annual reviews of #

OTHER SEARCHING AIDS:

NEWS (F8 key) - Enter this to obtain the latest library user news.

HELP (F9 key) - Enter this to obtain online help with database searching commands, tips, files, etc. When the Main Menu appears, choose one of the information options offered.

? -- Enter this to obtain a summary of library commands which may be used in the Cougalog database.

Holland Library, Washington State University

12 *fc l,* Searching by call number

fc d,

desc

You can find any item in the database by using its exact call number.

EXAMPLES

1a. For a Library of Congress call number
(beginning with a letter) type *fc l,*.   *fc l,nk1165j471984*

1b. For a Dewey Decimal call number
(beginning with numerals) type *fc d,*.   *fc d,813c88t*

2. Type the complete call number. No spaces
are necessary. Include any decimal point
between numerals; no other punctuation is
necessary within the call number. If there
is a date at the end of the call number,
include it.

3. Press RETURN key and proceed as in Box 2.

If the response is "Zero hits on search," use the DESC command to search a
temporary circulation file:

EXAMPLES

1. Type *desc* followed by a space.   *desc nk1165j471984*

2. Type complete call number.   *desc 813c88t*

3. Press RETURN key and proceed as in Box 2.

- -

PLEASE NOTE: If you do not find the author, title, or subject you are looking
for in the database, BE SURE TO CHECK THE CARD CATALOG. For periodical titles
check the list of WSU Journals and Serials on microfiche. The database does
not contain all holdings. Consult the reference librarian for further assistance.

Holland Library, Washington State University

LUIS

SEARCH HIM!

Meet

LUIS

Your Library User
Information Service

SEARCH HIM!

a=author

LUIS will tell you what books and recordings are owned by the Library and where you can find them.

To look for a book by its author:
1. Type a=author's last name [and first name(s) if you wish]
examples: a=dickens
    a=dickens c
    a=dickens charles
2. Press **ENTER** key

For assistance:
1. Type a and press **ENTER** key for help screen
2. Check the card catalog
3. Ask a librarian for help

White Plains Public Library
100 Martine Ave., White Plains, N.Y. 10601
Information Center: (914) 682-4480
Children's Library: (914) 682-4476

Meet

LUIS

Your Library User
Information Service

SEARCH HIM!

t=title

LUIS will tell you what books and recordings are owned by the Library and where you can find them.

To look for a book by its title:
1. Type t=(title of book)
examples: t=war and peace
    t=war and
2. Press **ENTER** key
(IMPORTANT: Do *not* type the articles a, an, or the. at beginning of title)

For assistance:
1. Type t and press **ENTER** key for help screen
2. Check card catalog
3. Ask a librarian for help

White Plains Public Library
100 Martine Ave., White Plains, N.Y. 10601
Information Center: (914) 682-4480
Children's Library: (914) 682-4476

Meet

LUIS

Your Library User
Information Service

SEARCH HIM!

s=subject

LUIS will tell you what books and recordings are owned by the Library and where you can find them.

To look for a book by its subject:
1. Type **s**=(subject)
Type **sm**=(subject for children's books)
examples: s=television
    sm=alphabet
2. Press **ENTER** key

For assistance:
1. Type s and press **ENTER** key for help screen
2. Check card catalog
3. Ask a librarian for help

To find out what subject headings are used by LUIS, check the *Library of Congress Subject Headings* books.

White Plains Public Library
100 Martine Ave., White Plains, N.Y. 10601
Information Center: (914) 682-4480
Children's Library: (914) 682-4476

Introduce yourself to **LUIS,** our online computerized catalog, who will let you know what books and other materials are in the Library. He will find information for you whether you're starting with an author. a title or a subject.

Look for him on one of our easy-to-use computer terminals. Just type e and press the **ENTER** key. and **LUIS** will give you instructions on how to use him.

LUIS is available during regular library hours. If you have any problems or questions, just ask at the Information Center for help.

White Plains Public Library
100 Martine Ave., White Plains, N.Y. 10601
Information Center: (914) 682-4480
Children's Library: (914) 682-4476

White Plains Public Library

THE WHOLE PICTURE

LUIS is part of **NOTIS,** a total, computerized library management system which we are gradually implementing. He's the part the public sees and uses. Behind the scenes, **NOTIS** *(Northwestern Online Total Integrated System)* will provide a rapid, efficient circulation system, keep track of items as they are ordered and received, tell you what books you can expect to find on the shelves, be used for checking in current periodicals and serve many of the business functions of the Library. Most important, **NOTIS** will gather the important data that will help us make the decisions on how to provide optimum service to you, our public.

CALL US

Information/Reference Center	682-4480
Library & Holiday Hours	682-4400
Children's Library	682-4476
Overdue & Reserve Notices	682-4490
Program Information	682-4480
Meeting Room Reservations	682-4493
Public Relations	682-4493
TTY	682-4491
Library Director/Orrin Dow	682-4407

The City of White Plains

Alfred Del Vecchio, Mayor

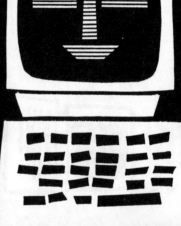

LUIS

SEARCH HIM!

White Plains Public Library

THIS IS LUIS — SEARCH HIM!

We'd like to introduce you to **LUIS.** His formal name is Library User Information Service. He's ready and eager to go to work for you, to help you search for what you want in the White Plains Public Library.

HE'S AS EASY AS a, t, s

LUIS is our new computerized public access catalog. He can find information for you, whether you're starting with **a**=author, **t**=title or **s**=subject (**sm**=children's subject). He'll let you know which books and other materials are in the library, where you can find them and which books are on order. You can find data on adult, young adult, and children's books all in the same place. He's fast and easy to use. You can talk with him on one of our computer terminals. Just type **e** and press the **ENTER** key. **LUIS** will give you instructions on how to use him.

WE'RE GLAD TO HELP

We know you'll like **LUIS** as you get to know him. He loves searching out data for you, but if he doesn't seem to co-operate at times, remember the library staff knows how to bring out the best in him. Just ask at the Information Center for help if you need it.

LUIS IS TOUGH

Nothing you type on the terminal will break **LUIS**, so don't be afraid to experiment, to try different searches and commands. Be adventurous.

LUIS KEEPS GROWING

LUIS can be used instead of the card catalog to help you find what you want in the Library. But he doesn't know everything yet. If you don't find it in **LUIS**, check the card catalog. We keep feeding **LUIS** information. He's growing byte by byte. Someday, he'll contain everything the card catalog does, and more.

HE'S A HARD WORKER

LUIS is friendly and loves to work for you. He's here to help us better serve you, the public. He's online with information at your fingertips during library hours.

Adult Services:

Monday-Thursday	9am-9pm
Friday	9am-6pm
Saturday	9am-5pm
Sunday (Oct.-May)	1pm-5pm

Children's Room:

Monday	9am-9pm
Tuesday-Friday	9am-6pm
Saturday	9am-5pm
Sunday (Oct.-May)	1pm-5pm

White Plains Public Library

Online Catalog Guides:

Bibliographies

Library Orientation and Instruction-1984

Hannelore B. Rader

This annotated list of materials provides library users with orientation to facilities and services, and instructs them in library information and computer skills. It is the eleventh annual review of this literature published in *RSR* and covers publications from 1984. A few items have been included from 1983 because of their significance and because they had not been available for review last year. Several items were not annotated because the compiler was unable to secure them.

The list includes publications on user instruction in all types of libraries and for all types of users from children to senior citizens. Publications in foreign languages have been excluded. Arrangement is by type of library.

The number of publications related to user instruction in 1984 increased by 50 percent over 1983 as follows:

-	academic libraries	91%
-	public libraries	100%
-	school libraries	6%
-	special libraries	37%
-	all types	35%

The largest increase in number of user instruction publications occurred in academic libraries - 91 percent and in public libraries - 100 percent. The number of items related to school and special libraries showed a decrease.

It is noteworthy that the publications dealing with theory and research related to user instruction are increasing, and that many more of such writings are being published in discipline-oriented publications, a clear result of the increased endeavors

Rader is Director of Libraries at the University of Wisconsin-Parkside.

of the Association of College and Research Libraries to build closer coalitions with other professional associations. Several other observations may be of interest:

- An increasing number of publications are concerned with the place of microcomputers in user instruction.
- Several items address teaching patrons the use of online catalogs and training them to do online searching.
- There is an increase in the number of books on user education for the school and college level user.
- A number of library journals have added bibliographic instruction columns while both the ALA Library Instruction Round Table and the ACRL Bibliographic Instruction Section are now publishing newsletters.
- The trend to have joint librarian/faculty presentations of user instruction at professional conferences is growing.
- Several articles deal with special types of users such as the handicapped, foreign students, disadvantaged students, and others.

ACADEMIC LIBRARIES

ACRL-BIS Clearinghouse Committee. *The Bibliographic Instruction Clearinghouse: A Practical Guide.* Chicago: Association of College and Research Libraries, 1984.

This work provides guidelines and information on bibliographic instruction clearinghouses.

Anderson, David, et al. "Patron Use and Understanding of the COM and Card Catalog at Georgia State University." In *Academic Libraries: Myths and Realities*, ed. by S. Dodson and G. Menges, 207-214. Chicago: Association of College and Research Libraries, 1984.

The authors summarize a survey of Georgia State University to determine patron use and understanding of a frozen card catalog and a COM catalog. Preference for the latter was indicated.

Arp, Lori L. and L.A. Wilson. "Library Instructor's View--Theoretical." *Research Strategies* 2 (Winter 1984): 16-22.

The authors provide the theoretical framework for the undergraduate bibliographic instruction program at the University of Illinois-Urbana. They discuss parts of the program, such as a three-step research strategy, taxonomy of library skills, the student body, and students' needs.

Baldwin, Claudia. "Fast and Furious: A Weekend Session in Bibliographic Instruction." *College and Research Libraries News* 45 (May 1984): 234-235.

Baldwin describes a concentrated, two-weekend course on library skills taught at California State University-Dominguez Hills. Grades are based on individual projects. Students have generally liked this type of instruction.

Bales, Jack. "Library Instruction Course for Credit." *LIFLine News* 26 (September 1984): 3-5.

Benson, Stanley H. "The Library's Status in Undergraduate Instruction: Far from the Heart of Things." In *Academic Libraries: Myths and Realities*, ed. by S. Dodson and G. Menges, 215-221. Chicago: Association of College and Research Libraries, 1984.

Benson reviews the history of libraries in higher education and its place in undergraduate instruction. He advocates the development of stronger relationships between faculty and administrators.

Bhullar, Pushpazit and P. Timberlake. "Library Skills: An Undergraduate Course at the University of Missouri-Columbia." *Show-Me-Libraries* 36 (October/November 1984): 70-74.

The authors describe a formal course in library use for one credit, taught by reference librarians in cooperation with the School of Library and Information Science. Several sections are offered each year, and a workbook is used; pre- and post-tests are given.

"Bibliographic Competencies for Music Students at an Undergraduate Level." *Music Library Association Notes* 40 (March 1984): 529-532.

Minimal bibliographic skills are identified for the undergraduate majoring in music.

"BI Line: A Column on Bibliographic Instruction." *Colorado Libraries* 10 (March 1984): 57-59.

In this column, C. Woo and D. Fink discuss an audiocassette walking tour of the library.

"BI Statistics Tips." *College and Research Libraries News* 45 (February 1984): 86-87.

Guidelines to keep BI statistics are provided. These guidelines were developed by the ACRL Bibliographic Instruction Section Research Committee.

"BI Tip Sheet for Academic Administrators and Support Staff." *College and Research Libraries News* 45 (November 1984): 546-548.

The tip sheet reproduced here was developed by the ACRL Education and Behavioral Sciences Section, Bibliographic Instruction for Educators Committee, to plan user instruction programs for college and university departmental secretaries, clerks, and administrative assistants.

Blazek, Ron. "The Administrative Climate for Bibliographic Instruction in Large Academic Libraries." *The Reference Librarian* 10 (Spring/Summer 1984): 161-179.

Blazek provides a comparison of attitudes of top level managers with those of middle managers to examine the administrative climate for bibliographic instruction. A study of fifty-one academic libraries is summarized. It was found that there is more support for bibliographic instruction than previously assumed.

Bodi, Sonia. "Relevance in Library Instruction: The Pursuit." *College and Research Libraries* 45 (January 1984): 59-65.

Bodi reports on the bibliographic instruction program at North Park College in Chicago, where a self-instruction workbook is used. Faculty and students were surveyed as to students' ability to use the library. Library instruction to freshmen is not course-integrated; librarians use worksheets with students. Other parts of the program are also described.

Bohning, James J. "Integration of Chemical History into the Chemical Literature Course." *Journal of Chemical Information and Computer Sciences* 24 (May 1984): 101-107.

The author describes a traditional chemical literature course, which should also include fundamentals for personal growth, a developmental history of chemistry, and information retrieval techniques to make retrospective literature searches more meaningful.

Bruce, Norton. "Why BI or LI: A Forum." *Reference Services Review* 12 (Spring 1984): 59-66.

Bruce presents a forum on why to have a library instruction program. William Fisher from the University of California-Los Angeles responds that library instruction is fundamental to the role of the library, while Thomas Kirk from Berea College notes that integrated library instruction helps to develop abilities and qualities of a rational mind. Bruce Morton from Carleton College discusses subject/discipline information as a focus of library instruction, and Cerise Oberman from the University of Minnesota talks about the library's role in higher education and how the teaching of information structure gives library instruction its purpose. Topsey N. Smalley from SUNY-Plattsburgh comments on the importance of library instruction to teach students the workings of information systems, and Barbara A. Schwartz from the University of Texas-Austin discusses the teaching of library skills in a large research university.

Budd, John. "The Question of Questioning: On the Coexistence of Library Instruction and Reference." *The Reference Librarian* 10 (Spring/Summer 1984): 93-100.

Budd discusses the merits of combining reference and library instruction.

Cable, Carol. "The Object, the Signal, the Information." *Research Strategies* 2 (Spring 1984): 60-64.

A fine arts librarian at the University of Texas-Austin describes an assignment involving the description, comparison, and stylistic analysis of a piece of art as part of an art course and the help librarians can give students undertaking such coursework.

Carlson, David and Ruth H. Miller. "Librarians and Teaching Faculty, Partners in Bibliographic Instruction." *College and Research Libraries* 45 (November 1984): 483-491.

The authors discuss course-integrated bibliographic instruction and its inherent problems, such as dependence on faculty cooperation, the consistency of instruction programs, and transference of library knowledge from one course to another. Good faculty/librarian relationships are essential to successful library instruction programs.

Carpenter, Don A. *Focus: A Forum on Teaching and Learning in Utah Community and Technical Colleges. Volume III*. ERIC Reproduction Service, 1984. ED 247 976.

This is a collection of articles on various aspects of curriculum and instruction at Utah's community colleges. It includes a paper on the "need for library instruction in 2-year colleges."

Chittenden, Carol B. "New Signs in Old Buildings." *Research Strategies* 2 (Winter 1984): 45-46.

Chittenden describes the remodeling of an old library building at the University of Kansas and the planning and implementation of a new sign system.

Coleman, Kathleen. "Library Instruction and the Advancement of Reference Service." *The Reference Librarian* 10 (Spring/Summer 1984): 241-252.

Coleman discusses some major sources of conflict between teaching and nonteaching librarians and identifies theoretical and practical contributions of library instruction to reference service.

Coniglio, Jamie W. "Bibliographic Counseling: The Term Paper Advisory Service." *Show-Me-Libraries* 36 (October/November 1984): 79-82.

Coniglio discusses library instruction at Iowa State University where all students must pass a for-credit, half-semester course on the use of the library. This is followed by the Term Paper Advisory Service using an appointment structure.

D'Aniello, Charles. "A Basic Bibliography of Readings and Course Materials for Bibliographic Instruction in Undergraduate and Graduate History Programs." *The History Teacher* 17 (May 1984): 408-444.

The author presents an annotated, comprehensive bibliography of materials useful to prepare a course or module on bibliographic instruction for history majors or history graduate students. Several appendixes provide a review of scholarly journals, factual verification in historical editing, pathfinder exercises, and the course syllabus.

_____. "An Historical Bibliography and Methods Course: The SUNY at Buffalo Experience." *The History Teacher* 17 (May 1984): 396-404.

D'Aniello discusses a required semester course on history bibliography/methodology at SUNY-Buffalo from the librarian/bibliographer's point-of-view. This course is co-taught with a history professor.

Davidson, Nancy. "Government Documents: An Integrated Part of the BI Program in Colleges." *South Carolina Librarian* 28 (Spring 1984): 19-20.

Davidson comments on including government documents in the library instruction program for freshmen writing courses.

Davinson, Donald. "Never Mind the Quality, Feel the Width." *The Reference Librarian* 10 (Spring/Summer 1984): 29-37.

The author presents a criticism of library instruction from the British point-of-view stating that the assumption continues to be that such instruction is good for the users. He advocates the need for user instruction cost studies with a view to saving money in higher education.

Davis, H. Scott. *An Introduction to Your College Library: Making It Work for You.* ERIC Reproduction Service, 1984. ED 253 254.

Davis presents the full text of a self-paced library skills workbook for freshmen English students at Georgia College. He includes an audiotape script for a tour, evaluation instruments, and a bibliography.

"Designing a Decathlon." Editorial. *Research Strategies* 2 (Fall 1984): 154-155.

This article provides a description of a possible bibliographic version of the Olympics decathlon for renowned scholars to test their skills in a research library.

Doelker, R.E. and P. Toifel. "The Development

of a Self-Guided Library-Based Materials and Methods Manual for Social Work Research." *Behavioral and Social Sciences Librarian* 3 (Summer 1984): 81-93.

Dougherty, Richard M. "Reallocating Resources and Reordering Priorities at the Reference Desk." Editorial. *Journal of Academic Librarianship* 10 (November 1984): 255.

This editorial highlights the dilemma of balancing new philosophies and technologies with traditional reference services and the frustrations this can cause. Dougherty advocates the use of priority setting to help with this dilemma.

Dougherty, Richard M. and W.P. Lougee. "What Will Survive?" *Library Journal* 109 (February 1985): 41-44.

This paper explores issues related to electronic publishing and implications for scholars, libraries, and publishers. It includes a brief discussion on the library's possible competition with the computer center for user education, reference assistance, and consultation.

Dykeman, Amy. "Betwixt and Between: Some Thoughts on the Technical Services Librarian Involved in Reference and Bibliographic Instruction." *The Reference Librarian* 10 (Spring/Summer 1984): 233-239.

The author discusses ways of incorporating more technical services librarians into bibliographic instruction programs.

Ellis, Steve. "Where to Find a Bibliographic-Instruction Corps." *American Libraries* 15 (September 1984): 592-593.

Ellis describes the library instruction program at the University of Washington, which is taught cooperatively by the library staff and the library school.

Engledinger, Eugene A. and Barbara R. Stevens. "Library Instruction within the Curriculum." *College and Research Libraries News* 45 (December 1984): 593-598.

The authors discuss a workshop/seminar for faculty on integrated library instruction at the University of Wisconsin-Eau Claire and its results in terms of the curriculum incorporating library research skills. A number of conclusions from the University of Wisconsin-Eau Claire are summarized.

Farber, Evan I. "Alternatives to the Term Paper." *New Directions for Teaching and Library* 18 (June 1984): 45-53.

The author discusses several alternatives to the term paper to engage students in library use such as annotated bibliographies and scholarship evaluation.

_____. "B.I. and Library Instruction: Some Observations." *The Reference Librarian* 10 (Spring/Summer 1984): 5-13.

Farber discusses the impact of bibliographic instruction on the design of the library building in reference to instructional and reference areas, reference desks, working space, and new technology.

Fleury, Bruce E. "Lectures, Textbooks and the College Librarian." *Improving College and University Teaching* 32 (Spring 1984): 103-106.

This article provides a criticism of the lecture/textbook teaching method supported by the library reserve system. It promotes course-integrated library instruction and its implementation in higher education.

Frick, Elizabeth. "Humanizing Technology through Instruction." *Canadian Library Journal* 41 (October 1984): 263-267.

Frick discusses the problem librarians have ensuring patrons direct access to the literature not only by being statistically effective, but also by providing a humanely effective, delivery system.

George, Mary and S. Hogan. "Information on Cards and What It All Means." *Research Strategies* 2 (Spring 1984): 88-97.

This article concludes a three-part discussion on teaching the card catalog to college students. It describes methodology to teach tracings, symbols, filing rules, subject headings, call numbers, locations, and various entries.

_____. "What's 3 x 5 and Full of Holes? Part 2." *Research Strategies* 2 (Winter 1984): 50-55.

The authors debate the virtues and problems of teaching the use of the card catalog to students. They discuss physical and conceptual features of the card catalog.

Goudy, Frank Wm. and Eugene Moushey. "Library Instruction and Foreign Students: A Survey of Opinions and Practices among Selected Libraries." *The Reference Librarian* 10 (Spring/Summer 1984): 215-226.

This article is a summary of a study of forty-four academic libraries and their service to foreign students with special emphasis on bibliographic instruction. No single dominant trend for bibliographic instruction to foreign students emerged.

"The Grad Versus Undergrad Debate: A Most Ingenious Paradox." Editorial. *Research Strategies* 2 (Winter 1984): 2-3.

Sharon Hogan and Mary George comment on the difficult dilemma facing many librarians, namely, whether to teach library skills to undergraduate or graduate students, given limited resources.

Griffiths, Pal and Roger Hines. "Use of CAL Programs for Instruction in the Use of the Microfiche Catalogue System at Sheffield City Polytechnic." *INFUSE* 8 (April 1984): 6-10.

The authors describe the development of a computer program for the IBM 4314 mainframe that supplements the teaching of new library users as related to use of microfiche. It turned out to be a costly program, but is used for students and new staff.

Gunjal, S.R. and A.Y. Asundi. "User Education and Training." *Herald of Library Science* 23 (January/April 1984): 16-23.

The authors explain the concept of user education and examine a variety of user education programs as related to students in universities in India.

Hales, Celia and D. Catlett. "The Credit Course: Reaffirmation from Two University Libraries. Methodology: East Carolina University." *Research Strategies* 2 (Fall 1984): 156-165.

This course is designed for students at the University of North Carolina- Charlotte. The self-paced workbook covers basic library skills needed to use a university library.

Hanson, Janet R. "The Evaluation of Library User Education with Reference to the Programme at Dorset Institute of Higher Education (DIHE)." *Journal of Librarianship* 16 (January 1984): 1-18.

This study examines theories of evaluation used in education as a vehicle to develop a system of evaluation for user education. Two models of evaluation are investigated, the objectives model and the illuminative model. Examples of evaluation instruments are appended.

Hanson, Janet. "A Survey of Library User Education for Students of Education." *INFUSE* 8 (June 1984): 5-11.

Hanson summarizes a 1981-1982 survey of user education in 100 higher education institutions in England and Wales to assess librarians' abilities to apply the principles of educational technology in their teaching activities. It was found that there are many user education activities among librarians in the field of education, but they are not firmly based in educational theory. The move toward use of cognitive perspectives on learning theory as used in the United States is being advocated for the United Kingdom.

Hare, A.R. "A Formally Taught Course of Bibliographic Instruction at Wolverhampton Polytechnic." *INFUSE* 8 (February 1984): 6-11.

Harris, Roma M. and C.L. Ross. "Teaching Research Methods: Students' Cognitive Complexity and Demand for Structure." *Journal of Education for Librarianship* 24 (Winter 1984): 189-198.

The authors discuss the relationship between cognitive style and structure in teaching research methods to students.

Hatchard, Desmond B. and Phyllis Toy. "Evaluation of a Library Instruction Programme at BCAE." *Australian Academic and Research Libraries* 15 (September 1984): 157-167.

The authors report that many studies have shown low use of the academic library by students, often because they enter universities unprepared for sophisticated library use. They summarize findings from a study at Bendigo College in Australia, which concurred with earlier studies.

Homic, Ronald J. "Library Use Instruction in Community Colleges." *Catholic Library World* 55 (April 1984): 398-401.

Homic examines the special nature of the needs and problems that students and faculty in community colleges have as related to library instruction.

Hostettler, John D. and M.B. Wolfe. "A Brief Introduction to the Chemical Literature with a Bibliography and Exercises." *Journal of Chemical Education* 61 (July 1984): 22-24.

The authors describe the design, content, and use of a set of materials that introduce students to the chemical literature.

Huber, Kris. "Biblical Exegesis." *Research Strategies* 2 (Summer 1984): 139-142.

Huber, Kris and P. Lewis. "Tired of Term Papers? Options for Librarians and Professors." *Research Strategies* 2 (Fall 1984): 192-199.

The authors describe a faculty seminar at St. Olaf College in Minnesota, where faculty and librarians explored alternatives to the term paper.

Jackson, William J. "The User-Friendly Library Guide." *College and Research Libraries News* 45 (October 1984): 468-471.

Jackson describes how librarians at the University of Houston-University Park have been attempting to make bibliographic guides less frustrating for users. The audience for these guides was profiled and the guides patterned after their needs.

_____. "The User-Friendly Library Guide." *Show-Me-Libraries* 36 (October/November 1984): 75-78.

The author discusses the library guides produced and used at the University of Houston-University Park. These guides are utilizing search strategy formats and are designed for a specific audience. Many tips for successful guides are given.

Janke, Richard V. "Online after Six: End-User Searching Comes to Age." *Online* 8 (November 1984): 15+.

Janke evaluates end-user search services at the University of Ottawa, one of the first such services anywhere.

Johnson, Eric W. "Library Instruction for Faculty Members." *The Reference Librarian* 10 (Spring/Summer 1984): 199-213.

Johnson provides several ideas for working with faculty in the area of library instruction.

Johnston, Bill and D. Nicholson. "Managing the Introduction of a Sign System for the Andersonian Library, University of Strathclyde: A Case Study." *INFUSE* 8 (December 1984): 4-9.

The authors provide a detailed description of a signage development project for a British university library.

Katz, William. *Your Library. A Reference Guide.* 2d ed. New York: Holt, Rinehart & Winston, 1984.

This is a revised edition of an earlier work that teaches students to learn how to use the library. A chapter on the research paper has been added. "Check your knowledge" sections have been added at the end of chapters to help students understand and find reference materials. The book may be used independently by students or in a classroom setting. An index is included.

Kennedy, Mary Ellen. "Bibliographic Instruction in the Academic Library: Looking at the Adult Student." *The Reference Librarian* 10 (Spring/Summer 1984): 205-213.

Kennedy discusses adult teaching and learning theories that provide bibliographic instruction to adults of all ages. She uses the example of "Elderhostel."

Kenney, Donald J. "Publishing BI Articles in Discipline Journals Social Sciences." *Reference Strategies* 2 (Summer 1984): 119-127.

Kenney, Patricia A. and J.N. McArthur. "Designing and Evaluating a Programmed Library Instruction Text." *College and Research Libraries* 45 (January 1984): 35-42.

This article is a description of a program of course-integrated user instruction using a programmed textbook at the University of Houston-Victoria. It includes a summary of a statistical study comparing this programmed text method with a lecture method. The article concludes that the programmed text method was more successful in teaching lower-level cognitive skills, and students preferred it. Also included is a description of teaching upper-level cognitive skills.

King, James R., et al. *Integrating Study Skills and Orientation Courses. College Reading and Learning Assistance Technical Report 84-07*. ERIC Reproduction Service, 1984. ED 248 760.

The authors describe a college-level, integrated study skills and orientation course providing students with learning experiences within the university setting. Course outline and materials are appended.

Kirk, Thomas G. "Concluding Comments." *New Directions for Teaching and Learning* 18 (June 1984): 85-92.

Kirk gives a rationale for incorporating a bibliographic instruction program into the liberal arts curriculum.

Kirkendall, Carolyn. "Accommodating International Users: How Much Is Too Much?" *Research Strategies* 2 (Spring 1984): 85-87.

Kirkendall discusses programs and materials for library instruction for foreign students. Comments are provided by Peter Wood of Boston University, Raymond DeSoto of UCLA, and Judith Avery of the University of Michigan.

_____. "BI Liaison Project Update." *College and Research Libraries News* 45 (January 1984): 10.

The author summarizes academic librarians' involvement in discipline associations in higher education through program participation.

_____. "BI Liaison Project Update." *College and Research Libraries News* 45 (March 1984): 132-133.

Kirkendall reports on the opportunities for academic librarians to become involved with other professional associations and documents several such involvements.

_____. "BI Liaison Project Update." *College and Research Libraries News* 45 (April 1984): 185-186.

Kirkendall summarizes library-related papers and programs presented at other professional conferences and meetings. She also discusses the pro-

ject's traveling exhibit.

_____. "BI Liaison Project Update." *College and Research Libraries News* 45 (October 1984): 481-483.

The author presents the final report of the program officer for the ACRL Bibliographic Instruction Liaison Project and a variety of recommendations to continue BI Liaison Project activities.

_____. "Do Faculty Members Have Fragile Egos?" *Research Strategies* 2 (Winter 1984): 47-49.

Responses to a statement about faculty's attitudes toward library instruction provided by librarians are given by Wendy Culotta from California State University-Long Beach, Jo Ann Lee from Lake Forest College, and Laura Osegueda from San Jose State University.

_____. "Frustrations of the Bibliographic Instructor." *Research Strategies* 2 (Fall 1984): 188-190.

Comments on this statement are provided by Susan Varca from the University of Georgia, Sandra Ready at Mankato State University, and Pam Englebrecht at Virginia Polytechnic University.

_____. "Improving Teaching: How a Clearinghouse Helps." *New Directions for Teaching and Learning* 18 (June 1984): 79-84.

Kirkendall describes the effectiveness of the national clearinghouse on bibliographic instruction in helping library instruction librarians provide better instruction programs.

Kirkendall, Carolyn A. *Bibliographic Instruction and the Learning Process: Theory, Style and Motivation*. Ann Arbor, MI: Pierian Press, 1984.

These papers were presented at the 12th Annual Library Instruction Conference held at Eastern Michigan University on 6-7 May 1982. Cerise Oberman from the University of Minnesota discussed the application of learning theory, while Rao Aluri and Mary Reichel from Emory University and Georgia State University respectively, addressed delineated learning theories for bibliographic instruction. Megan Lilly of the Chisholm Institute talked about "Learning Library Skills in Australia-Where to Now?" and Morell D. Boone from Eastern Michigan University discussed "Motivation and the Library Learner." David N. King of the Houston Academy of Medicine, assessed behavior for diversified instructional programming, while Jon Lindgren from St. Lawrence University presented a paper on "Library Use Instruction and the Basic Learning Processes: Reasoning, Writing and Research." "Systematic Development for Library Instruction Programs: Issues of Design and Change" was the title of Constance A. Mellon's presentation; she is at the University of Tennessee at Chattanooga. Constance P. Mulligan from Northern Kentucky University talked about "BI in Britain: Comp 102, Where Are We?" and Sally Wayman from Pennsylvania State University addressed "The International Student in Your Library: Coping with Cultural and Language Barriers." The topic of Barbara Brock from the University of Toledo was "Library Skills for International Students: From Theory to Practice." The volume concludes with a 1981 review of library orientation and instruction literature by Hannelore B. Rader from the University of Wisconsin-Parkside.

Kline, Eugene A. "A Practice Approach to the Use of Literature Early in a College Career." *Journal of Chemical Information and Computer Sciences* 4 (August 1984): 190-192.

Kline discusses use of chemical literature in freshman- and sophomore-level courses and its relationship to organic chemistry and laboratory work.

Kline, Laura S. and C.M. Rod. "Library Orientation Programs for Foreign Students: A Survey." *RQ* 24 (Winter 1984): 210-213.

The authors summarize a survey of fifty-four U.S. colleges and universities, which have large foreign student population, to obtain information about library orientation programs for foreign students. Fifty-six percent of the libraries in the institutions surveyed offer special library instruction programs for these students. Included are rationale and guidelines for such programs.

Koch, Hans-Albrecht. "Library Research in the Federal Republic of Germany." *Library and Information Science Research* 6 (April/June 1984): 133-153.

Koch summarizes the current state of research in academic librarianship in the Federal Republic of Germany. He includes a section on user research and user education.

Kohl, David. "Large-Scale Bibliographic Instruction: The Illinois Experience." *Research Strategies* 2 (Winter 1984): 4-5.

Kohl summarizes the background for the planning process of a revised bibliographic information program for undergraduates at the University of Illinois-Urbana/Champagne.

Kupersmith, John. "Breaking the Cost Barrier." *Research Strategies* 2 (Spring 1984): 82-84.

Kupersmith provides hints and information on funding sources, design sources, and different versions of signage.

_____. "A Design Model for Instructional

Graphics." *Research Strategies* 2 (Summer 1984): 136-138.

_____. "Don't Do This! Don't Do That!" *Research Strategies* 2 (Fall 1984): 185-187.

The author discusses the use and misuse of signs in libraries.

Lester, Linda L. *Faculty Perceptions of Students' Knowledge and Use of Libraries.* ERIC Reproduction Service, 1984. ED 247 949.

Lester summarizes a survey of faculty at the University of Virginia that assesses their perception of student's knowledge and use of the library. Sixty significant relationships were found and discussed. Improving library skills was among them.

Lolley, John. "University Night Students and the Online Library Catalog." *Research Strategies* 2 (Fall 1984): 172-178.

Lolley summarizes a survey of 133 night students at Central State University in Oklahoma that assesses their attitudes toward use of and success with automated and card catalogs. Preference for the online catalog was indicated.

Love, Barbara. "Coping with Stress: The 14th Annual Workshop on Instruction in Library Use." *College and Research Libraries News* 45 (September 1984): 407-410.

Love summarizes the 14th Annual Workshop on Instruction in Library Use in Canada. The focus was on "Coping with Stress" and presented information on crisis management, stress reduction mechanisms, burnout, and job sharing.

Lubans, John, Jr. "Library Literacy." *RQ* 23 (Spring 1984): 263-265.

Daniel Boyce from the University of South Carolina explores the etymological antecedent of "library orientation."

_____. "Library Literacy." *RQ* 23 (Summer 1984): 389-391.

Lubans discusses a rationale for testing of library skills especially as related to curriculum reform and basic competencies. He reviews briefly the out-of-print, out-of-date Feagley test on library skills. Readers are invited to comment on needs for new tests.

_____. "Library Literacy." *RQ* 24 (Fall 1984): 11-13.

Ilene Nelson discusses effective ways of presenting library use instruction, being a teacher, and communicating with students. She outlines a series workshop to train librarians in "presenting skills."

_____. "Organizational Change: A Public Services Application." *The Reference Librarian* 10 (Spring/Summer 1984): 15-25.

Lubans presents a planning process for user education that includes nine phases within the framework suggested. The article discusses the first three phases: identifying the problem, forming a task force, and finding out.

Lutzker, Marilyn. "Legal Reference Sources and Undergraduate Library Instruction in the Social Sciences." In *Academic Libraries: Myths and Realities*, ed. by S. Dodson and G. Menges, 222-229. Chicago: Association of College and Research Libraries, 1984.

Lutzker advocates the importance of teaching undergraduates the use of legal reference materials to help them with contemporary research topics.

Machalow, Robert. *Computer Based Library Orientation*. ERIC Reproduction Service, 1984. ED 252 239.

The author presents computer-based lessons that teach library skills to students at York College of CUNY. A word processor, disks, and Apple IIe are used.

Malley, Ian. "User Education." In *College Librarianship: The Objectives and the Practice*, by A.R. McElroy, 271-284. London: Library Association Publishing, 1984.

Markiewicz, James and L.G. Stewart. "Quicksearch Computer Searching for Undergraduates at Cornell University." *Journal of Academic Librarianship* 10 (July 1984): 134-136.

The authors describe a program that provides computer-generated bibliographies to undergraduates at Cornell University and teaches them computer literacy.

Martell, Charles R., et al. "A House Divided: Public Services Realities in the 1980's." In *Academic Libraries: Myths and Realities*, ed. by S. Dodson and G. Menges, 85-101. Chicago: Association of College and Research Libraries, 1984.

This section addresses the contemporary scene as related to public services and their fragmentation. The four papers by Gunning, Swanson, Jaynes, and Martell include views on bibliographic instruction.

McArthur, Judy and Pat Kenney. *Researching a Paper in the Library. A Programmed Text Business Version*. ERIC Reproduction Service, 1983. ED 244 643.

This is a programmed text that teaches the methodology of doing business research papers to college upper-classmen. Sample sources and self-tests are included.

In addition, the authors also compiled a programmed text for education, the humanities, and psychology. (ED 244 644, ED 244 645, and ED 244 646.)

McDonald, Susan P. "Writing Program: Administrator's View." *Research Strategies* 2 (Winter 1984): 38-44.

McDonald describes the bibliographic instruction program at the University of Illinois-Urbana as viewed by the faculty member responsible for the freshman writing program.

McInnis, Raymond G. "Mental Maps and Metaphors in Academic Libraries." *The Reference Librarian* 10 (Spring/Summer 1984): 109-120.

The author presents arguments in favor of using geographers' literature on mental maps to provide better understanding of scientific literature's formats, conventions, processes, and formulations. He continues to discuss scientific literature in terms of publications resulting from a systematic collective effort in the production of knowledge.

McQuistion, Virginia F. "The Credit Course: Reaffirmation from Two University Libraries. Measurement: Millikin University." *Research Strategies* 2 (Fall 1984): 166-171.

McQuistion describes a one-credit library skills course required for all freshmen at Millikin University in Illinois. She includes information on pre- and post-tests.

Meisel, Gloria B. and R. Kalick. "Marketing Bibliographic Instruction Through Improved Communication." *Community and Junior College* 2 (Spring 1984): 21-30.

The authors provide various ideas on how librarians can communicate with faculty and other campus groups to build support for user instruction.

Mellon, Constance A. "Process Not Product in Course Integrated Instruction: A Generic Model of Library Research." *College and Research Libraries* 45 (November 1984): 471-478.

Mellon describes the generic model of library research development at the University of Tennessee-Chattanooga Library. It includes pre-library, library awareness, and library competence components; all of these parallel a stage in the writing of the research paper process. Students learn to search, retrieve, evaluate, and summarize materials.

Mosely, Patricia and R. Jackson. "A Console That Loves to Teach Library Basics." *American Libraries* 15 (September 1984): 593.

The authors describe computer controlled video presentations that instruct patrons in library use at Roosevelt University.

Muehlbauer, Bill. "Solving the Riddle of Bibliographic Instruction at the 2-Year College." *Community Junior College Libraries* 3 (Fall 1984): 47-52.

Muehlbauer provides information about a structural bibliographic instruction program without the constraints of credit or noncredit courses at Columbia State Community College in Tennessee.

"Mum's Not the Word." Editorial. *Research Strategies* 2 (Spring 1984): 58-59.

This editorial describes a library instruction conference for academic librarians in Maryland that focused on effective instruction and how to communicate problems and solutions.

Oberman, Cerise. "Patterns for Research." *New Directions for Teaching and Learning* 18 (June 1984): 35-43.

Oberman describes the teaching of search strategy as a basic part of library instruction.

O'Hara, Molly. "Bibliographic Instruction for Foreign Students." In *Academic Libraries: Myths and Realities*, ed. by S. Dodson and G. Menges, 230-233. Chicago: Association of College and Research Libraries, 1984.

O'Hara discusses approaches which teach foreign students in U.S. academic institutions, library use skills based on bibliographic instruction materials already developed and using information from English as a foreign language literature.

Olson, Linda A. "Reference Service Evaluation in Medium-Sized Academic Libraries: A Model." *Journal of Academic Libraries* 9 (January 1984): 322-329.

Olson discusses instruction in library use as one of four reference services.

Ormondroyd, Joan L. "Bibliographic Instruction in an Undergraduate Library." *Catholic Library World* 55 (April 1984): 395-398.

The author describes the nine-year-old library instruction program in the undergraduate library at Cornell University that features course-related and course-integrated instruction for 3,000 students each year.

Pastine, Maureen. "Library Instruction and Reference Service: Administration of a Bibliographic Instruction Program in the Academic Library." *The Reference Librarian* 10 (Spring/Summer 1984): 181-189.

Pastine focuses on the advantages and disadvantages of centralizing the administration of a bibliographic instruction program in the reference department. She provides various alternatives and lists guidelines for successful bibliographic instruction programs.

Pausch, Lois M. and C.B. Perka. "Reference/Technical Services Cooperation in Library Instruction." *The Reference Librarian* 10 (Spring/Summer 1984): 101-107.

Peele, David. "Librarians as Teachers: Some Reality, Mostly Myth." *Journal of Academic Librarianship* 10 (November 1984): 267-271.

Peele discusses the relationship between reference work and teaching. He examines the concept of considering technical services librarians as teachers and finds fault with that. Peele concludes that teachers are an originating force while academic librarians are primarily a responding force.

Peroni, Patricia A. "A Book Review Assignment to Introduce Freshmen to the College Library." *Exercise Exchange* 30 (Fall 1984): 26-28.

Peroni describes the library component of a summer program for new minority freshmen. The library component is built around book reviews.

Phillips, Linda L. "More Information: Bibliographic Instruction Resources." *New Directions for Teaching and Learning* 18 (June 1984): 85-94.

The author provides a guide to the bibliographic instruction literature combining specific sources with information on subject access, personal contacts, and current awareness.

Pickert, Sarah M. and A.B. Chwalek. "Integrating Bibliographic Research Skills into a Graduate Program in Education." *Catholic Library World* 55 (April 1984): 392-394.

The authors describe a bibliographic instruction program involving graduate education research courses at Catholic University of America.

Plum, Stephen H. "Library Use and the Development of Critical Thought." *New Directions for Teaching and Learning* 18 (June 1984): 63-78.

Plum views library instruction as a discipline and shows how it can teach the independent inquirer to develop patterns of critical thought.

Rader, Hannelore B. "Bibliographic Instruction Programs in Academic Libraries." *New Directions for Teaching and Learning* 18 (June 1984): 63-78.

Rader describes eleven successful library instruction programs in academic libraries in the United States. She gives criteria for their successfulness.

_____. "Teaching Library: Myth or Reality." In *Academic Libraries: Myths and Realities*, ed. by S. Dodson and G. Menges, 234-237. Chicago: Association of College and Research Libraries, 1984.

Rader defines and discusses the concept of a teaching library. She provides a case study of such a library, the University of Wisconsin-Parkside, from the director's point-of-view. She points out how advances in technology can enhance this role model.

Rader, Hannelore B. and D.L. Horne. "Preparing Students for Academic Library Use." *Wisconsin Ideas in Media* 6 (September 1984): 6-8, 30.

The authors discuss the "Discovering Research" program at the Library/Learning Center of the University of Wisconsin-Parkside, which aims to prepare area high school students for library research projects in an academic setting.

Ramey, Mary Ann and A. Spanjer. "Video-Taping Bibliographic Instruction: A Confrontation with Self." *Research Strategies* 2 (Spring 1984): 71-75.

The authors promote video-taping for improvement of teaching techniques and practice for instruction libraries. Such taping will analyze problems, change behavior, create confidence, and assure immediate feedback. They also describe a program of freshman English library seminars at Georgia State University.

Ravilious, C.P. "Microcomputers for User Education." *INFUSE* 8 (October 1984): 8-11.

Ravilious describes user education experiments using microcomputers at the University of Sussex in Great Britain. Such attempts included online information retrieval training, orientation-type information, subject guides, and bulletin board information.

Ready, Sandra K. and L.E. Saltzman. "Collaboration on Integrated Library Instruction: A Reaction." *Research Strategies* 2 (Spring 1984): 76-81.

The authors describe a cooperative program between a librarian and a sociologist at Mankato State University, which integrates bibliographic instruction into a course entitled "Careers in Criminal Justice." Continuous evaluation and revision are a necessity to assure a successful experience.

Ready, Sandra K. "Putting the Online Catalog in Its Place." *Research Strategies* 2 (Summer 1984): 119-127.

Reeder, David. "User Education: Historical Devel-

opment and Current Practice." *Australian College Libraries* 2 (February 1984): 3-12.

Reeder describes user education growth in academic libraries in the United States, United Kingdom, Australia, and the University of New South Wales. He discusses user education in terms of the overall education of students and the necessary commitment of teaching faculty.

Reichel, Mary. "Bibliographic Education and Reference Desk Service--A Continuum." *The Reference Librarian* 10 (Spring/Summer 1984): 191-198.

Reichel discusses the interaction of four reference areas (bibliographic instruction, reference desk service, online searching, and interlibrary loan) to provide the user with the best service.

Reid, Bruce J. "Aston Intro-Active: A Library Game for New Undergraduates." *Research Strategies* 2 (Summer 1984): 108-118.

Richardson, Larry L. "Teaching Basic Library Skills: Past Tense, Future Perfect." *Reference Services Review* 12 (Spring 1984): 67-76.

Richardson discusses the importance of continuing the teaching of basic library skills to students and promotes a new approach to this teaching in the form of comprehensive self-instruction. He provides various examples of this approach.

Ridgeway, Trish. *Library Orientation Methods, Mental Maps, and Public Services Planning.* ERIC Reproduction Service, 1984. ED 247 942.

Ridgeway summarizes a study to compare two methods of freshman library orientation, a self-guided cassette walking tour, and a slide-tape program. Results indicate that the walking tour was more effective.

Rippey, Donald T. and C. Truett. "The Developmental Student and the Community College Library." *Community College Review* 11 (Winter 1983-84): 41-47.

The authors lament the fact that library instruction proponents have tended to ignore the needs of educationally disadvantaged students in community colleges.

Rosenberg, Jane A. "New Ways to Find Books: Searching, Locating, and Information Delivery." *The History Teacher* 17 (May 1984): 387-390.

Rosenberg considers the effect of technological change, such as online searching, online catalogs, and electronic publishing, on library users and use instruction.

Rosselet, Start. "Course Instructor's View." *Research Strategies* 2 (Winter 1984): 33-37.

Rosselet presents an English instructor's point-of-view of bibliographic instruction experiences at the University of Illinois-Urbana.

Rudnik, Sister M.C. "Bibliographic Instruction: Make It More Than Bibliographic First Aid." *Catholic Library World* 55 (April 1984): 388-391.

The author advocates better understanding of users' needs on the part of librarians in order to provide the best services including bibliographic instruction. She provides various marketing techniques.

Simon, Rose A. "The Faculty/Librarian Partnership." *New Directions for Teaching and Learning* 18 (June 1984): 55-61.

Simon discusses methods to promote and improve library instruction programs through effective faculty/librarian cooperation.

Skolnik, Herman. "Relevancy of Chemical Literature in the Educational Process." *Journal of Chemical Information and Computer Services* 24 (May 1984): 95-97.

Skolnik discusses the need for a basic course in chemical literature with special emphasis on aspects of literature in inorganic, organic, and physical chemistry.

Smalley, Topsy N. *Bibliographic Instruction for Undergraduates: An Example of a One-Unit Required Library Research Skills Course.* ERIC Reproduction Service, 1983. ED 232 656.

Smalley describes the required bibliographic instruction course at SUNY-Plattsburgh and its emphasis on learning experiences within the context of a conceptual framework.

Smith, Rita H. and L.L. Phillips. "Search Helper: An Online Service for Undergraduates." *Reference Services Review* 12 (Fall 1984): 31-34.

The authors describe how Search Helper and In-Search are used at the University of Tennessee-Knoxville. The services help teach undergraduates online database searching.

Soskin, Mark D. and N. Eldbolm. *Integrating the Term Paper into Economics Courses at Liberal Arts Colleges: Industry Case Studies Papers at SUNY-Potsdam.* A Preliminary Study.

The authors explore problems and benefits of a term paper for upper-level economics courses in a three-year study. They promote a closer relationship between faculty and librarians and discuss evaluating bibliographic instruction in this area.

Stamps, Dorothy C. "Out of the Woodwork: Orienting the 'Invisible' Faculty." *Georgia Librarian* 21 (November 1984): 90-92.

Stamps describes a faculty library orientation program at Southern Technical Institute in Georgia and provides some innovative tips for such an endeavor.

Stark, Marcella. "Using the Online Catalog Effectively." *College and Research Libraries News* 45 (June 1984): 301-305.

Stark describes a seminar for faculty that uses the online catalog at Syracuse University. She focuses on search techniques to the online catalog.

Stoan, Stephen K. "Research and Library Skills: An Analysis and Interpretation." *College and Research Libraries* 45 (March 1984): 99-109.

This study examines relationships between teaching faculty and librarians regarding library use and research and the different skills involved. It points out that library and research skills are often learned in isolation from one another. Implications of this finding are discussed both for bibliographic instruction and library policies.

Stoffle, Carla J., et al. "Teaching Research and Service: The Academic Library Role." *New Directions for Teaching and Learning* 18 (June 1984): 3-14.

The authors explore the virtue of a teaching library in terms of the value of bibliographic instruction.

Stringer, Roger. "Integrating Library User Education with Teaching English as a Second Language: An Experiment at Gweru Teacher's College, Zimbabwe." *INFUSE* 8 (October 1984): 5-8.

Stringer describes a special user instruction program at Gweru Teacher's College in Zimbabwe where language skills were integrated with traditional library user education since most library materials are not in the students' native language.

Swierenga, Robert P. "Bibliographic Instruction in Historical Methods Courses Kent State University." *The History Teacher* 17 (May 1984): 391-396.

Swierenga discusses the bibliographic instruction component of a historical methodology course at Kent State University. The professor's point-of-view is given.

Thomas, Joy and P. Ensor. "The University Faculty and Library Instruction." *RQ* 23 (Summer 1984): 431-437.

The authors describe a survey of teaching faculty at the California State University, Long Beach, that measures the attitude toward bibliographic instruction. Course-related instruction provided high satisfaction with library services and instruction to those faculty members using it. Twenty-nine percent of faculty did not request library instruction. Librarians need to promote instruction in library use and try to place it directly into the curriculum.

Thompson, Glenn J. "Computer Use in LMED100, How to Use the Library." *College and Research Libraries News* 45 (February 1984): 83.

Thompson describes an undergraduate credit course for library orientation, which utilizes computer-assisted instruction using BASIC programs on a microcomputer.

Tiefel, Virginia. "Creating a Comprehensive Library User Education Plan." In *Academic Libraries: Myths and Realities*, ed. by S. Dodson and G. Menges, 238-242. Chicago: Association of College and Research Libraries, 1984.

Tiefel describes the Ohio State University Library's program planning for user education. The plan is comprised of eight stages and incorporates an online catalog and various libraries.

Tierney, Judith. *Basic Library Skills: A Self-Paced Workbook.* ERIC Reproduction Service, 1984. ED 247 941.

This workbook is designed to introduce college students to library resources and basic library research.

Tobin, Carol, et al. "The Computer and Library Instruction." *Reference Services Review* 12 (Winter 1984): 71-78.

This article presents three different perspectives on how the computer relates to library instruction. Carol Tobin from Princeton University discusses the impact of access to online databases on a library instruction program. Harriet Tippet from Lawrence University talks about the use of word processing for producing instructional materials and the use of the computer to manage library instruction data. Patricia Culkin and Elizabeth Walker address computer-assisted instruction in user education.

Trzebiatowski, Elaine. "End User Study on BRS/After Dark." *RQ* 23 (Summer 1984): 446-450.

The author summarizes a study at the University of Wisconsin-Stout of twenty, first time end-users.

Tucker, John M. "Emerson's Library Legacy: Concepts of Bibliographic Instruction." *New Directions for Teaching and Learning* 18 (June 1984): 15-24.

Tucker discusses bibliographic instruction in terms of liberal education.

Tucker, Melvin J. "Comments on Cooperative Instruction: The SUNY at Buffalo Experience." *The History Teacher* 17 (May 1984): 404-408.

The author discusses, from the professor's point-of-view, a required history course on bibliography/methodology at SUNY-Buffalo taught by the history professor and a librarian.

_____. "Historians and Using Tomorrow's Research Library: Research Teaching and Training." *The History Teacher* 17 (May 1984): 385-387.

Tucker discusses the need for library instruction for graduate students in history and outlines various approaches to doing that.

Tuckett, Harold W. and C.J. Stoffle. "Learning Theory and the Self-Reliant Library User." *RQ* 24 (Fall 1984): 56-88.

The article reviews the pedagogical model used by librarians to instruct users. The authors describe a new, emerging model that incorporates cognitive learning theory into teaching methodology and course content while teaching students problem-solving skills.

Vincent, C. Paul. "Bibliographic Instruction in the Humanities: The Need to Stress Imagination." *Research Strategies* 2 (Fall 1984): 179-184.

Vincent discusses the importance of imagination as an attribute of a good reference librarian. This quality is even more important when dealing with bibliographic instruction in the humanities in order to inspire and guide students.

Volker, Joyce. "Practice Makes Perfect--I Hope. Library Skills Tutorials at the ANL Library." *Australian Academic and Research Libraries* 15 (March 1984): 16-22.

Volker describes the formal reader education program for undergraduates developed at the Australian National University. Specific information is given for the library skills tutorial, exercises, learning objectives, and evaluations.

Ward, James E. "Trends in the Growth of Bibliographic Instruction in 20th Century American Academic Libraries." In *Reference Services and Library Education: Essays in Honor of Frances Neel Chaney*, 79-94. Lexington Books, 1983.

Watson, Melissa R. "No Royal Road." *The Reference Librarian* 10 (Spring/Summer 1984): 227-232.

Watson describes a freshman English composition library instruction program at Northeastern Oklahoma A & M College.

Webster, Duane, et al. "Public Services in Research Libraries: Today's Realities." In *Academic Libraries:*

Myths and Realities, ed. by S. Dodson and G. Menges, 102-123. Chicago: Association of College and Research Libraries, 1984.

The authors summarize several ARL self-studies of public services under the auspices of the Office of Management Studies. Haka, Kaufman, Huling, Seibert, and Swanson each contribute a paper on various aspects of public services. All papers include information on bibliographic instruction.

Wilen, Samuel H. "Unresolved Problems and Opportunities in Chemical Literature Teaching." *Journal of Chemical Information and Computer Sciences* 24 (May 1984): 112-115.

Wilen discusses problems with teaching formal chemical literature courses. Included in these problems are a lack of appropriate exercises, time limits, unavailable key search tools in libraries, and professor/librarian interaction.

Williams, Ester. "Introduction to Science Literature: A Library Assignment for General Biology Students." *Research Strategies* 2 (Spring 1984): 65-70.

Williams discusses an assignment at the State University of New York-Purchase that teaches biology students library use through exposure to biological literatures, periodicals, research papers, and popular science literature.

Wilson, Lizabeth A. and L.L. Arp. "An Overview of the Undergraduate Library Instruction Program." *Research Strategies* 2 (Winter 1984): 12-15.

Wilson describes the various courses served by the library instruction program at the University of Illinois-Urbana.

_____. "Library Instructor's View--Practical." *Research Strategies* 2 (Winter 1984): 23-32.

This paper discusses the practical implications of implementing a library instruction program based on student need, the heterogeneousness of the student body, and hierarchically structured information at the University of Illinois-Urbana. The authors describe how very few librarians can provide quality, individualized, and responsive instruction to 6,000 students.

Wolman, Y. "Incorporating Chemical Literature and Information Retrieval into the Chemistry Curriculum at the Hebrew University." *Journal of Chemical Information and Computer Sciences* 24 (August 1984): 135-139.

Wolman describes a chemical literature and information retrieval program at Hebrew University in Jerusalem. The program is part of the undergraduate chemistry curriculum and emphasizes end-users.

Wood, Fiona. *Evaluation of a University Library's Catalogue. Patron Usage, Problems and Policy Direction. ANU Library Occasional Paper no. 4.* ERIC Reproduction Service, 1984. ED 247 947.

Wood summarizes a study at the Australian National University to determine any problems of users with the library's catalogs. Various problems were documented.

Wood, Richard J. "The Impact of a Library Research Course on Students at Slippery Rock University." *Journal of Academic Librarianship* 10 (November 1984): 278-284.

The author summarizes a study at Slippery Rock University of a one-credit library research course using a workbook and exercises to teach students bibliographic skills. It was found that students learned the skills and improved their attitude toward the library.

"Working with Associations: A Tip Sheet." *College and Research Libraries News* 45 (May 1984): 240-241.

This article provides guidelines developed by the ACRL Bibliographic Instruction Section Cooperation Committee on library promotion through subject disciplines.

PUBLIC LIBRARIES

Beilke, Patricia F. "Library Instruction in Public Libraries. A Dream Deferred, a Goal to Actualize." *The Reference Librarian* 10 (Spring/Summer 1984): 123-133.

Beilke relates library instruction in public libraries to adult education theories and programs.

Bortner, Ada. "Orientation for Children at the Public Library." *New Jersey Libraries* 17 (Fall 1984): 21-23.

Carbone, Jerry. "Library Use Instruction in the Small and Medium Public Library: A Review of the Literature." *The Reference Librarian* 10 (Spring/Summer 1984): 149-157.

Carbone identifies problems affecting library instruction in the small public library and provides relevant summaries of some writings.

Dietrich, J.M. "Library Use Instruction for Older Adults." *Canadian Library Journal* 41 (August 1984): 203-208.

Dietrich describes a model for instructing and assisting older adults in their use of libraries.

Hendley, Margaret. "User Education: The Adult

Patron in the Public Library." *RQ* 24 (Winter 1984): 191-194.

The author discusses guidelines for public libraries that want to initiate library use instruction for adult patrons. Ten questions are posed and answered to help public librarians plan a good program.

Reilley, Jane A. "Library Instruction Through the Reference Query." *The Reference Librarian* 10 (Spring/Summer 1984): 135-148.

Reilley stresses the helping relationship of a trained professional reference librarian to the library user. She provides several hints and guidelines. A brief annotated bibliography is included.

SCHOOL LIBRARIES

Atwater, Deborah F. *The 4-H Debate Project: Getting Adults and Children Involved in Communication* .ERIC Reproduction Service, 1984. ED 248 562.

Atwater includes a module on increasing 4-H members' knowledge of library skills through research among various other communication skills.

Avann, Patt. "Information Skills in Primary Schools." *Education Libraries Bulletin* 27 (1984): 1-14.

A task force in Coventry, England, composed of teachers and a librarian, suggests that information skills should be taught from infant level through primary grades with a sense of purpose.

Beck, Jean C. "Information Technology for School Children." *IFLA Journal* 10 (1984): 145-150.

Beswick, Norman W. "The School Library. What Should We Tell the Teachers?" *School Librarian* 32 (1984): 13-18.

Beswick discusses methodology for informing teachers about the importance of information skills for students to obtain their support.

Buckingham, Betty Jo. *Library Media Skills Sampler. Volume I: A Sharing of Ideas from Practicing School Library Media Specialists in Iowa.* ERIC Reproduction Service, 1984. ED 247 927.

Burdenuk, Gene. "Measuring Student Information Use." *Emergency Librarian* 11 (November/December 1983): 39-40.

The author discusses the work called "Measuring Student Information Use" and its importance in overcoming several problems with research in school librarianship.

Craver, Kathleen W. and L.H. Quanian. "The Introduction to Online Bibliographic Searching for High School Students." *Educational Technology* 24 (June 1984): 39-41.

The authors provide information on a one-semester course for high school seniors to teach them search strategy and online searching for research projects.

_____. *Teaching Online Bibliographic Searching to High School Students.* ERIC Reproduction Service, 1984. ED 244 633.

Craver and Quanian describe a project to introduce high school students to the concepts, terminology, and search strategy of online database searching.

Gibbs, Sally. "Computer in the Library as Indispensable Hub of the School." *Library Association Record* 86 (February 1984): 71-72.

Gibbs discusses, from the British point-of-view, the role of the school library in the age of information explosion. She proposes elimination of boundaries between teachers and librarians similar to the library college movement.

Heather, Pauline. "Research on Information Skills in Primary Schools." *The School Librarian* 32 (September 1984): 214-220.

Heather describes research on information skills for primary grade pupils in Great Britain. Use of the school library and its significance to the curriculum is related to the teaching methods in the school. Several recommendations are provided.

Hendley, Gaby G. *Using the Microcomputer to Generate Materials for Bibliographic Instruction.* ERIC Reproduction Service, 1984. ED 252 190.

Hendley describes a high school setting where guide/worksheets are developed by a word processor for library skills instruction in English and social studies.

Hopkins, David and J. Rudduck. "Academic Sixth-Form Courses, the Library and Prospectives on Independent Study: A Report on a Project." *Educational Research* 26 (June 1984): 137-141.

Howlett, Barbara. "Communication Skills and Strategies for Teacher-Librarian." *Emergency Librarian* 11 (November/December 1983): 14-19.

Howlett discusses how the teacher-librarian relationship can be improved through communication. Various strategies are provided to school librarians to obtain a more positive image.

Library Skills Curriculum Activities/Objectives, K-12. ERIC Reproduction Service, 1984. ED 252

222.

This work contains a list of general skills for a school library media curriculum by grade levels. Sample teaching units and a bibliography are included.

Mancall, Jacqueline. "Training Students to Search Online: Rationale, Process, and Implications." *Drexel Library Quarterly* 20 (Winter 1984): 64-84.

Mancall provides rationale and methodology for librarians to teach online searching to students in school media center settings.

Marshak, David. "Study Skills: Their Values and Why They Should Be Taught." *NASSP Bulletin* 68 (January 1984): 103-107.

Marshak describes a study skills program for secondary school students and its importance as related to teaching and learning basic skills.

Micetich, Barbara J. "Librarian, Do I Ever Need Your Help!" *Catholic Library World* 56 (November 1984): 187-190.

The author discusses the need for study and reference skills for junior high and high school students and how librarians could be part of the instructional team to design appropriate learning activities. Comments by other librarians supplement this opinion.

Morante, Rosemary, et al. *Instruction in Library Media Skills. Supplement to a Guide to School Library Media Programs.* ERIC Reproduction Service, 1984. ED 252 210.

This guide is for library media specialists and teachers to improve the teaching of library skills. It addresses curriculum development, sample lessons and units, goals, and specific skills for grades K through 12.

Moss, Dee. "Meow...a Whatalogue?" *Library Association Record* 86 (February 1984): 73.

A British school librarian describes a novel method of teaching pupils the use of the library through a specially produced videotape.

Perry, Penelope. "A Training Scheme for Pupil Librarians." *School Librarian* 31 (December 1983): 332-335.

Perry discusses library training for teenagers in a British school to serve as pupil librarians. Approximately 96 students are thus trained to serve a school with 1,000 enrollees.

Robbins, Wendy H. "Library Instruction: A Partnership between Teacher and Librarian." *Catholic Library World* 55 (April 1984): 384-387.

Robbins highlights the importance of user

instruction in secondary schools and offers various suggestions for the creation of a viable and effective program.

Rogers, Douglas B. "Assessing Study Skills." *Journal of Reading* 27 (January 1984): 346-354.

Rogers discusses reference and study skills as part of study skills education.

Ross, J.E. "Microsoftware for Library Skills Instruction." *School Library Journal* 31 (November 1984): 68-73.

Schon, Isabel, et al. "Effects of a Special School Library Program on Elementary Students' Library Use and Attitudes." *School Library Media Quarterly* 12 (Spring 1984): 277-231.

The authors describe a special program on library use, library attitudes, and reading attitudes among elementary school students in Phoenix.

Schon, Isabel and K.D. Hopkins. *Students' Attitudes and Use of the School Library (Eighth Grade) Procedures.* ERIC Reproduction Service, 1984. ED 247 956.

This is a packet of materials for school librarians to teach library skills to eighth graders. It features a six-week module with varied activities.

Seaver, A.R. *Library Media Skills; Strategies for Instructing Primary Students.* Littleton, CO: Libraries Unlimited, 1984.

Smith, Lotsee and K. Swisser. "Microcomputers in School Library Media Centers." *Drexel Library Quarterly* 20 (Winter 1984): 7-15.

In addition to various other uses, microcomputers can also enhance library skills instruction provided by school media centers.

Sorenson, R.J. "School Library Media Programs and Basic Skills." *Indiana Media Journal* 6 (Spring 1984): 3-5.

Stripling, Barbara. "What Price ID? A Practical Approach to a Personal Dilemma." *School Library Media Quarterly* 12 (Summer 1984): 290-296.

Stripling discusses instructional development as related to the library media center in high schools. She provides positive and negative aspects of instructional development and implications for the media specialist. Some cost reduction solutions are also given.

Tabberer, Ralph. "Introducing Study Skills at 16-19." *Educational Research* 26 (February 1984): 1-6.

Tabberer summarizes the report of the "Teaching

Study Skills Project" for students ages 16 to 19 in both schools and colleges in Great Britain.

Telford, Doris. "Evaluation of a Tape-Slide Presentation: An Introduction to Study Skills." *Education Library Bulletin* 27 (1984): 22-37.

Trask, Margaret, et al. *South Pacific Region Pilot Project on School Library Development: Training Programmes for Teachers.* ERIC Reproduction Service, 1984. ED 247 938.

The authors summarize two courses to train primary and secondary teachers and librarians. They seek to stimulate teachers to encourage students to use library resources. The work also trains student teachers in a similar manner.

Van Vliet, Lucille W. *Media Skills for Middle Schools.* Littleton, CO: Libraries Unlimited, Inc., 1984.

This work provides strategies for media specialists and teachers to help them teach library media skills as an integral part of the curriculum. It includes seventy sample lessons as well as philosophy and goals, characteristics of middle school students, and their needs.

Wehmeyer, L.B. *The School Librarian as Educator.* 2d ed. Littleton, CO: Libraries Unlimited, 1984.

This is a revised and updated edition of the 1976 publication.

Zlotnick, Barbara B. *Ready for Reference. Media Skills for Intermediate Students.* Littleton, CO: Libraries Unlimited, Inc., 1984.

This work suggests practical strategies and activities for establishing an information skills program within the curriculum. It includes a discussion of essential skills needed, presents an integrated instructional model, various activities, and worksheets.

SPECIAL LIBRARIES

Allegri, Francesca. "On the Other Side of the Reference Desk: The Patron with a Physical Disability." *Medical Reference Services Quarterly* 3 (Fall 1984): 65-76.

Bader, S.G. "A Library Skills Workshop: One Library's Experience." *Medical Reference Service Quarterly* 3 (Winter 1984): 67-70.

Ben-Shir, R. "Library Instruction Integrated with Patient Management." *Bulletin of the Medical Library Association* 72 (July 1984): 310-311.

This paper discusses an individualized library instruction program for residents in training at MacNeal Memorial Hospital associated with the University of Illinois. Library information is part of the patient management conference program.

Gray, Rosemary. "Legal Research Education in an Online Age." *INFUSE* 8 (August 1984): 6-11.

Gray summarizes a research study comprised of a detailed comparison of four major commercial legal research systems available in the United Kingdom; a two-year survey of the growth in legal research systems in British law schools and the provision of instruction in legal research skills; and the evaluation of an experimental Legal Research Methods course at North East London Polytechnic.

Jonas, E.S. "Preparation of a Slide-Tape Program for Biological Abstracts: Harvard University." *Science and Technology Libraries* 5 (Fall 1984): 63-67.

King, D.N. "Beyond Bibliographic Instruction." *Medical Reference Service Quarterly* 3 (Summer 1984): 75-80.

Schwartz, D.G. "Bibliographic Instruction: A Public Relations Perspective." *Medical Reference Service Quarterly* 3 (Summer 1984): 43-49.

Ward, S.N. and L.M. Osegueda. "Teaching University Student End-Users about Online Searching." *Science and Technology Libraries* 5 (Fall 1984): 17-31.

ALL LEVELS

ALA. LIRT. Continuing Education Committee. "Continuing Education for Bibliographic Instruction Librarians." *LIRT News* 6 (June 1984): 1-20.

This article lists an annotated bibliography of selected items to help librarians stay informed about bibliographic instruction.

Agrawal, S.P., et al. "User Education for Information Seeking: Eureka versus Despair." *Library Herald* 22 (January 1984): 176-182.

The authors discuss user education in terms of its value, methodology, and assessment. They describe user education in India and internationally. The formation of a national policy on user education and an agency to administer appropriate programs are proposed.

Dalrymple, Prudence W. "Closing the Gap: The Role of the Librarian in Online Searching." *RQ* 24 (Winter 1984): 177-185.

Using a review of the literature, the author discusses key aspects of the changing role of librarians related to online searching and instructing users in this process.

David, Agnes. "A Bibliography. User Education for the Online Catalog." *LIFLine News* 26 (September 1984): 5-8.

Davidson, Nancy M. "Bibliographic Instruction Roundup." *South Carolina Librarian* 28 (Fall 1984): 18-19.

Jan Presseau describes a workshop called "Perspectives on Bibliographic Instruction" held in Columbia, South Carolina. Descriptions of the instruction program at Presbyterian College, at Brookland-Cayce High School and at Spartanburg County Public Library are included.

Dlin, E. Deborah. "Teaching a Library Skill to Severely Retarded Students at Northwest Louisiana State School." *LLA Bulletin* 47 (Summer 1984): 11-14.

Dlin describes special problems evident in teaching library skills to the profoundly retarded (IQ of 39 or below). The skill, which was taught in this case study, was "to retrieve a book from the shelf." A detailed description is provided for the lesson including evaluation.

Ellsbury, Susan H. and R. Rafferty. *Reach Out and Teach. Library Instruction in Mississippi Libraries. Script for Slide-Tape Presentation.* ERIC Reproduction Service, 1984. ED 245 699.

The LIRT prepared a library instruction program for school, public, and academic libraries using slides, a script, and a follow-up discussion for a 1984 regional meeting sponsored by the Mississippi Library Association.

Eng, Sidney. "CAI and the Future of Bibliographic Instruction." *Catholic Library World* 55 (May 1984): 441-444.

Eng discusses the capabilities of the computer as an instructional tool in user education as well as the effect microcomputers will have on instruction librarians.

Figueiredo, Nice. *User Education and Marketing of Information Services in Brazil.* ERIC Reproduction Service, 1984. ED 253 253.

The author advocates the importance of marketing to create users' needs for information and to attract users to library. The current status of library education in Brazil is discussed and information on the state of user education in Brazil is included. The author gives a description of the education program at the Central Library of the University of Rio Grande do Sul, which is preparing instruction librarians.

Harris, Robert. "The Compleat Library Patron." *Reference Librarian* 10 (Spring/Summer 1984): 51-54.

Harris discusses how patron self-reliance and universality of the need of library skills as a result of bibliographic instruction cannot be supported.

Heck, Thomas F. "Flow Charts as a Tool in Bibliographic Instruction." *Comments On Library User Education* 11 (September 1984): 1-4.

Laburn, C. "User Guidance and Training." *South African Journal of Library and Information Science* 52 (August 1984): 93-98.

Lester, Ray. "Clues or Answers? Which Response to Library Users' Questions?" *The Reference Librarian* 10 (Spring/Summer 1984): 85-92.

The author discusses reference situations which require the reference librarian to give an answer to the user and others that require a "clue," such as a guide to the user to solve the problem him or herself.

_____. "User Education in the Online Age." *Aslib Proceedings* 36 (February 1984): 96-112.

Lester discusses the need for and complexities of successful user instruction. He describes the needs of different types of users as defined in "Discussion Paper on User Education" by the British LISC group.

Lubans, John, Jr. "Library Literacy." *RQ* 24 (Winter 1984): 135-137.

Lubans discusses the impact of computers on user instruction. He describes some of the problems computers will cause. It will be up to librarians to teach library users to use computers in information searches.

Lyon, Sally. "End-User Searching of Online Databases: A Selective Annotated Bibliography." *Library Hi Tech* 2 (July 1984): 47-50.

Lyon reports on literature related to end-user online searching. She discusses the librarians's role, cost-effectiveness, and training methods.

Malley, Ian. *Basis of Information Skills Teaching.* London: Bingley, 1984.

Markey, Karen. "Offline and Online User Assistance for Online Catalog Searches." *ONLINE* 8 (May 1984): 54-66.

Markey reports on an OCLC study of six libraries using online catalogs and how they train users.

M'Queen, I. "AVSCOT Viewing Session, Glasgow, Wednesday, 29 February, 1984." *AV Librarian* 10 (Summer 1984): 151-152.

User education programs from around the United Kingdom are summarized.

Pearce, R. "Functions of Visuals in Tape-Slide Instructional Programmes." *AV Librarian* 10 (Winter 1984): 18-23.

Rader, Hannelore B. "Librarian Orientation and Instruction--1983." *Reference Services Review* 12 (Summer 1984): 59-71.

The annual review of the library instruction literature in English provides short annotations for articles and books published in 1983.

Rice, James. "Library-Use-Instruction with Individual Users: Should Instruction Be Included in the Reference Interview?" *The Reference Librarian* 10 (Spring/Summer 1984): 75-84.

Rice reviews the literature on the benefits of library instruction in reference service to users. He discusses how instruction fits into the reference interview, whether or not it infringes upon the rights of the user, or detracts from the effectiveness in satisfying the user's needs.

Robert, Anne F. "Training Reference Librarians Using Library Instruction Methods." *Reference Librarian* 10 (Spring/Summer 1984): 67-74.

Robert advocates the use of library instruction methodology and objectives for reference librarians' staff training programs.

Swan, John C. "The Reference Librarian Who Teaches: The Confessions of a Mother Hen." *The Reference Librarian* 10 (Spring/Summer 1984): 55-66.

Swan discusses the role of the reference librarian in library instruction based on various bibliographic instruction and teaching/learning theories.

"User Education." *Texas Library Journal* 60 (Summer 1984): 58-60.

This article is a discussion of library guides, how to organize and write them for the best effect on users.

"User Education." *Texas Library Journal* 60 (Spring 1984): 22-23.

This article provides a discussion of bibliographic instruction in the information age and some of the implications for the future.

Vincent, A. Paul. "Bibliographic Instruction and the Reference Desk: A Symbiotic Relationship." *The Reference Librarian* 10 (Spring/Summer 1984): 39-47.

Vincent lobbies for the confirmation and strengthening of sophisticated reference desk service with or without strong library instruction programs.

Instructing the Online Catalog User:

A LOEX Bibliography

Arends, Mark W. "Designing Effective Instruction Brochures for Online Catalogs." *Library Hi Tech News* 21 (November 1985): 17.

Baker, Betsy. "A Conceptual Framework for Teaching Online Catalog Instruction." *The Journal of Academic Librarianship* 12 (May 1986): 90-96.

_____. "A New Direction for Online Catalog Instruction." *Information Technology and Libraries* 5 (March 1986): 35-41.

Baker, Betsy and Brian Nielsen. "Educating the Online Catalog User: Experiences and Plans at Northwestern University Library." *Research Strategies* 1 (Fall 1983): 155-166.

Bhullar, Pushpajit. "LUMIN User Education." *Show-Me-Libraries* 36 (August 1985): 13-18.

Coppola, Elaine. "Who Trains the Trainer? Library Staff Are OPAC Users, Too." *Library Hi Tech* 1 (Winter 1983): 36-38.

Council on Library Resources. *Training Users of Online Public Access Catalogs.* Report of a conference sponsored by Trinity University and CLR, 12-14 January 1982. ERIC Document ED 235 832.

Diskin, Gregory M. and Thomas J. Michalak. "Beyond the Online Catalog: Utilizing the OPAC for Library Information." *Library Hi Tech* 3 (1985): 7-14.

Farber, Evan. "Catalog Dependency." *Library Journal* 109 (15 February 1984): 325-328.

Ferguson, Douglas. "Online Catalogs at the Reference Desk and Beyond." *RQ* 20 (Fall 1980): 7-9.

Heinzkill, Richard. "Instructing Students in the Use of a Public OCLC Terminal." *PNLA Quarterly* 49 (Summer 1985): 14-16.

Herndon, Gail A. and Noelle Van Pulis. "Online Library: Problems and Prospects for User Education." In *New Horizons for Academic Libraries*, 539-544. New York: Saur, 1979.

Hildreth, Charles R. *Online Public Access Catalogs: The User Interface.* Dublin, OH: OCLC, 1982.

See Chapter 10.

Jarvis, William E. "Integrating Subject Pathfinders into Online Catalogs." *Database* (February 1985): 65-67.

Kenney, Donald and Linda Wilson. "Education for the Online Access Catalog: A Model." *Research Strategies* 3 (Fall 1985): 13-18.

Larson, Mary E. and Dace Freivalds. *Penn State University Libraries: A Final Report from the Public Services Research Project: The Effects of an Instruction Program on Online Catalog Users.* 1985. ED 255 223.

McDonald, David R. and Susan Searing. "Bibliographic Instruction and the Development of Online Catalogs." *College & Research Libraries* 44 (January 1983): 5-11.

Masters, Deborah. "Library Users and the Online Catalog: Suggested Objectives for Library Instruction." Presented at the ACRL New England Chapter Spring Conference, 19 March 1982; Wellesley, MA.

Nielsen, Brian, et al. *Educating the Online Catalog User: A Model for Instructional Development and Education, Final Report, Revised.* 1985. ED 261 679.

Nielsen, Brian. "What They Say They Do and What They Do: Assessing Online Catalog Use Instruction through Transaction Monitoring." *Information Technology and Libraries* 5 (March 1986): 28-34.

Ready, Sandra. "Putting the Online Catalog in Its Place." *Research Strategies* 2 (Summer 1984): 119-127.

Seiden, Peggy and Patricia Sullivan. "Designing User Manuals for the Online Public Access Catalog." *Library Hi Tech* 13 (1986): 29-35.

Senzig, Donna. "Teaching the Use of Online Catalogs." *Wisconsin Library Bulletin* 78 (Summer 1983): 84-86.

Stark, Marcella. "Using the Online Catalog Effectively." *C&RL News* 45 (June 1984): 301-305.

Sullivan, Patricia and Peggy Seiden. "How Should We Educate Online Catalog Users?" *Library Hi Tech* 10 (1985): 11-19.

Turnage, Martha. "User Education." *Texas Library Journal* 61 (Winter 1985): 128-129.

Van Pulis, Noelle. *User and Staff Education for the Online Catalog*. 1985. ED 257 478.

_____. "User Education for an Online Catalog: A Workshop Approach." *RQ* 21 (Fall 1981): 61-68.

Wilson, Linda. "Designing Point-of-Use Instruction for Online Catalogs." *LIRT News* 7 (September 1984): 5-6.

_____. "User Education for Online Catalogs." *LIFline News Sheet* 24 (January 1984): 3-4.

The Online Library Catalog:

User Reactions and Responses:

A LOEX Bibliography

Bishop, David F. "The CLR OPAC Study: Analysis of ARL User Responses." *Information Technology and Libraries* 2 (September 1983): 315-321.

Broadus, R.N. "Online Catalogs and Their Users." *College & Research Libraries* 44 (November 1983): 458-467.

Dowlin, Kenneth. "Online Catalog User Acceptance Survey." *RQ* 20 (Fall 1980): 44-47.

Ferguson, Douglas, et al. "The CLR Public Online Catalog Study: An Overview." *Information Technology and Libraries* 1 (June 1982): 84-88.

Gouke, Mary Noel and Sue Pease. "Title Searches in an Online Catalog and a Card Catalog: A Comparative Study of Patron Success in Two Libraries." *Journal of Academic Librarianship* 8 (July 1982): 137-143.

Kinney, Karen. "Online Catalogs: A Public Services Point of View." *Library Hi Tech News* 1 (July-August 1984): 1+.

Larson, Ray R. "Users Look at Online Catalogs. Part 2: Interacting with Online Catalogs." Berkeley, CA: Division of Library Automation and Library Studies and Research Division, Office of the Assistant VP. *Library Plans and Policies* U CA System-Wide Administration, 1983.

Lolley, John. "University Night Students and the Online Library Catalog." *Research Strategies* 2 (Fall 1984): 172-178.

Markey, Karen. "Thus Spake the OPAC User." *Information Technology and Libraries* 2 (December 1983): 381-387.

Moore, Carol Weiss. "Reactions to Online Catalogs." *College and Research Libraries* 42 (July 1981): 295-302.

Pease, Sue and M.N. Gouke. "Patterns of Use in an Online Catalog and a Card Catalog." *College and Research Libraries* 43 (July 1982): 279-291.

Senzig, Donna. "Library Catalogs for Library Users." *RQ* 24 (Fall 1984): 37-42.

Steinberg, David and Paul Metz. "User Response to and Knowledge about an Online Catalog." *College & Research Libraries* 45 (January 1984): 66-70.

University of California Division of Library Automation. "Users Look at Online Catalogs: Results of a National Survey of Users and Non-Users of Online Public Access Catalogs." Final Report to the Council on Library Resources, Inc. Berkeley, CA, 16 November 1982.

Welborn, V., et al. "Card Catalog and LCS Users: A Comparison." In ASIS Conference Proceedings, Columbus, OH 1982. *Proceedings* v. 19; *Information Interaction*. Knowledge Ind. Pubs. for ASIS 1982: 330-334.

Online Catalog Guides:

List of Participants from
Second Annual LOEX
Library Instruction Workshop

SECOND BIENNIAL LOEX LIBRARY INSTRUCTION WORKSHOP

Hoyt Center-Eastern Michigan University--9-10 May 1985

Participants

Anderson, Gail Calvert
   Education Coordinator
Medical College of Georgia
Augusta, GA 30912

Anderson, Kari D.
   Reference
E. Lee Trinkle Library
Mary Washington College
1301 College Ave.
Fredericksburg, VA 22401

Austin, Donald E.
   Reference-Grad Library
University of Michigan
Ann Arbor, MI 48109

Betsy Baker
Reference/Instruction
Northwestern University
Evanston, IN 60201

Baker, William S.
   Ass't Humanities Librarian
King Library
Miami University
Oxford, OH 45056

Balsiger, Linda
   Public Services Librarian
College Library
University of Wisconsin-Madison
Madison, WI 53706

Barnard, Robin
   Instructor
Newman Library
Virginia Tech
Blacksburg, VA 24061

Bell, Richard
   Reference Librarian
Wm. D. McIntyre Library
University of Wisconsin-Eau Claire
Eau Claire, WI 54701

Benson, Elizabeth
   Reference Librarian
Library/Learning Resources Center
University of Minnesota-Duluth

Duluth, MN 55812

Bhullar, Goodie
   Library Instruction Coordinator
Ellis Library
University of Missouri
Columbia, MO 65201

Birkner, Robin Wagner
   Library Instruction Coordinator
Baker Library
Dartmouth College
Hanover, NH 03755

Bjorkland, Lucy A.
   Public Services Librarian
Beeghly Library
Ohio Wesleyan University
Delaware, OH 43015

Bobay, Julie
   Instruction Librarian
Indiana University
Indianapolis, IN 47405

Brady, Anna
   Coordinator of Instructional Services
Paul Klapper Library
Queens College
New York, NY 11367

Brancolini, Kristine
   Media Librarian
Media Center
Indiana University
Bloomington, IN 47405

Bright, Alice
   Serials Librarian
Hunt Library
Carnegie-Mellon University
Schenley Park
Pittsburgh, PA 15213

Brown, Cecelia
   Librarian-Specialist
College Library
University of Wisconsin
Madison, WI 53706

Cameron, Lynn
    Coordinator of Library Instruction
Carrier Library
James Madison University
Harrisonburg, VA 22807

Carter-Lovejoy, Steven
    Reference Librarian
Tompkins-McCaw Library
Virginia Commonwealth University
Box 582 - MCV Station
Richmond, VA 23298

Cash, Michele
    Bibliographic Instruction Coordinator
Indiana University at South Bend
PO Box 7111
South Bend, IN 46634

Chisholm, Clarence
    Social Sciences Librarian
Center of Educational Resources
Eastern Michigan University
Ypsilanti, MI 48197

Christianson, Marilyn
    Library Instruction Librarian
Cunningham Memorial Library
Indiana State University
Terre Haute, IN 47809

Clougherty, Leo P.
    Reference/Extension Librarian
University of Arkansas for the Medical Sciences
Library - Slot 586
Little Rock, AR 72205

Coffey, Helen
    Reference Librarian
Douglas Library
Queen's University
Kingston, Ontario
CANADA K7L 5C4

Crofts, Jayne
    User Education Coordinator
Welch Medical Library
Johns Hopkins University
Baltimore, MD 21205

Dantin, Doris
    Associate Reference Librarian
Middleton Library
Louisiana State University
Baton Rouge, LA 70808

Davidge, Lyn
    Reference Librarian

Hatcher Graduate Library
University of Michigan
Ann Arbor, MI 48105

Davidson, Nancy
    Coordinator: Bibliographic Instruction
Dacus Library
Winthrop College
Rock Hill, SC 29733

Dawkins, Willie Mae
    Reference/Instruction
Library/Learning Center
University of Wisconsin-Parkside
Kenosha, WI 53141

Donahue, Thomas J., Jr.
    Librarian/Instructor
Pullen Library
Georgia State University
100 Decatur St. SE
Atlanta, GA 30303-3081

Eichelberger, Susan
    Bibliographic Instruction Librarian
Cullom-Davis Library
Bradley University
Peoria, IL 61615

Eide, Marge
    Social Sciences Coordinator
Center of Educational Resources
Eastern Michigan University
Ypsilanti, MI 48197

Engeldinger, Eugene
    Head Reference Librarian
Wm. D. McIntyre Library
University of Wisconsin-Eau Claire
Eau Claire, WI 54701

Ernest, Doug
    Ass't Reference Librarian
Morgan Library
Colorado State University
Fort Collins, CO 80521

Feldman, Beverly
    Head Reference Department
Undergraduate Library
State University of New York-Buffalo
Buffalo, NY 14260

Evans, Nancy
    Reference Department
Hunt Library
Carnegie-Mellon University
Schenley Park

Pittsburgh, PA 15213

Haka, Cliff
   Head Information/Reference
Michigan State University
East Lansing, MI 48823

Hamilton, Dennis Clark
   Associate Librarian-Cataloging
University of California
Santa Barbara, CA 93106

Hannon, Christine
   Coordinator of Library Instruction
Bracken Library
Ball State University
Muncie, IN 47206

Hayes, Paula
   Head of Reference
McKeldin Library
University of Maryland
College Park, MD 20742

Hensley, Randall B.
   Bibliographic Instruction Coordinator
Libraries
University of Washington
Seattle, WA 98195

Jesudason, Melba
   Public Services Librarian
College Library
University of Wisconsin-Madison
Madison, WI 53706

Jones, Glenn Ellen S.
   Library Instruction Coordinator
Belk Library
Appalachian State University
Boone, NC 28608

Kohler, Jane B.
   Librarian
Community College of Allegheny County
Pittsburgh, PA 15237

Leget, Max
   Reference Librarian
Weeks Library
University of South Dakota
Vermillion, SD 57069

Leysen, Joan
   Monographic Cataloger
Parks Library
Iowa State University
Ames, IA 50011

Magdol, Lynn
   Reference Librarian
Memorial Library
University of Wisconsin
Madison, WI 53706

Masters, Deborah C.
   Head Reference & Instruction Department
Gelman Library
George Washington University
2130 H St., NW
Washington, DC 20052

Max, Patrick
   Instruction Coordinator
Memorial Library
University of Notre Dame
Notre Dame, IN 46556

Mayo, Lynn
   Reference/Instruction Librarian
Burke Library
Hamilton College
Clinton, NY 13323

Miller, Doris A.
   Coordinator-Library Instruction
Founders Memorial Library
Northern Illinois University
DeKalb, IL 60115

Miller, Marilyn
   Reference Librarian
Coe Library
University of Wyoming
Laramie, WY 82071

Miller, William
   Acting Dean
Libraries/Learning Resources
Bowling Green State University
Bowling Green, OH 43403-0170

Moore, Kathryn
   Bibliographic Instruction Coordinator
Jackson Library
University of North Carolina at Greensboro
Greensboro, NC 27412

Moyer, Anna Jane
   Readers' Services Librarian
Library
Gettysburg College
Gettysburg, PA 17325

Nixon, Henriette
   Reference/Bibliographic Instruction
Solomon R. Baker Library

Bentley College
Waltham, MA 02254

Nowakowski, Frances C.
    Reference Librarian
Killam Library
Dalhousie University
Halifax, Nova Scotia
CANADA R3H 4H8

Oberman, Cerise
    Acting Director
Walter Library
University of Minnesota
Minneapolis, MN 55455

Okada, Emily M.
    Reference/Instruction
Undergraduate Library
Indiana University
Bloomington, IN 47405

Poff, Doug
    Area Coordinator-Information and Reserve
Centre
Libraries
University of Alberta
Edmonton, Alberta
CANADA T6G 2J8

Radde, Laurie
    Reference Librarian
Carl B. Ylvisaker Library
Concordia College
Moorhead, MN 56560

Ready, Sandra K.
    Instructional Services
Library
Mankato State University
Mankato, MN 56001

Ream, Dan
    Coordinator-Basic Skills Instruction
Undergraduate Library
University of Tennessee
Knoxville, TN 37996

Roske, Peggy
    Reference/Instruction
Joint Libraries
St. John's University-College of St. Benedict
Collegeville, MN 56321

Sager, Harvey
    Instructional Services
Hayden Library
Arizona State University

Tempe, AZ 85287

Sandore, Beth
    Reference/Bibliographic Instruction
Illinois Institute of Technology Library
Chicago, IL 60616

Schichtel, Sandra Nan
    Serials/Data Base Librarian
Woodhouse Learning Resources Center
Aquinas College
1607 Robinson Rd. SE
Grand Rapids, MI 49506

Seiden, Peggy
    Educational Software Librarian
Hunt Library
Schenley Park
Carnegie-Mellon University
Pittsburgh, PA 15213

Schobert, Tim
    Head Public Services
Olson Library
Northern Michigan University
Marquette, MI 49855

Sheets, Janet
    Head Reference Services
Moody Memorial Library
Baylor University
Waco, TX 76706

Shonrock, Diana D.
    Ass't Professor: Library Instruction
Parks Library
Iowa State University
Ames, IA 50010

Sikora, Judith
    Automation Project Coordinator/Reference
Alfred C. O'Connell Library
Genesee Community College
Batavia, NY 14020

Skekloff, Susan D.
    Reference
Helmke Library
Indiana University-Purdue University at Fort
Wayne
2101 Coliseum Blvd. E
Fort Wayne, IN 46805

Smith, Karen V.
    Information Services
Southwestern College Library
900 Otay Lakes Rd.
Chula Vista, CA 92010

Snow, Marilyn
    Coordinator: Library Instruction
University of Central Florida Library
Orlando, FL 32816

Somer, Deborah A.
    Bibliographic Instruction Coordinator
Libraries
University of Georgia
Athens, GA 30602

Sperring, Beverly A.
    Assistant Head Reference
Regenstein Library
University of Chicago
Chicago, IL 60637

Stanger, Keith
    Orientation Librarian
Center of Educational Resources
Eastern Michigan University
Ypsilanti, MI 48197

Stark, Marcella
    Coordinator-Instructional Services
E.S. Bird Library
Syracuse University
Syracuse, NY 13210

Swain, Richard H.
    Ass't Director: Public Services
Libraries
Cleveland State University
Cleveland, OH 44115

Takeuchi, Carolyn
    Reference Librarian
Owen Science & Engineering Library
Washington State University
Pullman, WA 99164-3200

Tate, Vicki L.
    Reference Librarian
Milner Library
Illinois State University
Normal, IL 61761

Thomas, Mary Ellen
    Information Services Librarian
Cabell Library
Virginia Commonwealth University
901 Park Ave.
Richmond, VA 23284

Tuckett, Harold
    Reference/Instruction Librarian
Library/Learning Center
University of Wisconsin-Parkside

Kenosha, WI 53141

Van Balen, John
    Public Services Librarian
Weeks Library
University of South Dakota
Vermillion, SD 57069

Van Pulis, Noelle
    Systems Librarian-Automation Office
Libraries
Ohio State University
1858 Neil Avenue Mall
Columbus, OH 43210-1286

Violette, Judith L.
    Ass't Director: Public Services
Helmke Library
Indiana University-Purdue University at Fort
Wayne
Fort Wayne, IN 46805

Waltz, Mary Anne
    Anthropology/Geography/Maps Librarian
E.S. Bird Library
Syracuse University
Syracuse, NY 13210

Ward, James E.
    Director
Crisman Memorial Library
David Lipscomb College
Nashville, TN 37203

Warmann, Carolyn
    Ass't General Reference Librarian
Newman Library
Virginia Tech
Blacksburg, VA 24061

Wells, Margaret R.
    Library Instruction Coordinator
E.H. Butler Library
State University College at Buffalo
1300 Elmwood Ave.
Buffalo, NY 14222

Wenner, Sandra
    Bibliographic Instruction Coordinator
Draughan Library
Auburn University
Auburn, AL 36849

Whitaker, Constance
    Reference Librarian
Beeghly Library
Ohio Wesleyan University
Delaware, OH 43015

Wiggins, Marvin E.
  Library-Use Instruction Librarian
Lee Library
Brigham Young University
Provo, UT 84604

Wilson, Barbara
  Education/Information Services Librarian
Houston Academy of Medicine-Texas Medical
Center Library
Houston, TX 77030

Wilson, Linda
  Project Manager for User Education
Newman Library
Virginia Tech
Blacksburg, VA 24061

Wittkopf, Barbara
  Bibliographic Instruction Coordinator
114 Library West
University of Florida
Gainesville, FL 32611

Wright, Marie
  Reference/Orientation

Library
Indiana/Purdue University at Indianapolis
Indianapolis, IN 46202

Yee, Sandra
  Head of Access Services
Center of Educational Resources
Eastern Michigan University
Ypsilanti, MI 48197

Young, Judith
  Head of Access Services
Library
University of Central Florida
Orlando, FL 32816

Young, Vicky
  Science Library
Bowling Green State University
Bowling Green, OH 43404

Zaporozhetz, Laurene E.
  Library Instruction Coordinator
Library
University of Oregon
Eugene, OR 97403